Christopher D. Call

The Hymnal

The Hymnal

A READING HISTORY

Christopher N. Phillips

Johns Hopkins University Press
Baltimore

2 4 6 8 9 7 5 3 1

Johns Hopkins University Press
2715 North Charles Street
Baltimore, Maryland 21218-4363
www.press.jhu.edu

Library of Congress Cataloging-in-Publication Data

Names: Phillips, Christopher N., author.
Title: The hymnal : a reading history / Christopher N. Phillips.
Description: Baltimore : Johns Hopkins University Press, 2018. |
Includes bibliographical references and index.
Identifiers: LCCN 2017046428 | ISBN 9781421425924 (hardcover : alk. paper) |
ISBN 9781421425931 (electronic) | ISBN 1421425920 (hardcover : alk. paper) |
ISBN 1421425939 (electronic)
Subjects: LCSH: Hymns, English—History and criticism—18th century. | Hymns,
English—History and criticism—19th century.
Classification: LCC BV312 .P45 2018 | DDC 264/.230973—dc23
LC record available at https://lccn.loc.gov/2017046428

A catalog record for this book is available from the British Library.

*Special discounts are available for bulk purchases of this book. For more information, please
contact Special Sales at 410-516-6936 or specialsales@press.jhu.edu.*

Johns Hopkins University Press uses environmentally friendly book materials, including
recycled text paper that is composed of at least 30 percent post-consumer waste,
whenever possible.

For Richard B. Phillips
and Elizabeth A. Phillips,
lovers of hymns,
lovers of books,
living hymns of love

Any history of reading is also a meditation on the reading of a particular writer.

—*Leah Price*

CONTENTS

PART III   HOME

A Word to Readers of This Book

To begin with, thank you. This book has been many years in the making, and while we may never know each other, your choice to read this book (including the easily skippable front matter) gives us a chance to share a mental world together. I hope you enjoy.

Now, a caveat: This is a book written for interested readers who may or may not have an academic or church professional background. It is a work of scholarship presented to engage readers beyond the fields of literary studies, hymnology, and history of the book. I hope that scholars in those areas and others will find this volume useful, and the notes are for their benefit: an alternative book experience that delivers the obligatory bibliography but also comments on side points and technical details, the things scholars enjoy exploring and arguing about. The notes are highly optional for readers who have less interest in such things. A glossary is provided for those non-bibliographers who may read this book; I hope the bibliographers will not find too much fault with my definitions.

Next, a declaration: For my scholarly readers, this book is an intervention in the field of historical poetics that seeks to bring together the study of poetry, book history, and lived religion. Despite the growing importance of specific poetic genres to literary history, the ubiquity of hymnbooks in pre-1900 print culture, and the importance of hymnbooks in the everyday lives of Christians, Jews, and other English-speakers, remarkably little work has been done on the history of the hymnbook. Louis Benson's magisterial *The English Hymn* (1915) is still the definitive work in the field, a 500-page survey of the production of hymnbooks and their place in their respective churches; J. R. Watson's more recent, similarly titled *The English Hymn* (1999) treats the hymn as a poetic form, offering an extended survey grounded in a close reading of the evolution of hymn writing in English.[1]

My study focuses on what one might call the "social lives of hymnbooks," to adapt a phrase from Michael Cohen. As objects as well as carriers of text, hymnbooks were part of the everyday social practices of hundreds of thousands of English-speakers across two centuries, and I seek in this book to articulate and analyze those practices.

The older scholarship on hymnody has tended to take the hymn's status as a sung text as its fundamental distinguishing feature from, say, religious poetry. This assumption effectively erases the complex of practices I reconstruct in this volume, and (as I will develop in a subsequent book) I find rather that what most distinguishes a hymn from other kinds of poetry, including song lyrics, is the expectation that the speaker and the reader will collapse into each other—that is, readers will read (including singing) rightly when they can voice the words as if they were their own. This has profound implications for the study of the history of poetry as well as the relationship between reading and belief, and I have been led to this idea through works by Wesley Kort, Paul Griffiths, Paul Ricoeur, Charles Taylor, Misty Anderson, Giorgio Agamben, Jean-Luc Marion, and John Henry Newman, among others.[2] Scholarship on hymnody, particularly by Claudia Stokes, Mary De Jong, David Music, and Dennis Dickerson, has helped me situate hymns and hymnbooks within larger discourses of poetry, sentimentalism, and denominational identity.[3]

My interest in "social practice," and my use of that term, has been influenced by sociologist Anthony Giddens's idea that the practice, not the individual or the family, is the foundational social unit. This idea has been further developed by Elizabeth Shove and her collaborators as a way of understanding humans, animals, objects, infrastructures, ideas, values, and habits as all participating together in performing relationships.[4] For the purposes of this volume, I have taken as an organizing principle the three most important spaces for the use of hymnbooks—church, school, and home—not to limit discussion of other sites and possibilities in each of my book's three main parts, but to highlight the ways in which each of these spaces has created, sustained, and at times revised expectations of what goes on there and why. Singing and reading from hymnbooks is obviously important in church, but the use of hymnbooks to carry things to and from church, to have silent conversations when speaking aloud is forbidden, and to remember departed loved ones are also significant practices: they rely to varying extents on the people, the things, the time, and the space involved to achieve their coherence and meaning.

In thinking about practice from a book history perspective, I am especially indebted to the work of Matthew Brown, Patricia Crain, M. O. Grenby, H. J. Jackson, and Leah Price; in lived religion, Lauren Winner, Candy Gunther Brown, Colleen McDannell, and David Hall have been particularly formative for me, as has the work of Michael Cohen, Edward Whitley, and Virginia Jackson in historical poetics. It is my aim that this book can further conversation across these fields, and potentially into others, as I pursue my own version of what D. F. McKenzie has famously called a "sociology of texts."[5]

ACKNOWLEDGMENTS

This book has been a joy to work on, not least because of the delightful interactions that have nourished and guided me over some seven years of research, thinking, and writing. The woman who has been there through the entire process, Emily Phillips, has given her listening ear, her quiet support, and her ability to keep me aware that the rabbit hole of a scholar's work is not the same as life or the world. We have traveled together, raised children together, talked and read and sung together; this project began while she was carrying our second child, and the first writing began when that child was only a few months old. Luke and his siblings, Joseph, Stephen, and Miranda, will have to adapt to life without this book consuming their father's thoughts, and I think they will find that an easy adjustment.

Friends and colleagues old and new have stepped in at the right time to help this project along. Some have done so in the form of writing groups, and I especially thank Anna Edlund, Ingrid Furniss, Lynda Yankaskas, Jeremy Zallen, Jeff Hotz, and Monica Najar for their insights and their collective faith in this book. Some have shared research space and conversation, always bringing me greater clarity and energy for this work. To Ed Whitley, Patty Roylance, Steffi Dippold, Zach Hutchins, Brett Hendrickson, James Woolley, Jane Giscombe, Michael Cohen, Joel Pierce, Ben Jahre, Wendy Roberts, Meredith Neuman, Sandra Gustafson, Michael Winship, Meredith McGill, Joe Rezek, Alex Black, Brendan Gillis, Abby Cooper, Ezra Greenspan, and Greg Nobles: you may recognize specific contributions you made to this book, or you may not, but they are real and appreciated all the same. Matt McAdam, Catherine Goldstead, and the reviewers for Johns Hopkins University Press have been consummate professionals who have offered much seasonable good advice, guidance, and reassurance.

A special thanks to those librarians and curators who have gone above and beyond, often repeatedly. The enthusiasm of Laura Wasowicz at the American Antiquarian Society (AAS) for children's literature and the many startling connections it has to, well, everything else has been inspiring and sustaining through my long surveys of children's hymnbooks (which she cataloged). Connie King at the Library Company of Philadelphia used her "spidey sense" for finding out-of-the-way materials that I might be able to use and showed great patience in long conversations with me about what I found. Jim Green, also at the LCP, made himself available for many consultations over music printing, hymnbook bibliographies, and the intricacies of Philadelphia's library world. Chris Wirth at the Longfellow House– Washington's Headquarters National Historic Site helped me navigate the multilayered worlds of the Longfellows as I explored the Samuel Longfellow Papers. Charlene Peacock at the Presbyterian Historical Society discovered nearly forgotten materials and guided me through the many finding aids of the PHS to piece together that library's astonishing hymnody holdings. Ashley Cataldo of the AAS was the first librarian to say, "Let's just get you a truckful of these things" and thus opened a whole new vista in this research for me; her continual encouragement, sharp questions, ready suggestions, and willingness even to read part of a late draft of this book have set a new standard for a librarian's involvement in my scholarly projects.

Dozens of libraries provided hymnbooks, expertise, working space, and answers to many questions over the course of this project, and in addition to those already mentioned, I would like to thank the staffs at the University of Edinburgh's New College Library; the Huntington Library; Special Collections at Stanford University; the Claremont Libraries; the Charleston Historical Society and the College of Charleston; the Pitts Theological Library at Emory University; the Methodist Library at Drew University; the Historical Society of Pennsylvania; the University of Pennsylvania Libraries; the Princeton Theological Seminary Library; Dr. Williams's Library; and of course, Lafayette College's Skillman Library.

Generous funding for research was provided by Lafayette in the form of a Richard K. Mellon summer research grant, an enhanced sabbatical grant, and a leave of absence, thanks in part to the support of John Meier, Robin Rinehart, Pat Donahue, the Academic Research Committee, and the Promotion and Tenure Review Committee. Other generous funding included the AAS's Lapides fellowship, a National Endowment for the Humanities postdoctoral fellowship at the LCP, and a Frederick Burkhardt fellowship from the American Council of Learned Societies, which allowed for the completion of this book while I was in residence at the AAS. My heartfelt thanks for all of this professional and moral support.

Portions of this book were published previously and are here presented, in revised form, with permission: parts of chapter 5 appeared as "Cotton Mather Brings Isaac Watts's Hymns to America; or, How to Perform a Hymn without Singing It," *New England Quarterly* 85.2 (2012): 203–21; and parts of chapter 1 appeared as "Versifying African Methodism; or, What Did Early African-American Hymnbooks Do?" *Papers of the Bibliographical Society of America* 107.3 (2013): 325–33.

Finally, my thanks to my sister, Britta, for great conversations, insights on Jewish liturgy in particular, and the opportunity to share my work with a larger audience at Calvary Presbyterian Church in South Pasadena. She and I learned our love of music, learning, reading, poetry, God, and much else from our parents, Richard and Elizabeth Phillips, who raised us singing hymns, reading good books, and enjoying the wonder of life. It is to them that this book is dedicated.

The Hymnal

Looking for Hymns

Who reads a hymnal? Hardly anyone today, and that has been the case for at least a century of English-language religious practice. Even singing from hymnals is now on the decline, as congregations increasingly move to projecting the lyrics of hymns and praise songs on large screens. Recapturing the importance of hymnals was apparently already a concern by 1978, when an issue of *Hymn*, the journal of the Hymn Society of the United States and Canada, included a public-service announcement intended for photocopying and including in church bulletins. Titled "Thirty Ways You Use Your Hymnal!" the one-page, somewhat tongue-in-cheek list included entries focused on the practical uses of a large book as an object: a doorstop, a booster seat for children, a toy to slide down a pew and crash to the floor. Some uses, such as singing, were clearly acceptable to do openly; others, such as passing notes in church, were not. The books could be stolen for home use, since they were not generally available for individual purchase—they were too expensive for most people to want to buy one anyway—and of course they could be used in worship. But beyond looking up information about a specific hymn, simply *reading* the books did not make the list. That was too far beyond the horizon of possibilities in 1978.[1]

A century earlier, however, the situation was far different. By the late 1870s, hymnals had begun to take the form we recognize today, with music and text appearing on pages together. That now seems intuitive, but worshipers in 1878 were in the middle of a generation-long struggle over the nature, purpose, and shape of a hymnal. Until the 1850s, books for congregational use had almost universally excluded music; instead, the hands of worshipers throughout North America and the United Kingdom cradled pocket-sized collections of hymn texts, and only the choirs and accompanists had printed tunes. These early collections, generally called "hymnbooks," were privately owned and carried from home to church and back again. They traveled to schools, to offices, to fields, and to markets. They provided devotional material and early literacy instruction; they forged bonds between friends and family members, and they proclaimed the identities of the churches that used them beyond the walls of their buildings.

Adding music changed all that. In an effort to improve congregational singing, reform-minded clergy, such as Henry Ward Beecher, introduced books that included music alongside the texts. In an attempt at a compromise between reading and singing, Beecher's *Plymouth Collection* and others like it gave only the first stanzas interlined with the music, leaving the other stanzas unbroken by musical notation. And yet these books proved so unpopular at first that even the most successful hymnals—the term attached to these new, music-filled books—also appeared in words-only forms. The price and weight of the books had increased dramatically, and the visual distraction of the music staffs threatened to undo a century and a half of a multifaceted reading culture that had built up around a book that sat beside the Bibles in hundreds of thousands of English-speaking households. By 1878, the singing reformers were gaining the upper hand, partly thanks to a generation of Sunday school graduates who had learned singing in their childhood classes (using the old hymnbooks) and who thus brought a new standard of musical literacy to congregations as adults. Those singers remembered a culture of reading that had followed them into many of their lives' most significant spaces and relationships. By 1978, that memory was gone.

This book reaches back to that older form of the hymnal—the hymnbook—the small companion that carried human-authored texts on divine subjects to and with their owners. Visiting the three sacred spaces of church, school, and home, in the chapters that follow I explore the rise and maturing of a robust reading culture. From the adoption of congregational hymns alongside older psalm-singing practices around 1700 to the appearance of the new style of hymnals, this culture merged older devotional traditions with new relationships to media, both sacred and secular, as hymnbooks went nearly everywhere print culture could reach. To speak of a "reading history" of the hymnal, as this volume's title does, thus means to search past the uniformly bound books in their pew racks, what we call "hymnals" today, to their older, smaller, more individuated forms.[2]

How do we undertake such a search? How do we find the history of hymnbooks? Descriptions of the details of use are few and scattered widely across letters, diaries, and memoirs. One place where we might find typical or idealized patterns of hymnbook use is in images from past centuries. Take the first image in this book, for instance. A rural family prepares to walk to church on a Sunday morning. Children and dogs circle around a patient donkey that will carry a grandmother down the path. The family members are wearing their finest clothes, including sashes and jewelry. And they also have their books with them. Three are visible in the picture. A large volume lies open on a bench on the left—almost certainly a Bible. The father, whose Bible this presumably is, has turned from his reading to help two of his children with a much smaller book, likely owned by at least one of the children. At the right edge of the family group, the mother prepares to lead the way, cradling a small leather-bound book in her hand. What are these smaller books? They could also be Bibles, which were available in a wide range of formats and sizes by the late eighteenth century. More likely, since the father has his Bible and will probably carry it with him, these other books are to help the family during the service.

This image has its origin in England; it was painted by William Redmore Bigg and engraved in London in the 1790s, which means the books depicted were probably copies of the Book of Common Prayer. But this particular version is an 1863 engraving by Philadelphia artist John Sartain, created for an American market in which Episcopalians with their BCPs were part of the religious landscape but by no means the dominant feature. By the 1860s, American BCPs generally included supplements of hymns, and the church also used its own hymnbooks by this time alongside the BCP, sometimes bound together. But if we do not assume an Anglican or Episcopalian identity here—many American denominations by the 1860s imitated the Gothic style of the church in the picture's background—the child's and mother's books are most likely hymnbooks. Until the late nineteenth century, churches adopted hymnbooks but did not provide them in the pews; families bought their own, often at a discount through the church, and they carried the books between church and home, as well as wherever else they wished.

Perhaps this analysis doesn't establish the presence of the hymnbook sufficiently. The next image gives us another angle, an interior scene of daily morning prayer. Again, the man of the house has a large book in his

William Redmore Bigg, *Sunday Morning* (1795), engraved by John Sartain.
Eclectic Magazine (1863). *Courtesy of American Antiquarian Society.*

possession, again presumably a Bible. He reads while the women in the room
listen. This family's wardrobe and decor indicate that they are wealthier
than the family in the first image, with fine carpets and furniture crowd-
ing them around the table holding the Bible. On the chair to the right is
another small book, handsomely bound but unidentified, though the structure of Protestant family worship gives us some clues. Scripture reading
was one of three main elements (alongside prayer and singing) in Protestant
domestic worship from the Puritan era. By the mid-nineteenth century, Bible reading and vocal prayer were generally understood as the man's purview, but women and children often led the singing.[3] A plausible narrative
for this scene is that, having led the family in a song at the start of their devotional time, the woman on the right has set her hymnbook down to listen to the next stage of the exercises, Bible reading. Hymnbooks played a
supporting role in biblical devotion in the eighteenth and nineteenth centuries, becoming increasingly indispensable as a source of devotional read-

Lucy Adams, *Morning Prayer* (n.d.), engraved by H. S. Sadd (1857). *Courtesy of American Antiquarian Society.*

ing and of song. They could even stand on their own as devotional works, as suggested by the image on page 9, in which a woman in a carefully furnished closet (a private reading room) reads a small volume, most likely a hymnbook, while what may be a large Bible rests unopened on a small table across the room. Hymnbooks were sources of solace, inspiration, guidance, pleasure, poetry, and even meditation in the time before printed music joined the words, generally before about 1870.

Some hymnbooks, especially those meant primarily for the home, sometimes included images suggesting how they might be used. The vignette

FAMILY HYMNS.

PUBLISHED BY

THE AMERICAN TRACT SOCIETY.

NO. 150 NASSAU-STREET, NEW-YORK.

1838.

....

Fanshaw, Printer.

Opposite, Title page with vignette of family singing with hymnbooks. American Tract Society, *Family Hymns* (1838). *Courtesy of American Antiquarian Society.*

Above, Frontispiece for Caroline Snowden Whitmarsh, ed., *Hymns for Mothers and Children,* 2nd ser. (1865). *Courtesy of American Antiquarian Society.*

on the title page of the American Tract Society's *Family Hymns* (1838) shows a middle-class family in their parlor, singing together from their individual copies of the book: father, mother, and children each holding their own. These books would likely have been some of the first the children owned, and the copy this image is taken from was inscribed to a young girl as a New Year's gift from her teacher. And while the most prevalent depictions of mothers reading to their children in the nineteenth century showed the mother holding a Bible, the frontispiece to the second volume of the series *Hymns for Mothers and Children* (1865) showed that mothers could just as easily read from hymnbooks—perhaps more easily, as the mother in this image would have had difficulty sharing lap space between a large-format Bible and her drowsy child. While perhaps not as obviously wealthy as the family in the morning prayer image, this family lives in a very comfortable home with capacious chairs, paintings on the walls, and books on the end table. This would be a perfect setting for a round of absorptive novel reading, but it turns out the hymnbook was just as at home in such a setting.

Hymnbooks, as these images tell us, were as much a family matter as they were part of the life of church worship. Their ability to inhabit spaces set aside for devotion, entertainment, worship, relaxation, education, and more made them one of the most lived with and the most reproduced of all print genres before the twentieth century. Not content to rest on shelves alongside a medley of other works, hymnbooks tended to stay ready-to-hand on tables, chairs, desks, pulpits, and pews. While designed to lead their readers to think on heavenly things, hymnbooks experienced more of the world than most other books did. Those experiences could leave traces that help us reconstruct the lives led by hymnbooks and their users before the hymn*books* became hymn*als* with music: heavier and pricier volumes that by the end of the nineteenth century people were content to leave at church.

As these visual examples show, however, even simply finding hymnbooks in images of reading is a challenge. The classic image of the solitary reader lost in a book generally implies, through the physical context and the relative size of the volume, that the book at which the reader gazes is either a Bible (in a devotional context) or a novel (in other settings). These are the two great genres of absorption in reading as we have imagined reading in

Unknown artist, *Get Wisdom* (1847–1851). *Courtesy of American Antiquarian Society.*

the West.[4] Yet only one of the images in this brief section actually depicts a solitary reader. Further, in the age of print especially, Bibles and novels dwell in worlds of books, and when an image gives us a glimpse of more than one book, we may start to understand what kinds of neighbors these books had and what their relationship might have been. This demands some careful looking, a bit of detective work, and some knowledge of the reading practices of English-speakers of the eighteenth and nineteenth centuries, which can help us see where these books might be in the pictures of the time and what they're doing there. Such is precisely what I seek to undertake in this volume: creating a multifaceted picture in words of the crowded, fascinating world in which the hymnbook flourished for well over a century.

Much of this book wrestles with the fact that reading itself is largely invisible. Even in the present day, the attempt to articulate what it is we actually *do* when we read—physically, cognitively, emotionally, spiritually—serves to show how enigmatic reading is. This mystery deepens when we look into reading of the past, since the marginal notes and written firsthand accounts of reading that survive are by definition anomalies; generalizing from these special cases is perilous work. Visual depictions of reading have the further challenge of being idealized scenes, ones that can tell us much about the values of artists and their cultures but may easily distort our ideas of what "really happened." And yet the desire to know—to connect with readers of the past and so understand something of our reading experiences today—draws scholars and book enthusiasts back to the special cases, the ideal images. Most of this book will focus on the book as artifact, evidence, and clue. And so let us meet the books that will guide us into that world.

A Reader's Hymnbook

The book stands barely three inches high, less than two inches wide, and nearly an inch and a half thick: a small brick of a book. The page block is skewed a bit, and the worn, cheap, leather-over-board covers don't quite close. The spine shows four lines originally meant to imitate the ridges of a fine binding, but they are now dull and partially worn out; one spot of the leather has rubbed away to show the scrap paper used to strengthen the binding. On the boards, swaths of lighter brown show where the oils of a smallish hand held the book, one along the center of the front board where the thumb and heel rested, a larger one near the hinge edge of the back board where four fingers supported the unwieldy page block. Wear to the corners along the bottom and unbound side edges suggest shelf wear as well as pocket or handbag travel. This book has seen considerable use, and in more than one place.

But for what use was it designed? And who would have been meant to use it? The title page begins to provide an answer, taking us to the early nineteenth century with an 1819 publication date and then to the early eighteenth century since the title reads *The Psalms of David, Imitated in the Language of the New Testament*, with Isaac Watts named as the author: the collection was exactly a century old at the time of this reprinting. This, then, is a religious collection, one that seems to have had some popular success to warrant a reprinting so long after the first edition. The contents would certainly have been considered public domain by 1819, but even in terms of attribution whose psalms these are is a bit of a mystery—are they David's, Watts's, or (according to Calvinist doctrines of the inspiration of scripture) God's? Let me defer that question for a moment and see what else the book reveals of itself.

The printer named on the title page is John I. Williams of Exeter, New Hampshire. Williams had only set up shop in Exeter the year before, and he would remain a partner with his brother, a bookbinder named Benjamin Williams, in the successful firm of J. and B. Williams for decades. According to one source, this firm specialized in "new editions of those [works] which were already favorites of the public," in both fine and cheap editions.[1] This Williams imprint was thus part of the business of reprinting books, particularly British works, which dominated the American book trade following the War of 1812.[2] And this business was robust enough to cross state lines: above the printer's name appears a line naming B. and J. Collins as the firm that made the stereotype plates for the edition. The year 1819 is early for American stereotyping, but the Collins firm, part of the Collins and Co. Bible-publishing empire begun by Isaac Collins in Burlington and New York in the 1790s, was stereotyping full Bibles as early as 1816.[3] The Collinses exemplify the religious publishing industry's status as the "early adopter" sector of American publishing, experimenting with stereotyping and steam-powered presses in the first third of the nineteenth century. The Williams firm in New Hampshire thus acquired the means of producing a cheap edition of Watts's book by way of a New York–based firm that specialized in steady-selling religious works, and the Williamses (who also are named as the book's publishers) had some sort of connection to a regional or even national distribution network, as I discuss below.

While the covers of this book indicate its devotional value for the owner, the first leaves tell a story of the hymnbook as commodity, from making the plates to pricing the final object for purchase. By turning from the title page to the unprinted flyleaves at the very front of the book, we can get some sense of what that pricing was. Just inside the front cover a flyleaf bears an inscription in oxidized ink from the early nineteenth century:

> Coral Woodford
> property Book
> Robeson County
> N. Carolina
> Price 34 1/2 cents[4]

Nothing more is known of this book's owner than what is given in this inscription. Coral Woodford most likely bought this book, since she (or he) knew the price of it, and the place of residence is identified by county and state, likely because Woodford lived in a rural area rather than in Pembroke or another town in Robeson County. This steady-selling British text, reproduced in New York and New Hampshire, traveled some thousand miles south and about ninety miles inland from the port of Wilmington, North Carolina, to spend countless hours in hands whose oils would combine with the Carolina humidity to leave a permanent impression of the time that person and book spent together. Today, that book sits in my hands, a relic of another time and a different world of book production and book use. I now mine the book for clues about itself, teasing out hints about its life while wondering what Coral's favorite texts were or if his or her hands ever tired of holding this small but hefty book.

Under what circumstances would the book have been held? For an answer to that, we have to extrapolate based on the time period, following a little more investigation of the book's contents. The title page mentioned above for Watts's *Psalms* only introduces half the pages, as it turns out. The volume's girth comes from two books being bound together, the second being Watts's 1709 *Hymns*, which has a separate title page with identical publication information, separate text numbering and pagination, and its own first-line index. *Psalms* has a separate first-line index in the back of that volume, the bare minimum a reader or singer would need to locate a text from memory or upon hearing the first line spoken or sung. Watts's original prefaces, including justifications for singing works of human composition (a controversial idea at the time Watts was writing) and directions for proper performance, are absent from Woodford's book. So are the later subject indexes that would be developed to aid preachers and others to quickly find texts suited to various moods, occasions, and topics. The printed text itself squeezes together, small type pushing to the margins; only Watts's original titles, meters, and larger initial letters offer any variety to the packed rows of verse. One of Watts's other paratextual elements survives: brackets (which Watts called "crotchets") pointing out which hymn verses could be omitted when sung, indicating the dual uses of reading and singing anticipated by the Williams firm as well as Watts. This is a stripped-down edition, designed to sell in bulk, travel easily in a pocket or bag, and provide "Watts entire"—the father of English hymnody's complete "System of Praise" that by 1819 had largely replaced the older psalmbooks in Reformed

Protestant churches and brought hymns into all but the most conservative Calvinist circles.

When Watts published the first version of his *Hymns* in 1707, the idea that these would be appropriate in worship services was radical; Calvin had taught that only texts from the inspired Word of God, the Bible, were allowed in such a setting. Thus Calvinists sang only psalms in church. Watts contended that texts that could speak to a New Testament church more directly than the Hebrew psalms did, in language that was suitable for the modern day and free from fashionable ornamentation, were a better means of obeying the scriptural command to sing "psalms, hymns, and spiritual songs." His startlingly free paraphrases of the book of Psalms were intended to bring the old together with the new, offering conservative congregations a middle ground between retaining what many admitted were increasingly rusty metrical translations of the book of Psalms and the controversial move of adopting hymns in worship, something that generally only the more enthusiastic congregations in the wake of the international Great Awakening of the 1730s and 1740s were willing to do. In New England, Watts's *Psalms* gained enough popularity by the time of the Revolution that poets such as Joel Barlow and Timothy Dwight—later known as America's first epic poets—were commissioned to revise Watts, removing references to Britain and its king that had become more difficult for American congregants to sing with conviction. As more congregations moved from the gateway commodity of the psalms to headier modern hymns, they developed supplements to help Watts fit their denominational views. Even when Watts was not adopted in full, churches as diverse as the Roman Catholic, Unitarian, and Latter-Day Saints reworded Watts's texts to fit their own devotional and theological ends. For those who had adopted "Watts entire" by 1819, this formerly polarizing collection was now the canon: all of Watts, and nothing but Watts, would be the hill that the Old School Presbyterians, for instance, would choose to die on when the split with the New School in the 1830s erupted into, among other things, a free-for-all debate over the future of the denomination's liturgy. Watts was one of the most important liturgical vehicles for the establishment of a congregational or denominational identity from the mid-eighteenth century to the mid-nineteenth. This use of Watts to establish an identity continues, as some churches in the rural South, particularly in the South Carolina Low Country, still sing their hymns "lined out" in a call-and-response structure, without accompaniment; this is often called "Wattsing" after the author of the books used to develop and preserve that practice.

Coral Woodford was likely a member of a Presbyterian congregation, or at the very least a Reformed one, that embraced the new idea of Watts as their liturgical heritage and that found all the psalms (or nearly all, often split into multiple song texts) and 365 hymns sufficient for their worship purposes. Like all churches of the time, Woodford's church would have adopted its hymnbook the way college professors today adopt textbooks: the leader would announce the choice, and it would be up to those in the seats to acquire their own copies. In poorer communities, this often meant only one book per household, and those books would be carried from home to church for each service. Some would also be carried elsewhere, into schools, fields, and other spaces where reading or singing might take place. The book could even become a visible mark of religious allegiance. Woodford's copy of Watts would have been a visible sign of congregational belonging, but it was also the site of personal practices that shaped an individual identity, and possibly a family's as well. Woodford's hands held still on the cover, but they were far from idle. They had learned how to build a spiritual life around a small book.

Now I pick up another book. A bit under six inches tall, this book settles lightly into my hand, my fingertips just reaching beyond the cover boards. It is much thinner than the Watts book and twelve years later. The quarter-calf binding still holds the book together well, revealing text on the printed board covers that has survived years of handling and storage. The black leather shows a few gilt lines on the spine and the very brief title *Infant Hymns*. The printed cover gives the full title as *Hymns for Infant Minds* and names the publisher as Dorr and Howland of Worcester, Massachusetts, with agents in Boston and New York—a major name in children's and religious publishing by 1831, the book's year of publication and copyright. But who wrote the work?

The answer to that question is a bit complicated. The title page only says that these are *Taylor's Hymns for Infant Minds*, with an "analysis to each," so as to "assist mothers and teachers in developing the infant mind." This is a book, then, to be taught and to be used together by readers of different generations and literacies. The name Taylor is assumed to be recognizable to any potential user or buyer as a stamp of public approval: no first name is necessary. The analyses are questions to be asked of the child reader to encourage comprehension as well as moral and spiritual development, anticipating the format that popular school readers such as the Worcester and McGuffey series would follow for decades. A brief, unsigned "advertisement" introduces the book's contents and its reading-and-question form. This advertisement is a rather odd one since it consists of a single paragraph followed by a one-paragraph note, the latter dated "Boston, March, 1831." The first paragraph refers to Isaac Watts's *Divine and Moral Songs for Children* (1715), stating that his collection was not to be surpassed in quality, but could be expanded in terms of subject matter. It also confesses that "to some of the pieces, the title of *Hymns* may not appear correctly applied; but for this inaccuracy, the nature of the subject will, it is hoped, apologize."[5] Indeed, following Watts's own distinction between the hymnic "divine songs" of his children's collection and the more lyrical and didactic "moral songs," some of the Taylor book's texts focus on inculcating moral principles without addressing any overtly religious topic. The note that follows this paragraph focuses on the analyses. The note is by the unnamed editor, referred to on the title page as the editor of *Lessons for Infant Sabbath Schools*, which is among the books advertised on the back cover; he was Henry Jenkins Howland of Dorr and Howland.

The front matter thus elides the author's and editor's roles, leaving both unnamed but giving prominence, strangely, to the editor with the date at the end. This practice was far from unusual in edited texts from the eighteenth and nineteenth centuries, and it was also fairly typical of the editorial treatment of the authors in question. Ann Taylor and Jane Taylor were sisters and the coauthors of a number of collections of children's poetry and hymnody in the early nineteenth century, sometimes joined by their relatives and friends, male and female. Though their names are nearly unknown today, nearly every child in the English-speaking world has likely encountered a Taylor text, the most famous being "Twinkle, Twinkle, Little Star," generally attributed to Jane. The Taylors were immensely popular, but though their works appeared in dozens of editions across the nineteenth century's English-speaking world, the sisters generally followed the practices of "poetesses" of their day by preferring anonymous publication, prefaces that downplayed the quality or originality of their work, and deference to canonical writers with whom they sought to compete (Watts, in this case). Following poets such as Anna Letitia Barbauld, the Taylors introduced a hymnody for children with an intensified attention to pedagogical use and child development. Their book was designed to be sung, read, and recited in Sunday schools and other social and pedagogical settings by children as young as three years old.

These hymns, as well as Watts's earlier contributions, worked so well as recitation texts that from the early 1700s—well before hymns were uniformly accepted in churches—hymn texts were anthologized in readers and spellers to teach literacy. There was considerable competition among hymnodic reading canons; the Taylors wrote poems for younger readers who could not understand or decode Watts, while Barbauld wrote "hymns in prose," arguing that children should master prose reading before moving to verse forms. Brief, accessible texts such as the Taylors composed could be rewritten, recombined, and published as full or partial collections—ideal for the growing industry in children's gift books and rewards of merit, genres used to mark milestones of achievement at school and church as well as birthdays and holidays at home. These books were meant to be read, memorized, treasured, and (this point cannot be overemphasized) owned by children. A child's relationship to this kind of book was bound by practices of giving, earning, and owning that made the entrance into literacy also an entrance into a material economy of leisure objects. Using these books often constituted a form of work, but through their texts and physicality, these books simultaneously enabled ways of imagining the rewards of work and a range of acceptable private activities (such as good reading) that a child could undertake outside work time.

The copy in my hands displays the marks of these practices across a number of decades. Between the well-worn boards, several texts have large penciled check marks next to them, a typical method for marking favorite texts as well as an overlapping group of texts: those that have been successfully memorized. Memorizing was often a reader's preferred way of keeping a favorite text, and teachers and parents frequently assigned children texts to memorize in the hope of creating favorites that reflected the adults' dearest values. Yet those values were not always strictly moralistic. In this copy, the checked hymns tend to revolve around specific worship settings, such as

Sunday services or morning and evening prayers; the development of spiritual disciplines, such as private prayer and Bible reading; family duties to parents and siblings (though most other "moral hymns" were left unmarked); and praise for mercy and the beauty of the created world. These texts suggest the shape of a child's faith, one more interested in the experience of the person of God than in the combating of vice or cultivation of virtue. One hymn recounts the story of the boy Samuel inviting the voice of God, expressing a child's longing to have a conversational relationship with God. In a similar vein, a hymn on the Bible's use in forging such a bond between God and believer opens with a celebration of literacy and of the book as gift, with God as the giver:

> This is a precious book indeed!
> Happy the child that loves to read!
> 'Tis God's own word, which he has giv'n,
> To show our souls the way to heav'n.[6]

What else can we learn about who used this book? A penciled inscription on the first front flyleaf gives the name "Sarah Louisa Martyn," who then wrote "Buffalo 1832." A year after the book's publication, Dorr and Howland's distribution network had reached a girl in upstate New York. Beyond the check marks, there is little else in this hand to indicate young Sarah's reaction to the book, but the next flyleaf offers information about the book's place in a larger life narrative beyond childhood. That leaf bears the ink inscription: "Mrs. R. W. Wright / 161 Orange Street, / 1861." Beneath that, in a meticulous penciled script, appears: "To be given to <u>Grace</u> / I learned hymns out of this / book when a very little girl," and the hand is similar enough to the ink inscription to assume a link between the young Sarah Martyn and the grown Mrs. Wright who now plans to give the book to Grace, most likely a daughter. The reason for thinking this is that one more ink inscription in a different hand appears below the penciled words: "Mother gave me / this on the 4th of March / 1871." This was likely written by Grace.[7]

A remarkable cycle of ownership and memory has unfolded here. After performing a classic rite of book ownership in 1832, Sarah Martyn methodically made the book more internally her own through memorization, and the book stayed with her intimately enough that Sarah Martyn Wright used her childhood treasure to mark a stage in her married life. By doing so she turned the source of her own memories into an external repository of memory, not of the hymns but of the self brought into being by learning those hymns. Sarah received the book into her hands and the texts into her memory, and four decades later Grace received the book as a way of preserving the memory of her mother, the text's memorizer. The Martyn girl's relationship to the book enabled an added bond in her later relationship to her daughter, who chose to create her own memory by preserving the date and source of the gift inside it. The book's life as a guide to practical divinity (John Wesley's definition of a hymn collection) was likely near an end by 1871, as the well-worn cover's tight binding suggests that the book had periods of intense use and long periods of storage. Yet the combination of ephemeral wear and pious preservation has transformed this book into a relic, a memento of a life well spent and a family that guarded its memories.

Before setting this book down, it is worth pointing out that neither Sarah Martyn Wright's Taylor book nor Coral Woodford's Watts book have music in them. Mainly for reasons of production cost but also of portability, interlined music in hymnals was not viable in mass printing until the 1850s, and it was not the norm until at least the 1870s in either the United States or Great Britain. This necessity enabled these books to be read almost as if they were poetry anthologies, and the Taylor book certainly shows the influence of the miscellanies and anthologies that crowded the growing gift book market of the nineteenth century. Indeed, one of the key aspects I want to emphasize here is the hymn's fundamental role in teaching people across the eighteenth and nineteenth centuries how to read poetry, an overlooked but crucial element in understanding the formal evolutions and market expectations of English and American poetry. To begin that story, I turn to one more volume.

This is another Watts book. Even at first glance, it clearly does not share a shelf with the previous two books. The height is little more than the Taylor book (just under seven inches), but the thin page block draws attention to itself with gilding on the three free edges. The boards are bound in blind-stamped blue cloth, and the spine is gilt-stamped with the following golden words between matched ornaments: WATTS'S SONGS—ILLUSTRATED. The color of the spine is considerably lighter than the boards, and the entire binding is in admirable condition, suggesting that this book has spent most of its life displayed on a shelf, rather than being held and perused (some rounding on the free-edge corners might indicate it also did time in a box or crate at some point). The smooth, cream-colored front endpaper shows the single letter *A* in pencil, written hastily and not entirely straight. As with the previous book, the free half of the endpaper bears an inscription. This time, however, it is not in the owner's hand:

> Eliza Anne Walker
> from her dear Uncle Charlie
> on her fifth Birthday
> July <u>28th 1848</u>[8]

This inscription, executed in a confident, beautiful script, offers a clue as to the author of the *A* on the endpaper: could this be a trace of Eliza Anne Walker's early encounters with her present from Uncle Charlie? M. O. Grenby has commented on the tenuous relationship between the contents of books owned by children and the marks made in those books by their young owners;[9] the black ink doodles in Coral Woodford's Watts might suggest that the book found itself in smaller hands than the inscribed owner's at some point.

Unlike Woodford's volume of Watts, this book was designed with children in mind, but with an original price of seven shillings and sixpence (a later bookseller's price on a flyleaf, twenty-five pounds, approximates the modern equivalent), the book was more than seven times the price of the earlier Watts. This was not a cheap purchase but a decidedly middle-class gift for a young, barely literate or preliterate child, similar to a well-made hardcover picture book today. It is unlikely that this edition was intended to be read to death, but what then was its designed use?

The half-title page (a feature missing from the other books) offers some indication: these are "Songs, Divine and Moral: Attempted in Easy Language." The "easy language" is clearly targeted not only to reach early readers but to provide part of their education; Watts's original preface is included in this book, in which he explains that he had reading (aloud), understanding, and memorization in mind as the goals of his collection, which was one of the first of any kind made specifically for children when it appeared in 1715. By this book's publication in 1848, *Divine and Moral Songs* was still one of the most popular—perhaps the most popular—children's title on either side of the Atlantic. This edition displays a very familiar text then, and to the greatest possible advantage: the original designs for the fine wood engravings are credited on the title page to Charles West Cope, a painter of British history and domestic scenes who was elected to the Royal Academy in the same year that these illustrations appeared; Cope later recorded Prince Albert's admiring response to the artist's gift of a presentation copy of the Watts book.[10] Watts collector and bibliographer Wilbur Macey Stone singled out this version as "perhaps the most beautifully illustrated edition of this period,"[11] a combination of aesthetic ambition and shrewd business practice for a publisher whose list at the end of the book highlighted his offerings in architecture and natural history as well as his highly illustrated reissues of canonical works of literature. Watts appears here not as a religious steady seller but as a prestigious brick in the wall of British culture, ready to be consumed for pleasure and edification.

The layout of the text sets up the reading (or not-reading) experience. The large octavo pages offer ample white space on smooth, still-pristine paper; the engravings are liberally distributed throughout the work, some based on earlier stock designs (Elisha harassed by children, mothers reading the Bible with their children, curious children alongside their mother or guardian viewing bees working hives) and others depicting the kinds of scenes of domestic tranquility for which the genre painter Cope was already famous. The illustrations connect well with the texts, but the two media need not be read together; a perusal of the images provides its own pleasure, which may suit a preference either for devotion or for the joys of a good art album. A table of contents, separated along Watts's original division of divine and moral songs, lists the title of each poem, but no first-line or subject index is provided; indeed, these were rarely supplied for *Divine and Moral Songs*, since it was seldom marketed for clergy use and, even at the maximum number of texts, like this edition provides (forty-two), the need for a reference aid was not nearly as great as it was for the collection of hundreds of texts in Woodford's book.

This edition of Watts's book would have been a pleasure to read, or merely to look at, but in any case it was designed to be a gift, marking an important occasion and strengthening family bonds. Watts's original preface anticipated this in a way, since he recommended that parents and teachers let their charges memorize a poem each week as a reward, with the further reward of the volume itself after the children memorized a set number of verses.[12] The original edition was a small pocket volume, typical of early children's books through the end of the eighteenth century before advances in illustration technology would make more elaborate editions for children's use viable. The thingness of *Divine and Moral Songs*, as a site of reward and a token of love, combined with an emphasis on memorization to make this a book whose value lay in many contexts besides reading as we usually conceive of that action. If Coral Woodford's book directed the owner to do little but read it, Eliza Anne Walker's book encouraged her to do almost anything but read it. The canonization of Watts allowed for both the wide distribution of his words and the material bracketing of them.

Does this mean that the content of *Divine and Moral Songs* is beside the point? Hardly. Two of the songs—"The Sluggard" and "Against Idleness and Mischief"—were such popular recitation pieces in the nineteenth century that Lewis Carroll saw fit to parody them in his *Alice* books. One of the divine songs, "Praise for Creation and Providence," appears in many mainline hymnals today under the title "I Sing the Mighty Power of God." Watts's collection in fact proved to be the prototype for new collections of children's verse, coming a full generation before the decade usually accepted as the "rise" of children's literature (the 1740s) and remaining in print well into the twentieth century as a single title, not to mention hundreds of anthologizations, several of which I discuss below. What Watts set in motion in *Divine and Moral Songs* was a way for children to have their own hymnody, one much more closely aligned to poetry because of its separation from church services ("Praise for Creation" being the exception that proves the rule). This was a hymnody that could be read as well as sung, and over time publishers treated the collection and others like it increasingly like poetry. Scholars have pointed to the 1820s and the writings of James Montgomery and Reginald Heber as the key moments in the combining of hymn and lyric poem as literary categories, but those moments emerged from a long history of children's hymnody that rarely observed such genre lines and that were the first verses that many children encountered and memorized, establishing a kind of common-meter grammar for the style and substance of popular poetry quite through the nineteenth century and even beyond, in poets as diverse in style as Robert Frost, W. H. Auden, and Wallace Stevens. By the time Eliza Anne Walker received her Watts book, a new hybrid genre, the private hymnbook, had emerged, which offered liturgical texts—many of them from beyond Protestant traditions—exclusively for private, individual reading. This form had developed from children's collections and the layout that London publisher John Murray borrowed from his Byron volumes to set the first editions of Heber's *Hymns*. It paralleled the introduction, pioneered by Unitarian hymnbook compilers, of popular poetry into hymnbooks for congregational use. And this genre was very much in evidence in the home of a famously hymnic, and private, poet: Emily Dickinson.

Together, the three hymnbooks in this chapter offer a glimpse of the range of uses of hymnbooks in the lives of their owners and readers. A hymnbook could be a symbol for and an influence on who you were and who was with you; it could teach reading or preserve a self through various stages of its development; and it could open horizons in poetry as well as religion. In the three main parts of my book, the three most significant spaces for living with hymnbooks—church, school, and home—set the stage for practices of devotion, literacy, and poetry, though the individual embodiments of these practices move across spaces and intertwine with each other, often in surprising ways. Each of these areas is fleshed out in a series of linked chapters. They may be read separately and out of sequence, though reading in order will convey a thematic, if not chronological, thrust. It has been my privilege to take thousands of these fascinating, often unassuming, frequently tantalizing books into my hands after they have been carried down the years by loved ones and librarians. Now, reader, your turn comes: take, read.

The Wide, Wide World of Hymns

Susan Warner's *The Wide, Wide World* (1850) was one of the most popular American books of the nineteenth century and was greatly concerned with the act of reading. Throughout the novel, heroine Ellen Montgomery navigates the intricacies of purchasing a Bible, analyzing works of history and natural philosophy, selecting reading matter for her free time, writing appropriately worded letters (and parsing those she receives in turn), and developing the discipline to read the Word of God as her mother did before her early death. This fascination with reading has been commented on before, but one particular kind of reading—or, rather, a range of reading techniques revolving around a single book—can open our eyes to the place that hymnbooks held in the literate culture of mid-nineteenth-century America.

The hymnbook makes its first appearance in the novel in the wake of loss and shock; the morning that Ellen is forcibly removed from her parents' house to go live with her aunt, she meets a kind, nameless gentleman who extends solace and wise advice to the traumatized girl. After a serious spiritual conversation, the gentleman chooses to leave her to her thoughts, but not without direction. He takes "a little book from his pocket"—the title is never given—and walks away after asking her to "look over this hymn and think carefully of what I have been saying . . . and resolve what you will do."[1] Even as she cries, Ellen reads the words to Joseph Grigg's "Behold the Saviour at the Door," which turns into a prayer of her own and leads to her decision to seek a personal faith in Christ. Some hours after Ellen returns the book to its owner, she finds herself separated from him by another gentleman who engages the first in conversation; by way of making up for abandoning her, the hymnbook-bearing gentleman surreptitiously takes the book back out of his pocket and hands it to Ellen with a smile as he walks by. Having started as a prop for discussions of personal salvation, the hymnbook has now taken on a new status: as a symbol of the conspiratorial bond between Ellen and the unnamed man and as a substitute for an absent person, which the Bible will soon become for Ellen as she pines for her mother (77).

While the gentlemen continue their conversation, Ellen loses track of time while "studying" and "turning over" the hymnbook; she reads both intensively and discontinuously, not unlike the method of pious reading Matthew Brown has described.[2] When he returns to her, Ellen's new friend is surprised to hear how deep her reading has been. She admits to having memorized two hymns, including the Grigg text, during his absence. He asks if Ellen has a Bible, and on hearing that she does, he offers another present. Taking the hymnbook back, he marks several hymns with a special symbol intended just for Ellen (he explains the difference between it and his own marks for personal reference, already in the pages of the book) and gives her the book with the direction to heed well the hymns to which he has drawn her attention (78). This is a gift loaded with expectations, signs of forethought, and the sharing of favorite texts: the addition of the marks seals the book's status as a precious object in Ellen's eyes. Ellen places the gift in her pocket, and she draws it out again in a private moment that evening, left by herself in the hotel where she and her fellow travelers are spending the night. She seeks again to "refresh herself" with "looking at it"—is she reading or merely gazing at this treasure?—and uplift comes in the form of being "quickly and freshly" reminded of her friend, their "conversations," and her "resolve" (88), the memory of which leads her immediately into prayer, using the words of the hymn to supply the content. The book is returned to its hiding place when others enter the room, but once in her bed, Ellen places the book under her pillow, falls asleep with her hand on it, and wakes with her hand still on the hymnbook.

The hotel scene is not so much about reading as about memory, tracing connections between the hymnbook, its associated people, and the ideas and feelings conjured by those people. If Ellen seems to venerate the book at the expense of reading it, this is because she has already read deeply enough and absorbed enough of the language printed on the book's pages to realize a more immediate religious experience than even intensive reading can offer; she is making the transition to what Paul J. Griffiths calls "religious reading," the deeply attentive immersion of the self into a sacred text that often supersedes the physical need for viewing text.[3] Ellen is beginning to "get it," approaching the threshold of a spiritual gestalt shift she witnessed in her mother and in her new friend but that she has been mystified by when faced with the prospect of making the shift herself.

As Ellen settles into her new home with Aunt Fortune in a small upstate village, she consoles herself with reading when she can; however, her aunt keeps her so busy that she must instead simply think of "her Bible and hymn-book" (117), and the memories of her mother and the gentleman connected with those objects help Ellen maintain her resolve to seek the good despite growing tensions with her domineering aunt. Strangely, when Ellen tells of her encounter with the kind gentleman in a letter to her mother, she mentions him reading to her from the Bible and her resolve to learn to be a Christian, but she never mentions the hymnbook (111). Was this gift too private to be shared even with her beloved mother? Is Ellen unsure of whether her mother will approve of an unknown gentleman—even a devoutly evangelical one—giving her young daughter a gift? If the Bible as object and text brings her closer to her mother, at least mentally, the hymnbook does the complex work of bringing her further in line with her mother's piety while allowing the young Ellen to set herself apart as her own woman.

If the hymnbook fails to grow the bond between mother and daughter, it does provide the occasion for other relationships to blossom. While recovering from an illness, Ellen sits in bed too weak to read but "clasp[ing]" her book since "she felt the touch of it a solace to her" (207). When her friend Van Brunt, her aunt's farm manager, visits her room, she asks him to read from the book to her, just as Ellen read to her mother before their separation. Caught off guard and fumbling through the book, Van Brunt reads to her John Newton's hymn "Poor, Weak, and Worthless though I Am." Ellen exclaims, "Oh . . . how lovely that is!" and weeps silent tears as the farmer reads (214). After Van Brunt returns the book, Ellen notices one of the gentleman's marks next to the Newton text, and she then asks Van Brunt to read it again; it seems that part of her purpose is to begin memorizing the hymn. A few days later, when her new friend Alice Humphreys comes to visit, Ellen is holding her hymnbook again, and she tells her friend that she "was learning that lovely hymn,—do you know it, Miss Alice?—'Poor, weak, and worthless, though I am?'" (222). Without hesitation, Alice completes the stanza from memory. The sharing of a memorized hymn helps to deepen their friendship, and learning hymns becomes Ellen's preferred entertainment during her ongoing recovery; she is doing exactly that the next time Alice visits, and she asks her friend to "talk over a hymn" with her (237). Alice does not understand at first, and Ellen clarifies that she wants Alice to explain a hymn to her as she reads it. Taking the Charles Wesley text "A Charge to Keep I Have"—one of Ellen's mother's favorites—Alice begins the process of turning Ellen herself into a sacred text. Explaining that the hymn calls the reader to serve others and act out the Gospel to the world, Alice tells her young friend, "I have heard it said, Ellen, that Christians are the only Bible some people ever read" (239). Ellen resolves by the end of the conversation to become just such a text, and her spiritual growth increases greatly from this point.

By the time Alice falls mortally ill, Ellen has grown into a consummate caregiver, living out her charge by caring for her aunt and her friend through a series of illnesses and injuries. Ellen cannot restore Alice, but she becomes her patient's "greatest comfort" (437); amid the roses, smiles, readings, and conversations that Ellen uses to ease Alice's sufferings, she sings hymns to her and comforts herself by recalling Alice's favorite lines concerning the glories of heaven.

The value of the hymnbook reaches its climax in the wake of Alice's death, as the Humphreys family's friend George Marshman—the unnamed gentleman who had given Ellen the book—arrives at the house to comfort the mourners. Soon after learning her old friend's identity, Ellen finds herself thinking of him as "like a piece of old music," as if he were a deeply remembered hymn (451). In the very next paragraph after this reflection, Alice's brother John asks Ellen if she would sing a hymn for his father. At this point, Ellen's interior monologue reveals how deeply she has absorbed her reading in the hymnbook and how she uses the memory she has built with it: "And what should she sing? All that class of hymns that bore directly on the subject of their sorrow must be left on one side; she hardly dared think of them. Instinctively she took up another class, that without baring the wound would lay the balm close to it" (451). The selected text, another Newton hymn, begins: "How sweet the name of Jesus sounds / In a believer's ear." A calm hush fills the room as she sings, and as the silence continues she searches for the next hymn: "She thought of the hymn, 'Loving Kindness,' but the tune, and the spirit of the words, was too lively. Her mother's favourite, ''Tis my happiness below,' but Ellen could not venture that; she strove to forget it as fast as possible" (452). The text she settles on is Cowper's "Hark My Soul, It Is the Lord," and as she sings this one, Ellen finds her "task" to be "no longer painful, but most delightful." The narrator comments, "It was very well she could not see the effect upon her auditors": the two Humphreys men, Marshman, and Ellen share the library in near-total darkness (453). And yet as the singing grows easier, "the choice of hymns gave her the greatest trouble." Searching through her memory and evaluating the tones of words and music as a proper fit for the audience and occasion give Ellen a set of remarkable cognitive challenges, and she continues to reject hymns before finding the next suitable one: "She thought of 'Jerusalem, my happy home,' but it would not do; she and Alice had too often sung it in strains of joy. Happily came to her mind the beautiful, 'How firm a foundation, ye saints of the Lord,' &c. She went through all the seven long verses" (453). Gaining further confidence through her own hearing of the words (which "had gone down into her very heart"), she finally chooses a hymn *despite* its being a favorite of her deceased mother as well as Alice: Wesley's "Jesus, Lover of My Soul." The next hymn is "a favourite hymn of them all," James Montgomery's "What Are These in Bright Array" (453). The closing of this hymn finally brings Ellen to tears, and her impromptu concert ends with thanks from Mr. Humphreys.

Ellen had promised Alice to take her place in the family, and hymn singing becomes a crucial way to deliver on her commitment. While Alice's own hymnbook, sitting unused in their pew at church, is a reminder of her absence, Ellen and Mr. Humphreys make evening hymn singing a new family tradition; on Sunday evenings Ellen "was very apt when the darkness fell to take to singing hymns; and it grew to be a habit with Mr. Humphreys when he heard her to come out of his study and lie down upon the sofa and listen, suffering no light in the room but that of the fire" (466–67). While this repeated scene is so reminiscent of the night of Alice's death as to indicate the continued mourning of the family, it has also become a source of pleasure and bonding for Ellen and her surrogate father. Ellen seeks out these opportunities and "made it her business to fill her memory with all the beautiful hymns she ever knew or could find, or that he [Humphreys] liked particularly" (468). Hymns have become a love language in the Humphreys house, and Ellen's work of memorization, which started years before, becomes a key source of her place in the affections of her adopted family.

The hymnbook disappears from the novel at this point, but Ellen's store of memorized hymns allows her to carry the book with her as she moves to Scotland to live with her relatives the aristocratic Lindsays. When asked by her fault-finding aunt, Lady Keith, what her musical accomplishments are, Ellen comments that she can sing hymns. Lady Keith, perhaps the least religious in a spiritually apathetic family, worriedly asks if she can sing anything else. Having recognized the Lindsays' deep Anglophilia, Ellen allows herself a rare moment of teasing by mentioning that she can also sing "Hail, Columbia" (508). Ellen's piety, which has seemed at various times in the novel to be defined by submission, becomes her sole vehicle of self-assertion in the Lindsay home as her grandmother takes her Bible away, she is discouraged from going to church, and the family continually ridicules her religion. Finding a sympathetic spirit in the Lindsays' old housemaid, a pious Presbyterian who knew Ellen's mother, Ellen shares her love of hymn singing with the maid and finds comfort in the memorized songs. Mr. Lindsay walks into her room one day to hear her singing "Rock of Ages" and asks her to sing another to him. Her choice of a Methodist revival song—"O Canaan, Bright Canaan," which Harriet Beecher Stowe would portray slaves singing in *Uncle Tom's Cabin* two years later—strikes Lindsay as sad, but Ellen explains that the content of the songs is what attracts her most (545–56). The words that used to take physical form in a small book given her by an unnamed friend have now become embodied in the reader herself. Ellen has become her hymnbook, and in so doing has fashioned a self that the Lindsays cannot wholly control, despite their best efforts.

PART I

CHURCH

CHAPTER I

How Hymnbooks Made a People

What if a hymnbook could be an article of attire? What if a book carried from home could be not merely a possession but an accessory, a badge, announcing something of the self to a passerby simply by its appearance? As it turns out, hymnbooks often worked in exactly this way beginning in the eighteenth century. An anecdote from Dr. Samuel Johnson's journal illustrates this well. At the 1764 Easter Eucharist, Johnson noticed a young woman approach the altar rail "in a bedgown," a sign of destitution that moved Johnson to give her "a crown—though I saw Hart's Hymns in her hand."[1] In the same glance, the woman's attire moves the habitual almsgiver, and the book in her hand annoys the stolid churchman. Johnson opposed devotional poetry on aesthetic grounds and cared little for the doctrines or politics of Dissent; a collection by the Baptist Joseph Hart in his church would be seen at best as a gross indiscretion. Books of Common Prayer were standard fare in Anglican churches, and indeed they often displayed fine bindings as a way for affluent parishioners to show their wealth and piety. They were used to guide singing, chanting, and corporate reading as well as silent reading in their official form; many copies also had supplements, such as catechisms (and later, hymns), bound in. The poorly dressed woman was likely using her Baptist hymnbook for devotional reading during the service and for demonstrating her right to be there by performing the ownership of a "good book" in a setting where displays of book use were normative. She was both fitting in and asserting her difference—at least to anyone who was in a position to scrutinize her as closely as Johnson apparently did.

Yet as much as the woman's hymnbook singled her out, as it frequently did for Methodists and Dissenters of her day, it also allowed her to announce her spiritual allegiance. Holding a hymnbook gave her visual membership in ecumenical evangelicalism while she kept one foot in the established church. As was true for virtually every other Calvinist church in the English-speaking world, the Church of England had only sung psalms since the Reformation, following Calvin's teaching that texts used in worship could only be inspired ones: hymns of human composition were out of bounds. By the time of Johnson's anecdote, hymns had been slowly making inroads in Dissenting churches (Baptist, Presbyterian, Congregationalist, Independent) for a half century, with interest in hymns greatly accelerating at mid-century with the rise of Methodism and the sweeping transatlantic revivals later known collectively as the Great Awakening. But much of the Dissenting leadership, as well as the Anglicans generally, still thought hymns too uncontrolled, too enthusiastic, and, oddly, too secular for their churches. Singing hymns made a statement not just about the theology and praise expressed in the words, but about one's spiritual identity by the very fact of using hymns, a traditionally private devotional form, in public.

The next several chapters tell a broad story of how hymnbooks moved from the private to the public, even as they continued to inhabit and shape private spaces. The chronological origins of the public hymnbook are part of that story, but the first narrative arc I focus on here consists of nineteenth-century examples of the hymnbook's importance as a mark of membership, a physical and symbolic center around which a worshiping community could declare its legitimacy and its values. Only the most ambitious and radical new communities made the effort to produce a new translation of the Bible, but every group seems to have shared an impulse to create its own hymnbook. These hymnbooks were meant, as the subtitle of a widely popular Baptist collection announced, "for the use of religious assemblies and private Christians."[2] The implications of this description of dual use will unfold across this book, but here I want to highlight what it tells us about the idea of the hymnbook's reader: readers can be both individual and corporate.

Even as Johnson and the woman he saw in church had their individual uses for and reactions to Hart's *Hymns*, they serve as representatives of larger interpretive communities that had their own assumptions and practices when it came to glossing this new liturgical genre, the hymnbook. The compilers of these books were particularly engaged and influential readers, as were congregations, denominations, and the governing bodies within them that decided on questions of the allowance and use of these books. The stakes involved in corporate, institutional acts of reading form the subject of this chapter and the one following, even as the involvement of "private Christians" and non-Christians intersect with those stories. The consolidations, schisms, and strategic choices of large denominations, such as the Church of England or the Methodist Episcopal Church in the nineteenth-century United States, are major parts of this practice, but to understand how the use of hymnbooks was involved in organizing new communities, I focus on more self-consciously marginalized groups to highlight more fully the importance of the hymnbook in the face of theological and cultural controversy. From African Methodists to Latter-Day Saints to Reform Jews, the production of a hymnbook was among the first official acts by community leaders to say to themselves and the world: we are now a people.

The preface to *The African Union Hymn Book* (1822) made this declaration explicit, quoting 1 Peter 2:10 to predict the result of the book's use among its church members: "Then will the high praises of God be set up from East to West, from North to South, and then it may be said, 'they that were not a people, have become the people of God.'"[3] Here the church's identity as God's people blends with the hymnbook's role in instantiating that identity. The book allows for right worship, and right worship brings about a people. By the time the Union Church of Africans in New Castle, Delaware, produced this book, the Philadelphia-based African Methodist Episcopal (AME) Church had already laid out in its *Discipline* (1817) a set of principles for using a hymnbook to ensure right worship, which could describe the approach taken by most—though not all—communities outside the white Protestant mainstream. This was an essential project to get right since it helped announce the new denomination: while the *Discipline* was the first publication of the fledgling AME Church, *The African Methodist Pocket Hymn Book* (1818) was the second. Church leaders' greatest concern was not with the dangers of overly enthusiastic singing but with "formality" in worship, and two of the means of avoiding formality were "choosing such hymns as are proper for the congregation" and "sing[ing] no hymns of your own composing."[4] Only those hymns that had previously been proven to fit the sensibilities and experiences of the congregation could work—not a ready-made book from outside or a homegrown book of new texts. In order to create a unique, legitimate tradition for congregational worship, the *Discipline* argued, a careful selection of existing sources, by definition external to the community, was the best approach for what one scholar has called "the achievement of corporate personhood."[5] The preface to the *Pocket Hymn Book* echoed this sentiment, explaining: "Having become a distinct and separate body of people, there is no collection of hymns, we could, with propriety adopt." A further goal of the hymnbook beyond the principles of the *Discipline* appeared at the end of the preface: "We exhort you to retain the spirit of singing. . . . When the spirit and the understanding are united, it is believed to be a service acceptable in the sight of God, and beneficial to the souls of the people."[6] This blending of spirit and understanding, using a phrase from 1 Corinthians 14, added ideals of knowledge and literacy to the free expression of worship.

The Pauline passage quoted above is one of the most commonly used in hymnbooks across centuries and traditions, and for African American churches in particular it encapsulated the deep desires in their community for maintaining spiritual authenticity while achieving recognition and respectability among their more affluent, generally white neighbors. Richard Allen and his AME associates had these goals in mind when they compiled and published their hymnbook. Allen had already earned the distinction of editing the first two known hymnbooks produced by an African American, both in 1801 to supply his Mother Bethel congregation in the years between their separation from the Methodist congregation of St. George in 1787 and the founding of the AME denomination following Francis Asbury's death in 1816. Those slim early volumes were likely intended for use as supplements to existing canons of Methodist hymnody; Allen used texts by well-known evangelicals like Isaac Watts (an Independent), Anne Steele (a Baptist), and John Newton (an Anglican) in addition to a number of spiritual songs that circulated in revival contexts across a wide stretch of the new nation, from Kentucky to New Hampshire.

At one level, Allen's efforts were dignified protests in a very Methodist vein. American Methodists had infuriated John Wesley years before by adapting their own hymn collections—which frequently included texts by writers like Watts and Steele—rather than using the collections that Wesley had himself crafted, which were in more or less uniform use among Methodists in Britain.[7] Allen's efforts took this American dissent from the Dissenters one step further with the idea that this individual congregation needed its own supplement, its own book. Few of the congregants at Mother Bethel would have been able to afford either the Methodist hymnbook or Allen's (though they would have been cheap books), and it can also be assumed that not all members would have been able to read the hymns even if they were to hold a book. Yet the books were highly usable by the Bethel worshipers because oral and literate practices could reinforce each other through exercises such as reading aloud, and the books' very existence assumed a market, a church, an imagined community united by shared texts and symbolized by a bound volume. The members of the AME Church could be a people of the book not only in their study and celebration of God's written Word but also in their chosen words to respond to God. The ties that bound were expressed in the binding of texts.

The Union Church of Africans showed the early AME Church's influence in its 1822 book, with an eclectic approach to the content and to the use of its hymnbook. A lay movement among Delaware free blacks led by Peter Spencer, the Union Church declared its independence from the local white congregation in 1813, making it the first fully independent black Methodist church in the country. Spencer and his colleagues, in their efforts to guide singing with the Spirit and with understanding, drew from traditional Wesleyan sources and from the revival songs that Allen's church was by the 1810s beginning to suppress. A key reason for this was the ongoing importance of formal, respectable worship services *and* revivalistic meetings in the life of the church. The Union Church's signature tradition was a tent meeting known as Big Quarterly, which drew thousands from as far away as Virginia, some of whom were enslaved people who were granted leave and safe passage to attend the meeting.[8] These meetings tended to shift over the weekend from standardized Christian worship services to social singing, with West African–style ring shouts at the closing. Outside observers frequently remarked on the good discipline of these meetings, especially compared to the raucous, white-led western revivals, and these impressions made by the opening orderly services reflected the presence of *The African Union Hymn Book* as well as its ideals. With standardized texts, to use during the most emotional parts of the service, and the imprimatur of a denominational publication, this hymnbook served as a shield from outside interference, a mark of collective self-control that allowed Big Quarterly attendees space to embrace the folk and even distinctively African roots of their religious experience. That a second edition of the hymnbook appeared in 1829 attests to the book's success within the community and the importance of keeping a steady supply available.

The more urban AME Church, with figures like Allen who could trace their ordinations back to Francis Asbury and his colleagues, took a different approach as it came into formal existence. The dissent inherent in Allen's early books morphed into adaptation, as *The African Methodist Pocket Hymn Book* drew much more on the white Methodist canon and abandoned the revival songs. This volume had the heft of a denominational book and was clearly designed to assert the church's legitimacy among its white peers. As subsequent editions of the book appeared throughout the nineteenth century, the need to demonstrate respectability in the choice and presentation of hymns kept the AME Church's books surprisingly in line with those of white Methodist Episcopal and Baptist traditions, leaving the revival songs out of the books even as such songs formed part of the core of African American spirituality beyond the confines of church services.

A remarkable feature of hymnbooks in African American churches and those of other minority communities is how frequently the most locally significant texts were not *written in* those communities but *read into* them. Not until the 1890s would the now-iconic "Amazing Grace, How Sweet the Sound" appear in an AME book, because its reputation as a revival favorite in the nineteenth century gave it a stigma among African American churches that lasted far longer than it did among white ones. The Union Church, with its easier embrace of revival songs, was the only black church to print "Amazing Grace" earlier—although not until its book's second edition in 1829. By contrast, the text was an early favorite in the Baptist-based *Southern Harmony* and *Sacred Harp* shape-note traditions from the 1830s and was available in all major Presbyterian and Baptist books by the early 1840s; it first appeared in a denominational book in 1789 as an illustration of a point in the Heidelberg Catechism in the Dutch Reformed Church's *Psalms of David, with Hymns and Spiritual Songs*. If revival favorites had an ambivalent place in African American hymnody, Charles Wesley texts, such as "O for a Thousand Tongues to Sing" and "A Charge to Keep I Have," quickly found cherished places in many American traditions. One of the more striking texts in early African Methodist hymnbooks is a text from *The African Union Hymn Book*, "On Afric's Land Our Fathers

Roamed." This hymn's narrative arc bears some resemblance to the enslaved poet Phillis Wheatley's "On Being Brought from Africa to America,"
moving from the ignorance of pagan Africa to conversion through the
Middle Passage and culminating in a vision of spiritual racial equality
through the universal doctrine of original sin. The song has been celebrated by some scholars as an "early example of a hymn written by a black
author that refers specifically to the black experience,"[9] but the text was
actually written by an unnamed white board member of the New York
Sunday School Union Society to give black adult learners recitation texts
that fit their life circumstances better than the juvenile speakers of Watts's
Divine Songs for children—such were some of the many different types of
reading, and readers, with which hymnbooks interacted at this time. *The
African Union Hymn Book*'s editors likely encountered this text in adult
learners' books produced by the New York Sunday School Union Society
in 1818, and they embraced the sentiments ventriloquized in the text, rewriting the original singular first-person perspective as plural first person
and thus rendering the hymn a statement of shared identity and aspiration.
Significantly, the text's white source could easily be ignored in a print culture that seldom attributed hymn texts to specific authors. The common
intellectual property of hymns made it much easier for texts to pass across
racial as well as denominational boundaries.

Yet many hymns, such as "Amazing Grace" and "O for a Thousand
Tongues," had known provenances, named authors as well as the communities that sang them, and hymn provenance often provided something of
a spiritual genome for emerging and established communities, one that
changed over time. Few of these genetic maps are as telling as the early
books of the Latter-Day Saints. Following the tradition of new religious
movements, Joseph Smith commissioned his wife, Emma Hale Smith, to
compile a hymnbook just as the LDS Church was organizing in 1830. By the
time the book finally appeared in early 1836, its journey to publication
echoed the physical and emotional journeys of the community: difficult
pregnancies for Emma Smith, and moves from Palmyra, New York, to
Nauvoo, Illinois, to Independence, Missouri (where an early partial imprint
was likely destroyed in the Mormons' printing office in an 1833 riot), and to
Kirtland, Ohio, where the *Collection* finally appeared.[10] The brief, unsigned
preface to the second edition of the *Collection* used a notably conventional

quotation to declare the church's readiness for a hymnbook: "In order to sing by the Spirit, and with the understanding, it is necessary that the church of Latter Day Saints should have a collection of 'Sacred Hymns,' adapted to their faith and belief in the gospel."[11] This book could communicate to Mormons and to outsiders what they believed, how they wished to convey those beliefs, and what continuities and contrasts existed with other traditions, since it included texts from the range of churches from which the early LDS members originated (Emma Smith, for example, had a Methodist upbringing).

Roughly half of the ninety hymns in the *Collection* were adapted or copied from the hymnbooks previously known to Smith and her circle. The opening text was of Baptist origin. "Know Then That Ev'ry Soul Is Free" had first appeared in 1805 in the Free-Will Baptist collection *Hymns, Original and Selected*, and it enjoyed modest success in Baptist circles through the 1820s. The Mormons, however, adopted the text as a foundational expression of their church; it appeared as the first hymn in Smith's second edition in 1841, remained among the first five texts in the collections through the 1860s, and is still present in current LDS hymnals. While most of Smith's pre-Mormon texts did not have such longevity, the embracing of a Baptist hymn on free will, Isaac Watts's "Joy to the World," a cento of Charles Wesley's "O for a Thousand Tongues to Sing," and other standards of evangelical hymnody indicate that part of the *Collection*'s purpose was to demonstrate the doctrinal and spiritual normality of the Mormons.

Although the composition of the book offered an outward show of Protestant pedigree, the timing of the book's publication reflected the urgency for community life among the Latter-Day Saints. With the destruction of the Mormons' printing press in 1833 and the subsequent move to Ohio, Emma Smith had apparently shown little desire to return to her lost work, but the LDS High Council insisted in 1835 that the book be available in time for the first Mormon temple's dedication in Kirtland. While it is not clear whether the book was in fact available for the temple's dedication service in March 1836, the six hymns sung that day all appear in the *Collection*. Most significant among them is "The Spirit of God like a Fire Is Burning," an original hymn written by Mormon poet William Wines Phelps for Smith's collection, which has been used in the dedication service of every Mormon temple worldwide.[12] The long-delayed hymnbook thus became a vital part of a landmark occasion in the church's history in addition to being an occasion in itself.

The link between book and occasion was also vital for another minority community, the Beth Elohim synagogue in Charleston, South Carolina. Charleston had long been the home of the largest and most assimilated Jewish community in the United States when Beth Elohim dedicated a new synagogue building on March 9, 1841, to citywide fanfare, an event that announced the first Reform Jewish congregation in the United States. Prominent Protestant clergy were invited to give speeches alongside Rabbi Gustavus Poznanski; a newly organized congregational choir, supported by the first organ in an American synagogue, performed several "odes in English" written by congregants at the invitation of the synagogue board. There had been so many submissions that the board was already making plans to gather the hymns offered for the consecration into a collection for congregational use, and the book was brought out the following year.[13] The publication of *Hymns Written for the Service of the Hebrew Congregation Beth Elohim* (1842) was both an event and the commemoration of an event, with a section headed "Hymns Sung at the Consecration of the New Synagogue" opening the book. The book's compilers seemed to treat their volume as a local collection since no preface explained the existence or intentions of the hymnal, but the book's design (hymn titles, stanzaic format, a first-line index for quick reference) made clear the members' desire both for liturgical unity and for cultural recognition as a legitimate faith community in an overwhelmingly Protestant city.

One somewhat unusual element of this book was the inclusion of attributions by providing the initials of the author following each text. Unlike the many-sourced books of the Latter-Day Saints and the African Methodist Episcopal churches, this was an original, homegrown hymnbook, written and published by the congregation for the congregation, and nearly all of the book's original users would have been able to identify the authors by this shorthand technique. Sixty of the texts were composed by one person, Penina Moïse, a nationally published poet. Her father, Abraham, was a trustee at Beth Elohim and was likely an advocate for adding English hymnody to the service; he was possibly a compiler of the book as well.[14] Penina Moïse had become the leader of the synagogue's newly formed Sabbath school in 1839, and her role at the center of Beth Elohim's liturgical and educational reforms made her unique among women in mid-nineteenth-century Judaism. Her role as the de facto author of the synagogue's hymn-book was consolidated in the second edition in 1856: 190 of her texts were included, and the Society for the Religious Education of Jewish Youth, the women's organization that administered the Sabbath school, paid for the 500-copy print run. With the new title *Hymns for the Use of Hebrew Congregations*, the 1856 book identified its readership as ranging well beyond Charleston, though the board's minutes suggest that such a readership was already in mind in 1842. For that earlier edition, the board's original plan for the print run was 400 copies, but as work on the book progressed this expanded to 500, including 22 presentation copies in fine bindings for the hymns' authors and choir members. Also, while the book was priced at thirty-seven and a half cents, 100 copies were distributed in the drawers underneath the seats in the synagogue—an unusual step at a time when Protestant churches routinely expected congregants to provide their own hymnbooks.[15] In a synagogue whose membership hovered near 200, this print run was not merely a matter of ensuring that books could be replaced as they wore out, and the inscriptions to Jews in Columbia, South Carolina, and other regional communities indicate that the book was something of a monument in the Reform movement. The establishment of new Reform synagogues, such as Har Sinai in Baltimore in 1842 and Emanu-El in New York in 1843,[16] provided some of the motivation for the 1856 edition, which sought to keep Beth Elohim and Charleston in the vanguard of Reform Judaism's expression in the 1850s as Charleston's demographic importance to American Judaism had begun to fade. At the same time, in a city that was among the first to elect Jews to positions of local and state government and even to the US House of Representatives, Beth Elohim could display its slim, stately, words-only hymnbook as a badge of integration among the Lutherans, Unitarians, and Episcopalians who had supported and provided models for Reform efforts.

For each hymnbook discussed in this chapter, the impetus behind it was at one level the desire to belong in ways that were literally legible within and beyond the communities that made them. These books were assembled from textual materials across several traditions; even with the unusual home-written book of Beth Elohim, Penina Moïse as the lead writer drew on her acculturation into the secular, sentimental magazine verse of her day and the norms of evangelical Protestant hymnody. In a way, these were efforts to create a fitting suit of clothes out of other people's fashions. For African Methodists, Latter-Day Saints, and Reform Jews, these efforts were largely a success; each community now has long-running practices of assembling and using hymnals that are firmly attached to their corporate identities. These practices were often fraught with conflict, as the situation at Beth Elohim illustrates. Efforts to translate the liturgy into English and introduce an organ into the new building were so controversial that the congregation split, with traditionalists organizing the synagogue Shearit Israel, named for the Conservative synagogue in New York. Although Beth Elohim and Shearit Israel eventually reunited, congregational minutes show that disputes over liturgical choices, hymnbook copyright (held in the synagogue's name), and the meaning of Reform Judaism continued throughout the century.

As churches grappled with questions of cultural accommodation, the politics of their religion, and the role of emotion in worship, hymnbooks often became the sites for proxy battles in denominations, as well as the means of expressing the hopes and anxieties of a community in crisis. The next chapter focuses on conflicts generated and managed with hymnbooks.

CHAPTER 2

How to Fight with Hymnbooks

Book historians, especially those attuned to the study of marginal annotations, have long noted how pointed, animated, and long-winded some readers of theological books could be.[1] More than almost any other topic, doctrine tended to elicit sarcasm, attacks on the author, and lengthy counterarguments in their margins at the hands of exasperated book readers. Yet the hymnbook, which John Wesley described as "a little body of experimental and practical divinity," could also be read in similar ways.[2] Such was the case in M. Bromhead's copy of *A Collection of Hymns for the Use of the Protestant Church of the United Brethren*, published in Bath, England, in 1801 and annotated by Bromhead in April 1814. While Bromhead's identity remains a mystery, his views of the theology expressed in the hymns of the United Brethren, or Moravians, are not. On the volume's front endpaper is a bit of numerical calculation, and the purpose for it becomes clear on the facing flyleaf, where Bromhead points out that 1,167 of the 1,200 hymns are expressed to Jesus Christ alone, who is "very frequently addressed as the All in All"; the hymns addressing the Trinity or the Spirit still unduly emphasize the second person of the Trinity, so that "it may be fairly question[ed] of what use the Trinity is, in their [the Moravians'] system." Apparently well versed in the history of religious error, Bromhead makes an inquisitorial pronouncement: "It is impossible to read the hymns in this volume without perceiving that their general tendancy [*sic*] inculcates Sabetianism & that Christ is the Sole Deity."[3] Bromhead referred here to the obscure Cabalistic sect of Sabbatian Judaism, which had adherents in Moravia and other places; the United Brethren had some interaction with them. However accurate Bromhead's assessment was of the Moravians' theological irregularities, he was sure that their hymns were both the sign and the source of heresy and thus needed calling out.

Bromhead continued his commentary throughout the text of the book, crossing out a line in the litany reading "by my reason and strength" and writing above it "without reason and [strength]"; adding at the end of the congregational response "This I believe" the phrase "to be incomprehensible"; and commenting next to part of a baptism prayer "Shocking." On the book's title page, below the usual printed epigraph quoting Paul's words about singing with the Spirit and the understanding, Bromhead summarized his view of the book with a quip: "it is literally impossible to read these hymns 'with the understanding.' "[4] For Bromhead, hymns could be fighting words, and they called for the same.

Hymnbooks did not need the obsessive theological counterpunches of readers like Bromhead to participate in some of the major conflicts, doctrinal and otherwise, of the churches that used them. The very creation, adoption, and promotion of these books often reflected, and at times drove, disagreements that often led to major schisms, particularly in American Protestantism. In the previous chapter I gave some account of the controversies surrounding the rise of Reform Judaism in the United States and the Beth Elohim hymnbook's role in that process; this chapter focuses on developments in American Presbyterian and Methodist churches in which hymnbooks were implicated and even weaponized in some of the most famous splits in American church history.

From its colonial days, American Presbyterianism had been a doctrinally and culturally diverse community, encompassing psalms-only conservatives, hymn-singing revivalists, and many gradations between. For the first fifty years after independence, the national General Assembly (GA) of the Presbyterian Church in the United States of America had taken a laissez-faire approach to hymnody, leaving the adoption of Watts's System of Praise in various forms as an option for local presbyteries and congregations to consider. After most other denominations had developed their own distinctive collections, the GA began studying "the present state of Psalmody in [their] church" in 1819, and a year later charged a committee with compiling a book,[5] a project that would take more than a decade and the rejection of an already-printed book at the 1829 GA before the book finally appeared in 1831. Separate psalm and hymn sections, as ordered by the GA, were present, as were a subject index and a first-line index. But otherwise there was virtually no organization, since the committee assumed that the indexes would help the book's users find whatever they were looking for. The choice to leave the texts unorganized seems to have been driven by Dr. Archibald Alexander, Princeton Theological Seminary's first professor and a member of the Committee on Psalmody through the entire process. While the committee members are not acknowledged in the official book, Alexander put his name to a related book, *A Selection of Hymns, Adapted to the Devotions of the Closet, the Family, and the Social Circle*, also published in 1831 and intended as a private counterpart to the GA's public book. In the preface to the *Selection*, Alexander explained his rationale for leaving both books unorganized: the arranging of hymns by subject "is incapable of being rendered perfect, or even satisfactory," and "in reading hymns, it is much more pleasant to have them placed promiscuously, than to have all of a kind collected into one place."[6] Alexander expected that most readers would prefer the experience of reading a miscellany, discovering new texts and juxtapositions they did not seek on the way to old favorites, to receiving stricter guidance from the book's design. This ideal of reading echoed the old practice of *sortes biblicae*, the act of opening the Bible at random and letting the eye fall on a text, which was thought to illuminate a reader's concern or question. But it also shared affinities with the burgeoning culture of annual gift books, which offered an array of miscellaneous poems (including hymns), prose, and pictures. This blend of leisure and serendipity, however much it might be appreciated in the parlor, did not seem to cross over easily to the devotional closet or the church sanctuary. Sales of both books were slow, and many readers found the volumes frustrating—so much so that one enterprising Presbyterian saw an unusual, and not strictly legal, opportunity.

In 1834 George Fleming, the leading publisher in Carlisle, Pennsylvania, brought out *Psalms and Hymns for Public Worship . . . Arranged according to Subjects*. This book included all the psalm and hymn texts of the GA's book but reordered them into thematic sections, provided an expanded subject index, titled each text, and added directions for musical performance (though no staff music). This use of the 1831 book's content was even in the 1830s a blatant violation of the denomination's copyright, yet Fleming had been careful to acquire his own copyright for his book, which he insisted was a new and beneficial work. In the preface, Fleming asserted that his edition had "been undertaken with other feelings, than a desire for innovation, or a desire to interfere with the pecuniary advantages which may accrue to the General Assembly . . . from their copy-right." He argued that he was actually trying to save the church from itself: "If it were practicable to make such improvements as would promote the circulation and use of their compilation, and exclude others which had not received the approbation of the Assembly, it was thought that these were considerations of more advantage to the Presbyterian Church than the pecuniary profits which might arise from a limited sale of the original work."[7] The "others" Fleming alluded to were commercially produced hymnbooks, such as Lowell Mason's *Church Psalmody* (1831) and Samuel Worcester's 1820s editions of Watts, which numerous Presbyterian congregations (as well as Congregational and Baptist churches) adopted in preference to the denomination's book. In Fleming's view, ensuring that Presbyterians used a Presbyterian book was more important than respecting copyright. Fleming was himself Presbyterian, a member of the influential George Duffield's First Presbyterian Church in Carlisle, and Duffield's involvement in the book remains an open question. Duffield had been tried and convicted of heresy by a denominational panel in 1833; the trial was highly publicized and helped accelerate the denomination's Old School–New School split.[8] Could the hymnbook have been Duffield's idea of revenge on the denomination? Was this a way to promote his own reforms through liturgical rather than theological means? In any case, Fleming's book quickly garnered enough sales to force a response from the GA.

A dilemma faced church leadership at the 1835 GA meeting. On the one hand, Fleming had clearly violated the denomination's copyright; on the other, Fleming's book was selling well, and there was no reasonable expectation that the official book would be able to recover its lost market share since Fleming had been too savvy in exploiting the most common complaints about the official book. The GA's solution was to buy Fleming's copyright and stereotype plates rather than assert the church's rights via a lawsuit or injunction.[9] Later that year the denomination brought out its own printings of Fleming's book, which came to be called "the arranged edition," alongside the original book (the two versions were printed by different Philadelphia firms). The denomination never publicly addressed the controversy, and the reprinting of Fleming's book even included his preface in which he admitted his unauthorized appropriation of the hymn texts.

This situation was clearly not sustainable, and other disputes over doctrine and polity led to a schism at the 1837 GA meeting into the Old School and New School factions. The struggle over the denomination's hymnbooks only intensified with this split, demonstrating the challenges of uniting even a single faction's hymnody as competing collections rapidly proliferated. At issue in the split was the fundamental question of the relationship between the church's Calvinist heritage and cultural change. And while most historians have focused on doctrine and polity in studying this schism,[10] hymnbooks were a major element in each side's self-definition, intentionally and otherwise.

The Old School, via Alexander and his allies, had controlled the production of the 1831 book, and while no record of public objections appear in the GA minutes, that faction considered the arranged edition to be an affront to the church. When the first Old School GA in 1838 created a new Committee on Psalmody to undertake immediate revisions of the 1831 book, one of the committee's first actions was to order that, while the church awaited its new book, only the plates of the 1831 *Psalms and Hymns* were to be used for new printings.[11] The arranged edition was expressly banned from the Old School churches.

Under the leadership of the energetic, highly opinionated Rev. Robert Jefferson Breckinridge of Kentucky, and in an effort much more focused than that of Alexander's committee in the 1820s, the new committee brought the new *Psalms and Hymns* to the GA in 1842 and published it the following year. A key feature of this book was the restoration of Watts, whose texts had begun to drop out of the 1830s books in favor of more recent compositions. In doctrine, the Old School favored conservative interpretations of salvation doctrine, pointing back to the example of Jonathan Edwards; in hymnody, Watts had become sacrosanct. Though many of their grandfathers had resisted introducing Watts into the worship service, the Old School leadership now generally considered excerpting from the System of Praise as bordering on heresy. Two great virtues of Watts for the Old School were his age and his having produced a nearly full version of the book of Psalms. A significant number of Old School churches were now in their second or third generation of using Watts's books in their services, and having *Psalms* and *Hymns* together made Watts a useful compromise between psalm singers (who were still making their voices heard in the denomination) and hymn singers. That a major denomination would choose to bring substantial numbers of Watts texts back into a hymnbook after 1840—some 130 years after *Hymns* had originally appeared—illustrates how great Watts's standing was in more conservative Reformed circles at midcentury. No longer perceived as controversial or innovative, the father of English hymnody was now firmly at the head of the canon of hymnody, part of the Calvinist heritage around which the Old School rallied.

The Committee on Psalmody, in fact, made early and concerted efforts for the restoration of Watts texts that had been rewritten in the 1831 version. Breckinridge used his position as chair to take a central role in this endeavor. A noted controversialist, he seems to have held Watts up as a symbol of Old School orthodoxy, yet even as the committee sought to restore the number as well as the words of Watts's texts, they also undertook to revise the psalm section using all available sources. The metrical psalm had fallen on hard times by the 1830s, as those interested in writing liturgical and devotional verse focused increasingly on the freer forms of hymnic expression and scriptural paraphrase instead of metrical quasi translation; this was actually following Watts's lead in taking a more personal, literary approach to the book of Psalms than previous writers had felt at liberty to do. Ultimately, the committee concluded that there was no satisfactory way to improve what they admitted was an imperfect psalm section and left the 1831 psalms intact, focusing instead on revising the hymns.[12] The title of the 1843 book, *Psalms and Hymns Adapted to Social, Private, and Public Worship in the Presbyterian Church in the United States of America*, reflects the committee's effort to create the impression that the book formed a united front with Alexander's vision in the 1831 *Psalms and Hymns*—but it would be the last time a major American Presbyterian hymnbook would include a separate psalms section. As the project neared completion, the GA directed the committee to include the Apostles' Creed, the Directory for Worship, and the Shorter Catechism in the back of the book, making the volume more fully a vehicle for Presbyterian pedagogy and uniformity.

Judging by the substantial print runs recorded by the Old School board of publication, the 1843 *Psalms and Hymns* sold quite well and was adopted widely.[13] If the Old School's reverence for Watts was a bit old-fashioned, it was evidently marketable. By contrast, the New School's search for a new hymnody that would reflect its constituents' wide range of attitudes toward

Panel binding in the shape of a St. Andrew's cross on a pulpit copy of *Psalms and Hymns Adapted to Social, Private, and Public Worship in the Presbyterian Church in the United States of America* (Philadelphia, 1843). *Courtesy of Presbyterian Historical Society.*

worship and sacred poetry invited chaos that would plague the denomination well past the Old School–New School reunion in 1870. The trouble
began when Nathan Beman, a pastor in Troy, New York, proposed that
the New School GA adopt a book he had prepared titled *Sacred Lyrics* (1832,
revised 1841) thus saving the denomination the delays, compromises, and
expenses of editing a new book by committee. Beman had powerful connections in the New School's administrative leadership, and the 1840 GA
adopted *Sacred Lyrics*, retitled *Church Psalmist*, without dissent—at least in
voting. A number of other New School delegates resented Beman's success
in self-promotion (he stood to make a considerable profit from the sale of
his copyright), and a group of dissenters prevailed on the board of publication to bring out a competing book, *Parish Psalmody*. As Louis Benson remarked, this led to "open war," involving lawsuits, a pamphlet battle in the
court of public opinion, and a denomination that, even once the GA reaf-
firmed its adoption of *Church Psalmist*, left its churches free to use whatever
they wanted; this freedom of choice had already been articulated in a reso-
lution at the same GA that had initially adopted Beman's book. From his
own investigations, Beman reported to the GA in 1863 that no fewer than
fourteen different hymnbooks were in use across the denomination.[14] The
Presbyterian Hymnal produced in 1874 following the denomination's reunion
still had its competitors, not least *The Church Hymn Book* (1873), compiled
by the leading Presbyterian hymnologist Edwin Hatfield, who resigned
from the *Hymnal*'s committee to make his own book.[15] If the Old School
had seen their 1843 book as an opportunity to consolidate church discipline
in a hymnbook, the larger story of Presbyterian hymnody across the nineteenth century was one of market forces and local preferences.

Regional differences often combined with the market to push the diver-
sification of hymnbooks. After rejecting John Wesley's *Collection* for the
Pocket Hymn Book after American independence, the Methodist Episcopal
Church (MEC) in the United States repeatedly included in the prefaces to
its hymnbooks statements urging American Methodists to buy and use only
the denomination's books—for there were others. In particular, the western revivals had cultivated a rapidly growing body of song texts, largely ignored in the official volumes compiled on the eastern seaboard, and these
texts filled numerous collections printed from New York to Cincinnati
and beyond. Divides between North and South struck all the major US

Protestant denominations in the nineteenth century, but the impact on the church and its hymnbooks was perhaps most dramatic in the MEC, the country's largest Protestant denomination by the 1840s. Pro- and antislavery factions in the MEC became increasingly frustrated with the church leadership's attempt to maintain neutrality regarding slavery, which resulted in such conflicting actions in the late 1830s as the Baltimore Conference's refusal to commission ministers who owned slaves and the New York Conference's suspension of clergy who attended abolitionist meetings or wrote in abolitionist publications.[16] The first major schism was the departure of a number of northeastern churches following the 1840 General Conference to form the Wesleyan Methodist Connection of America. Influenced by their New England Congregationalist neighbors, the Wesleyan Connection rallied around an antibishop, antislavery, and temperance platform.[17] Their social commitments quickly manifested in the church's hymnbook; after a hastily produced book appeared in 1843, the first General Conference in 1844 commissioned a new collection, which appeared the following year, complete with a full twenty pages of antislavery hymns followed by a similar section of temperance hymns.[18] These hymns would almost certainly have been used at prayer meetings and political events rather than during Sunday services, but their presence in the text made an unmistakable statement about the Wesleyan Connection's commitments.

Even with the most vocal abolitionist leaders now absent from the MEC, tensions continued to mount between northern and southern Methodists until a series of protracted debates at the 1844 General Conference resulted in the break into the Methodist Episcopal Church and the Methodist Episcopal Church, South (MECS). The southern church quickly assembled a new book, commissioning a committee of five at its first General Conference in 1846 and publishing in 1847 *A Collection of Hymns for Public, Social, and Domestic Worship*. From its opening pages, this book announced its difference from the old denominational book, claiming a return to the spirit of Wesleyan origins. The preface opened with the judgment that the "Hymn Book of the Methodist Episcopal Church" was "in many respects defective," requiring the committee's "year of laborious application." By contrast, according to the MECS bishops' preface, the new *Collection* was "truly Wesleyan, or rather *Scriptural* in its sentiments, and also in the prominence given to those subjects which are of the greatest importance in the

Christian life."[19] The editorial confusion and lyrical deadweight of the previous collection, the preface's authors argued, were now reformed into a more practical and consistent book, one that was thus truer to the systematic genius of John Wesley than the previous American books had been. At the same time, this was only the second official American Methodist book to unseat Charles Wesley's "O for a Thousand Tongues to Sing" from the number one place in the arrangement. John Wesley had placed the hymn, which has been called by one scholar the "national anthem" of American Methodism,[20] at the start of his 1780 *Collection*, and before the Wesleyan Connection's 1843 *Collection* every American book had followed this precedent. In the MECS *Collection*, however, the new, more intuitive arrangement of hymns began with the attributes of God as Trinity and thematically relocated the hymn that sings the "great Redeemer's praise" to the much later section "Christian Experience," where it led off at number 456. The perfection of one Wesleyan standard had led to the rejection of an old mark of Wesleyan heritage.

Even the name of the church had disappeared from the title; the previous book, first published in 1832, was *A Collection of Hymns, for the Use of the Methodist Episcopal Church*. The MECS had retained the same governing structure as the MEC, had kept the same emphasis on bishops (though they were at first limited to those who chose to secede with the southern churches), and—significantly for the hymnbook's future—had sought to retain the Book Concern. In the 1840s, the denomination's main source of income was its publishing wing, which had offices in several states (generally in the North, including New York and Ohio) and generated materials for church use ranging from hymnbooks to Sunday school curricula, tracts to magazines. The Book Concern was perhaps the thorniest issue in the wake of the North-South split, resulting in a cluster of lawsuits that eventually reached the US Supreme Court—what one bishop dryly referred to as the "appeal to Caesar."[21] Launching a viable Book Concern as soon as possible was obviously a top priority at the 1846 MECS General Conference, and the speed with which both the new hymnbook and the *Quarterly Review of the Methodist Episcopal Church, South* were brought out in 1847 indicates how aggressive the church leaders were about establishing their publishing wing. These two publications served to reinforce each other, and an anonymous author—quite possibly one of the hymnbook committee members—wrote a sixty-page review of the new book in the January 1848 issue of the *Quarterly Review*. The author described the logic of the book's arrangement at length, carefully tracking the omissions, additions, and revisions of individual texts and reiterating the preface's insistence on the previous book's "defectiveness."[22] Drawing on research into the Wesleys' eighteenth-century publications and on comparisons to British editions of Methodist hymnbooks, the reviewer displayed considerable erudition while also making an appeal for the historical continuity of Wesleyan hymnody. In explaining the choice of the epigraph from Milton on the book's title page—"There are no songs comparable to the songs of Zion"—the reviewer contrasted the Wesleyan Christianizing of the book of Psalms to what occurred in Presbyterian churches: "Neither the Wesleys nor their followers ever had the misfortune to engage in the ridiculous controversy which defaced the history of the Scottish Church. From the beginning, the Methodists sang their joys and their sorrows in the language of the inspired Psalms, judiciously appropriated to the Christian state and worship."[23] The reviewer's allusion to the Reformed churches' psalm-singing heritage served to highlight hymn singing as one of Methodism's distinguishing traits. The conflict that had necessitated the 1847 *Collection* was thus sublimated into the practical problem of a defective book and the celebration of a united, ongoing worship practice that traced back to the Wesleys themselves. The hymnbook became a way to emphasize a distinctive identity while denying the magnitude of the church's division.

The dual challenges of the hymnbook and its review in the *Quarterly Review* were clear to the northern church, which organized its own hymnbook revision committee at its 1848 General Conference. The committee included two laymen, one of whom, David Creamer, had recently published the first American hymnological treatise, *Methodist Hymnology*, in which he traced the history of Wesleyan hymnody through its various publications, authors, and texts, including the new books of the Wesleyan Connection and the MECS. In fact, Creamer's work was up-to-date enough to include the *Quarterly Review* article in his bibliographic summary. Yet Creamer's erudition went well beyond that of the MECS committee; obsessed with a years-long quest to determine the authorship of all of Charles Wesley's hymns, Creamer had amassed a nearly complete collection of the Wesleys' verse publications in addition to a substantial library of other hymnbooks.

The committee chair, Dr. James Floy, moved into Creamer's Baltimore home for several weeks in order to access the remarkable collection. The result was a book much more fully informed by textual scholarship than any previous Methodist book had been, restoring Wesleyan originals, including texts from other traditions, and giving newly established author attributions. If the southern *Collection* claimed a fuller embodiment of John Wesley's system, the 1849 *Hymns for the Use of the Methodist Episcopal Church* insisted on a purer presentation of the Wesleys' words, beginning with "O for a Thousand Tongues to Sing." The careful scholarship and attention to textual quality gave the northern church a chance to declare its respectability and sophistication at a time when the church's reputation in the North was compromised by the scandal of the schism. Related to this respectability was the committee's refusal to engage with social issues in its collection. In contrast to the forty pages of abolition and temperance hymns in the Wesleyan Connection's book, the MEC never once addressed either topic in its 1849 book. Floy's leadership likely had great influence here; Floy's brief suspension by the New York Conference in 1838 for attending an abolitionist rally would have left a lasting impression on him.[24] As each new faction of American Methodism was established, its hymnbook became the site for its symbolic self-image; the hopes and fears of the compilers and their conferences were manifested in what each of the books did, and did not, include.

With the onset of the Civil War, Presbyterian and Methodist books took on new meanings and shapes in the face of unprecedented pressures. The New School Presbyterians divided North and South over slavery in 1859, and while the Old School had avoided political controversy by all but ignoring the issue of slavery at GA meetings, the outbreak of war in 1861 led to the southern churches' reorganization as the Presbyterian Church in the Confederate States of America (PCCSA). The new body aimed to continue the pattern of creating a new hymnbook to suit its needs and assert its distinctiveness, passing resolutions to that effect at its first GA in 1861, but two main obstacles hampered the PCCSA's work on its hymnbook. First, committee members found themselves unable to meet due to the difficulties of travel in a war zone, and second, the board of publication was hard pressed to acquire enough paper and type to carry out the limited work their funds would allow. Without access to the stereotype plates of the old editions (which remained in Philadelphia) and with trade with northern suppliers cut off, the southern churches saw what books they already had wear to rags over the course of the war. The psalmody committee's annual reports repeatedly spoke of peace as a requisite for completing the book. To avoid making no progress in the meantime, the committee's chair, Benjamin Morgan Palmer, compiled a manuscript that he hoped would be a point of departure when the committee could convene. At the December 1865 GA, after the denomination had grown by its 1864 merger with the southern New School churches and restyled itself the Presbyterian Church in the United States, Palmer announced that the war had completely defeated the hymnbook: his manuscript and related papers had burned in Columbia, South Carolina, during General William T. Sherman's march that spring. The committee would have to start over. Palmer recommended that a new (less demoralized) committee be formed for the purpose.[25]

What the PCCSA had managed to produce during the war was *The Army Hymn-Book*, a pocket-sized pamphlet that initially included staff music, but as paper and type supplies declined, later editions dropped the music for an increased number of texts—including more hymns from other traditions, such as "Amazing Grace" (then favored among Baptists) and the Wesleyan favorite "Jesus, Lover of My Soul." This was the PCCSA's longest book (editions ranged between 88 and nearly 130 pages), as well as its most-reprinted one, with 15,000 recorded in the GA minutes for 1864.[26] Unable to provide hymns to its churches, the denomination settled for keeping hymns in the field, even while the annual reports indicated the depressed state of the congregations as both congregants and hymnbooks dwindled.

A similar situation developed within the MECS. Unable to maintain printing supplies, the denomination turned its publishing efforts to tracts and pocket hymnbooks for soldiers in the field; a sixty-four-page book, *The Soldier's Hymn-Book: For Camp Worship*, went into dozens of editions of a thousand copies each, while the *Collection* went without reprinting during nearly the entire war. Like the soldiers themselves, these books traveled in all weathers, getting used up at an alarming rate while thousands more came to replace them. Very few copies of the wartime hymnbooks of any denomination survive, and those that do offer a poignant reminder of the impact of the war on southern religion and print culture. In the North, the reprinting of denominational books continued apace, with new books for the soldiers added to the existing lists of publications. After the war, new congregational versions of the southern hymnbooks, particularly that of the newly styled Presbyterian Church in the United States (successor to the PCCSA), were smaller with less scholarship and paratextual material than their northern counterparts. A long-standing cultural divide between North and South had a reflection in the continuing different approaches to the design of denominational hymnbooks. Yet individual reactions to the events of the mid-nineteenth century were often much more forceful and dramatic than those of denominations, and these occasionally found their way into the hymnbooks with which their owners, overcome by the costs and horrors of war, continued to live. Perhaps no greater sign of hymnbooks' entanglement in this traumatic historical moment exists than a penciled comment in the margin of a copy of the 1849 MEC *Hymns* now held at Fuller Theological Seminary: "God the Rebels may they go to evry lasting ruin Amen."

CHAPTER 3

Hymnbooks at Church

On a raw day in late March 1838, Washington Irving sat in his pew, weighed down with grief. In his hands was his Book of Common Prayer, the constant companion of a good Episcopalian, a book that by the time Irving's copy was printed in 1829 offered an appendix of hymns in the back to aid its users' devotional reading (and, occasionally, singing). The small book's simple, stately black morocco binding gave reassurance to Irving's hands by its soft familiarity; his name, pew number, and church were gilt-stamped on the front, assuring that it could be returned to pew 101 at St. Paul's in Manhattan should it wander off. This day, though, Irving's focus was not on the words on the cover nor on those printed in the book. He was dwelling on the loss of his older brother, John Treat Irving, earlier that month. Perhaps this day he sat at his brother's funeral; perhaps it was just before or just after the day of that somber service. We cannot know the exact day, but what is known is that Irving, seeking some way to relieve or witness to his emotions, picked up a pencil, opened his book to a blank endpaper, and wrote simply: "John T Irving left us the 15 March 1838 at 11 Oclock - the Lord have mercy on his departing Spirit."[1] As if the reality of his loss had not yet had sufficient expression, Irving later turned to a rear flyleaf and wrote the same thing again. He left no other marks in the book except these tributes to his brother and to the occasion of that day of intense grief that cried out for some way to mark its presence and ease its passing.

Books of Common Prayer shared with Bibles, psalmbooks, and hymnbooks the status of being part of the furniture of the worshiping Christian in Irving's time. These books lived with their users, some traveling with them from home to church and beyond, others, like Irving's book, standing watch over a rented pew, waiting for its owner's return to his chosen place of worship. Later chapters in this volume follow hymnbooks into homes and schools; in this chapter I relate the practices that linked hymn-books, humans, and other participants in church. In what was known as "public worship" in the nineteenth century, the church service provided for the performance of hymns as read and sung texts, but the church also, through the semiprivate space of the pew, allowed for much more: conversations, memorializations, and the transporting of other texts and objects through the conveyance of a codex that moved with its owner. The question of how people sang together from books with no music in them is worth addressing here, but the answer to that question lies within a larger world of devotion, gossip, argument, reminding, and other actions that brought the worship of God together with life in the world in sacred spaces.

Irving's spontaneous, repetitious acts of memorializing his brother shared in a surprisingly widespread practice of noting significant events or reactions in church. Samuel May Jr., a Unitarian minister in Leicester, Massachusetts, recorded important occasions associated with the hymns in his copy of Francis W. P. Greenwood's *Collection of Psalms and Hymns*.[2] He marked one hymn sung for the anniversary of the Pilgrims' landing at Plymouth Rock as "Thanksgiving / Pilgrims' Day Decr 22nd." Next to a few of the funeral hymns he indicated the date of Unitarian leaders William Ellery Channing's and Aaron Bancroft's funerals. Before the funeral hymn "Clay to Clay, and Dust to Dust," May wrote: "S. J. M. at Grandfathers burial," indicating that May's cousin Samuel J. May presided at the funeral, presumably of Samuel's father, Colonel Joseph May, in 1841. Beside the hymn's third stanza, May recorded simply: "broke down here." May's annotations preserve echoes of the loss of family, the presence of a dear cousin, and the emotional force of a hymn stanza in a few short jottings. May's brevity is remarkable in a book he clearly lived with and marked over a number of years; many of the hymn texts have combinations of +, −, and o marks beside them, part of a private system May likely kept for remembering which hymns he used, or wished to.

A more widespread way of tracking the use of hymns was to record the dates when songs were sung in church, a practice usually done by laypeople rather than clergy. James Martineau, an influential British Unitarian compiler and hymnist, kept just such a record in copies of his hymnbooks.[3] For Martineau, there were particular motives for this date recording; he could visualize his own congregation's reception of his book and potentially use

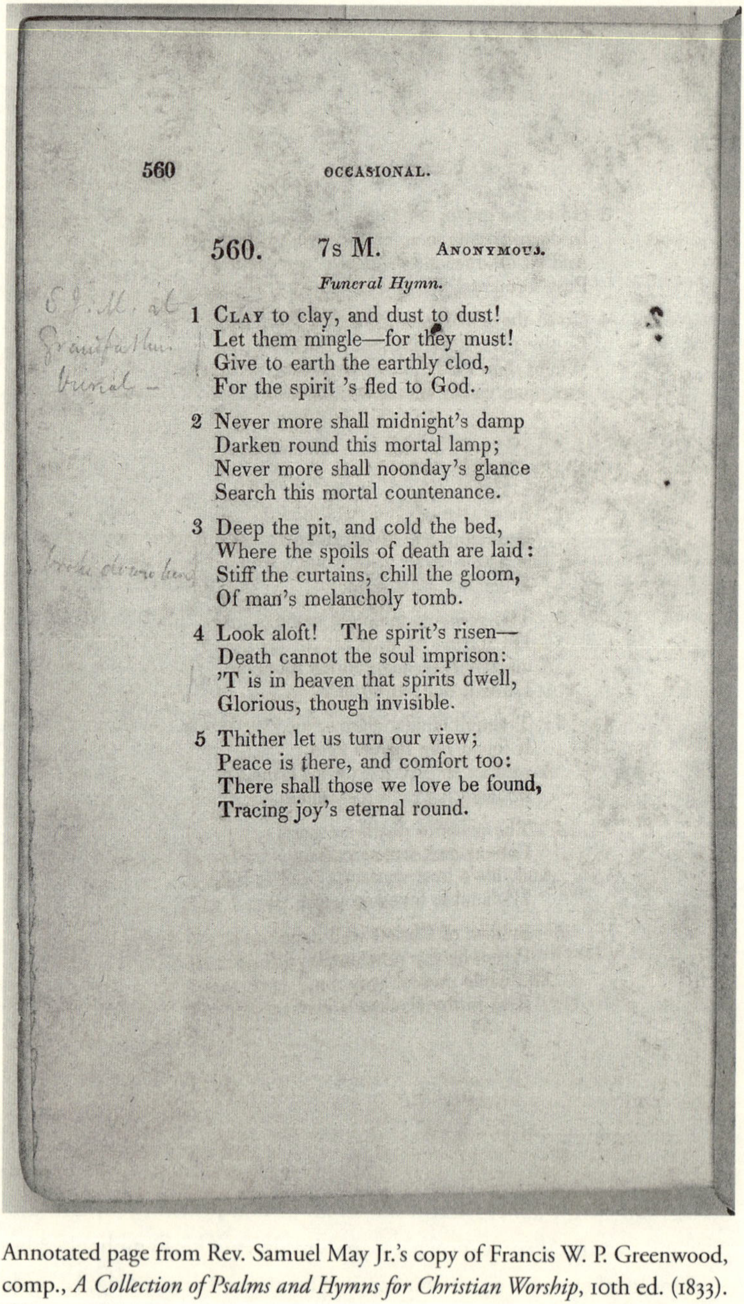

560.   7s M.   Anonymous.

Funeral Hymn.

[handwritten notes in left margin: "E. J. M. at Grandfather['s?] burial —"]

1 CLAY to clay, and dust to dust!
  Let them mingle—for they must!
  Give to earth the earthly clod,
  For the spirit 's fled to God.

2 Never more shall midnight's damp
  Darken round this mortal lamp;
  Never more shall noonday's glance
  Search this mortal countenance.

3 Deep the pit, and cold the bed,
  Where the spoils of death are laid:
  Stiff the curtains, chill the gloom,
  Of man's melancholy tomb.

4 Look aloft! The spirit's risen—
  Death cannot the soul imprison:
  'T is in heaven that spirits dwell,
  Glorious, though invisible.

5 Thither let us turn our view;
  Peace is there, and comfort too:
  There shall those we love be found,
  Tracing joy's eternal round.

Annotated page from Rev. Samuel May Jr.'s copy of Francis W. P. Greenwood, comp., *A Collection of Psalms and Hymns for Christian Worship*, 10th ed. (1833). *Courtesy of American Antiquarian Society.*

that information to guide revised editions. Thomas Wentworth Higginson, an American Unitarian minister and author, recorded his hymn choices in neat columns of paired numbers on the flyleaves of his copy of Longfellow and Johnson's *Book of Hymns*.[4] Most readers who recorded dates were not in the privileged position of the compiler, but through their practice they became self-declared historians of their churches—not of difficult board decisions, disputes, building campaigns, or changes in ministerial leadership, but of the mundane, influential, rarely remarked-on life of the church in its weekly worship. Some such historians also recorded who preached each Sunday and on what text, providing a holistic picture of the church's liturgical life over time.

This hymn historiography generally required the presence of writing implements, most frequently pencils, in the church along with the books and congregants; it thus required some foresight and often some means to keep these records since the larger-format hymnbooks were the best for marking in this way, rather than the cheaper and more popular pocket-size formats. Marking in the margins of these books created a new reading experience, one that gave more emphasis to the hymns that the community actually used, visualizing a canon of practice that led the eye through the book. Not everyone who handled these books appreciated the effect, however; the dates carried their own visual weight and could distract from the text. Tensions over this practice occasionally flared between Henry Onderdonk Jr. and his daughter Elizabeth at First Presbyterian Church in Jamaica, Long Island. The father was a noted antiquarian and a founder of the Long Island Historical Society, but it seems that the daughter was the historian in church. At one point, Henry seems to have lost patience with Elizabeth's practice of filling their book's margins with dates, for he wrote in the gutter of one page: "don't mark this book anymore." The hymn alongside it was Watts's "How sad our state by nature is! / Our sin how deep it stains!"[5] What Henry took to be the staining sin of his daughter's commentary had proven to be too much for him. Elizabeth's name appears in ink on the book's front endpaper in Henry's hand, facing his own signature in pencil on the front flyleaf—could she have taken what Henry considered undue liberty with his property? Or could the book have become her property after Henry considered it unusable?

In a larger-format copy of the same Presbyterian hymnbook, Henry signed his name on the title page with the date December 14, 1861 (at age fifty-seven, he may have preferred the larger print of this format). He also signed his name on the front endpaper, the same place he had written Elizabeth's name in the smaller book. Underneath, the name is repeated, but in a much more stylized form, with a type-style capital *H* and copperplate lettering, though all done in pencil. Was this Henry's idea of decorating his book? Was it Elizabeth's? In any case, on the flyleaf facing these signatures appear several lines in two different hands: "What are you / laughing at"; "Bumble Bee has struck / an atitude [*sic*]."[6] Father and daughter, restricted by the culture of silence during the church service, found that the hymnbook provided space to have a conversation. As annoyed as Henry was by Elizabeth's recordkeeping in the other book, he initiated this conversation, provoked by annoyance and curiosity over his daughter's lack of decorum in laughing (or stifling a laugh). Elizabeth's cryptic, witty response to her father's question uses the nickname for a fellow congregant, Bumble Bee, to pun on "beatitude," displaying a quick sense of humor reminiscent of Emily Dickinson. Indeed, it is difficult not to think of Elizabeth Onderdonk as a sharer in a cultural moment with the Amherst poet; born in 1829, only one year before Dickinson, Elizabeth would have been in her early thirties at the time of this written conversation (assuming Henry's 1861 date represents the start of his ownership). Like Dickinson, Elizabeth Onderdonk never married, and as of the 1900 Census she lived in Brooklyn with her brother Adrian's widow, Mary, and daughter, Charlotte; she died weeks shy of her eighty-eighth birthday in 1917, though if any fascicles of poetry were found in a drawer at that point, that fact has been lost to history.[7]

While striking, the Onderdonk example of conversing in hymnbooks is far from unique. One particularly chatty family was the Hagars of First Parish, Weston, in Massachusetts. The pew owner, Nathan Hagar (born Nathan Hager Jr.), had moved from his prosperous farm to become a partner in his father-in-law Isaac Hobbs's tannery and shoe factory, eventually taking over the business after Hobbs's death. Hagar was a pillar of the Weston community, representing the traditions of the town's old families. For the last fifteen years of his life, he served as town clerk, following his father, his father-in-law, and his grandfather-in-law in that office.[8] His son and four daughters shared a pew with Hagar and his wife, Mary Ann, and the family copy of Greenwood's *Collection of Psalms and Hymns* included dutiful notations of the dates when hymns were sung, who preached and on what texts, and brief passages for meditation, such as one headed "The Church" on the front endpaper: "The collective strength of disciple-ship which Christ might own on the earth."[9] Later excerpts included poetic calls to action, such as Sarah Bolton's "Awake to Effort," Robert Herrick's "To the Virgins, to Make Much of Time," and Adelaide Procter's "Now," suggesting the thin line between sentimental poetry and devotional verse in the mid-nineteenth century. The name Mary (Hagar's eldest daughter) appears below the "Church" passage, and then another hand writes length-wise: "That duet must remind Mr Baldwin of Miss Adams and Miss Adelia Ryan!" The hand of "The Church" passage responds: "Perhaps he thinks more of Cowper!" A conversation has broken out among marks of owner-ship and aids to devotion, with competing goals—a focus on the matter of the service or on the relationships among the congregants, with their memories, histories, and intrigues. While the former is greatly in evidence throughout the book, on the flyleaves the latter is at least as central. Com-ments on the service itself focus on style rather than content: "I wish Mr Sears [Rev. Edmund Sears] would pronounce to—2 not Ter." And when a neighbor brings their dog to church: "Fortunate he is accustomed to hear music—I am afraid he would howl!" Other comments focus on fashion ("Mrs Horatio Fisher has got a new bonnet!"), and a favorite game among the family seems to have been tracing clues in facial features for family connections: "Ellen Stearns looks at this distance like Mrs Frank Cutter" and "that lady in Hasting's pew next but one to the head looks like the Damon family."[10]

While there is evidence of erasure on several flyleaves and nearly all the writing on the rear endpaper has been crossed out, the Hagars' silent con-versations survived through the generations until the book entered the Damon family; Ann Hagar, the second daughter, married a Damon (had she been the one remarking on her future relation?), and her daughter Alice gave the book to the American Antiquarian Society in 1942. There is no way of telling what Alice Damon thought of her ancestors' hymnbook habits, but her willingness to preserve and donate the book suggests that she didn't entirely disapprove. Another copy of Greenwood owned by the Hagars contains further snippets of gossip about the identity of visitors, their professions, and their travels, as well as the underlined injunction: "<u>You ought to stay awake</u>."[11] While attention was not equally focused in the Hagar pew, the family's hymnbooks have left traces of the lively times they had in the silent, sacred space of the church pew.

These conversations were almost certainly *not* written for posterity; they survive likely in spite of the wishes of their participants, and a few hymn-books I have examined have had written-on flyleaves cut or torn out, indicating some censorship by mortified family. Other hymnbook conversations revolved around the issue of keeping children quiet in church. A copy of the 1849 northern Methodist *Hymns* owned by Mrs. A. P. Buss bears a single line written across the margin of a hymn in a child's hand: "I want to lay down."[12] The poet Henry Wadsworth Longfellow, who faithfully dog-eared his 1831 copy of Greenwood's *Collection* to keep track of hymns for devotional reading, drew humorous sketches in his 1840 Greenwood—happy and sad faces, a well-dressed man with smoke coming out of his hat[13]— likely to entertain his young son Charley and thus avoid disrupting the church service.

Faced with the prospect of boredom in church, hymnbook reading could become a game for adults and children alike. The poet-physician Oliver Wendell Holmes Sr., also a respected hymn writer, once explained to a friend his preferred form of play: "Sometimes when I am disinclined to listen to the preacher at church, I turn to the hymn-book, and when one strikes my eye, I cover the name at the bottom, and guess. It is almost invariably Watts or Wesley; after those, there are very few which are good for much."[14] Holmes's preference for the older, canonical hymns, along with his disinclination to listen to sermons, provided a means of textually engaging his Congregational-Unitarian tradition while disengaging from the preacher, the symbolic face of that tradition. For children, privately reading a hymnbook in church held higher stakes, often used as a last resort to avoid punishment for public misbehavior. Lucy Larcom, a popular poet and magazine writer best known for documenting her experience as a "mill girl" in Lowell, Massachusetts, dedicated an entire early chapter of her memoir, *A New England Girlhood* (1889), to "The Hymn-Book." There Larcom recalled fondly reading to her mother around the house, pleasing herself with the beauty of the hymns and her mother with the service of devotional reading she otherwise was too pressed by domestic work to enjoy. In church, however, Larcom's situation was different: "I was told to listen to the minister; but as I did not understand a word he was saying, I gave it up, and took ref-

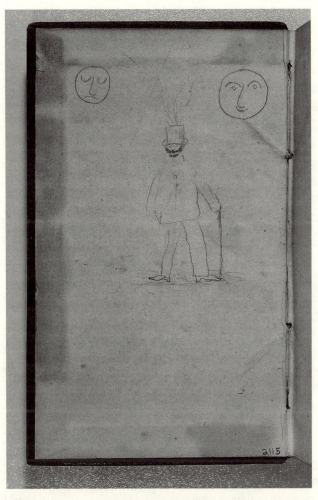

Front endpaper of Henry Wadsworth Longfellow's copy of Francis W. P. Greenwood, comp., *A Collection of Psalms and Hymns for Christian Worship*, 29th ed. (1840). *Courtesy of National Park Service, Longfellow House–Washington's Headquarters National Historic Site.*

uge in the hymn-book, with the conscientious purpose of trying to sit still. I turned the leaves over as noiselessly as possible to avoid the dreaded reproof of my mother's keen blue eyes; and sometimes I learned two or three hymns in a forenoon or an afternoon."[15] If the hymnbook was a play space for Holmes, it was a "refuge" for Larcom, providing an alternative liturgy of hymn texts whose cadences and images gave her more to work with than the prayers and sermons of the formal service did, and (as Larcom was the first to acknowledge) shaping her later career as a poet.

Such quietly rebellious acts of private reading pointed to a difficult fact of Protestant liturgical life. In the nineteenth century, Protestant seminaries generally trained ministers to think of the service in three parts: the prayer, the sermon, and the praise (meaning song). The first two categories were solely the minister's responsibility: the prayer an extended, improvised performance, the sermon a carefully honed feat of oratory. If done well, these could prove entertaining as well as edifying and were often credited with increasing church attendance. The third category, then, was the only part of the service in which the congregation took an active role, making it crucial for establishing worshipers' sense of engagement and investment in their religious rituals as well as anxiety-inducing for those ministers who feared the power of unruly forces in their congregation.

Standard practice since the English Reformation had been "lining out" songs in church, a practice involving a lay leader (called a precentor) singing the psalm line by line, with the congregation singing each line back. This was a way of compensating for the uneven access to literacy and book ownership among sixteenth-century English worshipers, but by the early eighteenth century, particularly in New England, access to reading and basic books was nearly universal.[16] The trade-offs in lining out were many: in relying on untrained precentors with a very limited repertoire of tunes, congregations were notorious for switching tunes halfway through a psalm or slowing a tune down to allow for improvised harmonies and cadenzas around individual notes, to the point where nobody was quite sure which words were being sung or what they meant. Such a situation allowed for the Spirit to guide individual singers, and many congregants treasured this element of worship. But if the participants could not get the point of the text being sung—which was God's Word, after all—the clergy feared that singing was damaging devotion rather than enhancing it.

In the 1720s, Cotton Mather and some colleagues instigated a campaign to educate congregations in reading musical notation so they could sing "regularly" or "by note" rather than merely by ear, an effort that would allow for the expansion of the tune repertoire at any church and bring everyone in musical line (literally) with each other. This reform met so much

congregational resistance that it became known as the "regular singing controversy," but the vehicle for the reform, the singing school, proved popular
enough to become a fixture in American musical life well into the nineteenth
century. Led by self-styled singing masters, either itinerant or locally based,
the schools would last several weeks at a time, concluding with a public
concert by the students and often a "singing lecture" preached by a local
minister for the occasion. All ages and genders mixed at these schools,
making them especially popular among adolescents and young adults, who
were rarely allowed to socialize with the opposite sex. And the music indeed
proved inspiring: recent singing school graduates often organized to peti-
tion their pastor to form a church choir. Not all pastors liked the idea of
bringing the best singers together in a space separate from the rest of the
congregation—before choir lofts became common, the front one or two
rows of pews generally became the choir's "singing seats"—but when the
clergy did allow choirs to form, the result was often mixed from a worship
standpoint, thanks to the addition of a new print genre: the tunebook.[17]

The singing masters' primary source of income was the sale of these
tunebooks, which were elongated volumes of engraved or typeset music with
perhaps a stanza or two of a well-known hymn to indicate the relationship
between text and tune. In practice, tunes and texts were highly interchangeable, and the indications of meter in both hymnbooks and tunebooks facilitated such mixing and matching. The students-turned-choristers carried
two worship books, their hymnbooks and their more expensive tunebooks,
giving them access to a much wider musical repertoire while still sharing a
supply of texts with the rest of the congregation. This new music was often
fun to sing, particularly as three- and four-part harmonies allowed for experiments in counterpoint and antiphonal singing—techniques that largely
mystified congregants who were used to singing their improvisations from a
baseline of unison. The result was that, unable to follow the more sophisticated music of the choir, congregations often retreated behind their hymnbooks, reading along in silence while a select group took over the singing.
While numerous congregations still managed to learn new tunes together
and the recurrence of old, familiar tunes invited vigorous participation
from all, the general rule was that the more musically adept the choir in early
America, the quieter the congregation became. The clergy's great liturgical
problem of the nineteenth century became how to get the congregation

singing again. Hymns had been private devotional reading before they became accepted for congregational song, as I explain in a later chapter. Yet
as congregational music became more impressive, private reading during the
singing, as well as during the sermon and other parts of the service, became
more common and important.

The public reading of hymns was also central to worship in the hymn-
singing church. A now-forgotten practice in worship services, the minister's
"giving out" of the hymn was so much second nature to clergy and congregants before the late nineteenth century that few mentioned it in accounts
of services, and those who did felt little need to explain that it was, as
Emily Dickinson put it, a "hymn from pulpit read." The idea that a minister
would read a hymn to a congregation before the text would be sung together
is so foreign now that accomplished Dickinson scholars have assumed that
the poet was merely referring to preaching.[18] Yet the practice of reading
songs from the pulpit predated the hymnbook, originating during the English Reformation as a first orienting step before a precentor led the lining
out of the song as a way of compensating for less than universal rates of
literacy and book ownership. This was a respected skill among clergy, one
that successful hymn readers advocated and handed down to their mentees,
as Samuel J. May recalled Dr. William Ellery Channing doing for him.[19]

While ministers generally owned their hymnbooks, and some enterprising publishers and editors marketed hymnbooks specifically for clergy use
in their personal devotions, in the nineteenth century many if not most
churches also purchased pulpit copies. These books, usually a larger format
than the pocket-size books preferred among congregants, were often the
only hymnbooks that belonged to the church building, and they were typically donated with a finer-than-usual binding in the manner of pulpit
Bibles. These books provided space for notes on slips of paper or blank pages
for hastily written reminders (one note in an 1843 Greenwood says simply:
"Speak to the boys").[20] Surviving pulpit hymnbooks tend to show signs of
heavy dog-earing, though the corners have generally been unfolded again;
folding down page corners was the easiest available marking system to allow ministers, including visiting preachers, quick reference to the texts for
a given service. This could occasionally cause confusion between preacher
and choir or musicians, as in the case of Unitarian minister Samuel Longfellow's first guest sermon. Having selected his hymns over Sunday break-

fast using an unfamiliar book, Longfellow gave out the hymn at the appointed time. The choir master, from his place behind the congregation, shouted across the church that the choir had no tune to fit that text's meter (indicating how accustomed choirs and congregations were to matching and rematching tunes to texts on the fly). Without a pause, Longfellow directed the choir to the next text, expecting it to be on the same topic—it wasn't.[21] This exception demonstrated the rule: reading the hymn from the pulpit, a poetic performance alongside preaching, praying, and singing, was experienced as a natural element of the flow of worship.

Hymn reading, whether through singing, private reading, annotating, or giving out the text, was a quietly central practice in Protestant worship for well over a century, so much so that the placing of the hymnbook in the pulpit could be considered as important a dedication-day action as placing the pulpit Bible. A well-worn, large-format 1842 copy of the Methodist *Collection of Hymns* tells just such a story about a new church opened that year in a small town on Maine's Kennebec River:

> Presented by Miss. Mary
> L. Trott, on the day of the
> Dedication. Oct. 20. 1842;
> For the use of this Pulpit,
> Of Woolwich ME. Sing with the Spirit
> And with the understanding.[22]

Mary Trott's gift reflected her Methodist congregation's commitment to singing, and the connections shaped by that gift highlight how much the hymnbook lived not merely as a commodity or an individual keepsake but as part of the ties that bind in a community. The hymnbook's role in building and remembering interpersonal relationships and community is the subject to which I now turn.

CHAPTER 4

Giving Hymnbooks, and What the Hymnbook Gives

Hymnbooks were practical things, a good like many others available in the general stores of the eighteenth and nineteenth centuries: they had key uses in home, church, and elsewhere, as I have shown. But they also had a talismanic power for many owners, creating a bond through hand, eye, and voice to God, to worshiping communities, to friends and neighbors, and to family and departed loved ones. Hymnbooks were big business by 1800, and they became a prime element in the gift economies of the industrial era. William S. Cuddy of St. Louis, Missouri, understood this well. Upon acquiring an 1856 pocket edition of the New School Presbyterian *Church Psalmist*, a book produced on steam-powered presses in New York and sold by the thousands from Providence to Cincinnati to San Francisco, he took this industrial object to a deeply personal level. Using a factory-made pencil, a breakthrough in nineteenth-century writing technology, he turned to the book's front endpaper and wrote in a wobbly but dramatic script: "Wm S Cuddy from hisself."[1] The spelling and orthography suggest that Cuddy's formal education was indifferent, but he knew enough to understand that it was in the nature of a hymnbook to be given, and in a parody of the convention of gift inscription—with which he was also clearly familiar—he marked his social relationship to a book that has long outlived him.

Cuddy's hymnbook highlights the interplay between the mass-produced and the personal, the common language of the gift, and the space for self-expression that typified the power of the hymnbook as gift. In its interpersonal manifestations as gift, the hymnbook shared in practices that involved Bibles, novels, rewards of merit, travelogues, devotional books, and by the nineteenth century the growing phenomenon of the ornamented gift book—some of the latter relying partly or exclusively on hymns for their textual content. Yet hymnbooks' ability to straddle the worlds of literary and religious reading, of song and private reflection, and of display and use made them particularly flexible and ubiquitous gifts by the dawn of industrial printing.

Recipients of hymnbooks tended to keep them for long periods of time, often for life, but layers of regifting could also accumulate in a single copy. Such is the case with a copy of *A Collection of Psalms and Hymns, for Social and Private Worship* (1820) in the Jay Fliegelman Collection at Stanford University. The minister Henry Devereaux Sewall edited the *Collection* anonymously to offer a more literary and theologically authentic hymnbook for Unitarians, who still largely relied on Watts—revised to avoid Trinitarian ideas—by 1820. The book's title suggests that it was meant for less formal venues ("social and private worship") rather than Sunday services (public worship), and this copy demonstrates the book's power in private circles. On a front flyleaf is a gift inscription from "the compiler" to Catharine Maria Sedgwick, who helped recruit contributions for the book from the recently discovered poet William Cullen Bryant and who would become a literary star with her first novel, *A New England Tale*, in 1822.[2] In her novels, Sedgwick declared her independence from her Calvinist upbringing in western Massachusetts, and her hymnbook speaks to the relationships she was forming among the Unitarians of her adopted city.

Sedgwick apparently read her gift, beautifully bound in red morocco with gilt tooling and a gilt page block, with sustained attention, judging by the "index" of favorite texts on the front endpaper (partly but not all in her hand) and a few annotations that reflect her wide reading in literary history, such as a note below an excerpt from Christopher Smart's "Song of David": "written by Smart on the walls of a Mad House."[3] However, the best evidence of how she read the book, and to what end, comes from the same flyleaf that bears Sewall's delicately written inscription. Filling the page below is a much longer, more rapidly written inscription from Sedgwick:

> To my friend Mrs
> Fitch—the faithful kind
> & dear friend of many
> years I give this book
> which has been my
> companion & solace thro'

the vicissitudes of many
years—May it go to
you my friend, with
the unction of a
Christmas & farewell gift
[signed] C M Sedgwick.[4]

Memorializing the event of the gift by dating it was not as important as calling to mind the scenes of friendship and reading that made these two women present to each other. For Fitch to hold this book was to recall her friend and the relationship Sedgwick had with this book, her "companion," by reading and living with it. Fitch was free to layer her own reading history onto Sedgwick's (and she may have contributed to the "index"), but the gift by no means demanded such reading. Possession was enough for it to be her companion as well.

There is no clear evidence of Fitch's reading the book, no marks that can with any confidence be identified as hers. It may very well be that she never read much beyond her friend's inscription, but the book records one important action she took with her gift. On the front endpaper below the handwritten index, an unnamed woman has written: "From Mrs Fitch I received the only birth-day gift ever made me."[5] Fitch may have written a note with the gift; perhaps she merely handed the book to its new recipient with a kind word, or an anecdote about Sedgwick. One possible reason for the absence of a third inscription was that the book was by now something of a relic in the devotional sense. Beyond its hymnic contents and denominational affiliation, it was marked as touching the life of one of the nation's most famous authors, a value that might compete with all others. If Fitch hesitated to overwrite this object, the new owner saw fit to memorialize the act of receiving a book that certainly meant more to her than to the giver.

Sedgwick had received the book as a literary and intellectual equal, from a writer to a writer (though neither was widely known at the time). She had given the book on equal footing through the conventions of middle-class female sociability. Something different seems to have been at work in Fitch's gift; she may have known the recipient as a lower-ranked volunteer at one of her societies or maybe even as an object of charity. In any case, the book was received this final time not as charity nor as a Sedgwick relic but as a birthday gift—a gesture demonstrating recognition, if not equality. This last recipient was not accustomed to being recognized, and her name is lost to history. But her tribute to the beauty of a gift in an economy of scarcity indicates how much had changed in the book's meaning as a gift over the years—the book's power within the gift economy was multidimensional and malleable.

If the last recipient of the Sedgwick book is anonymous to us, we can guess who Fitch was. One likely candidate is Mrs. Anna J. H. Fitch of New York, whose name appears with Sedgwick's among the members of several ladies' charitable societies in Manhattan.[6] Given Fitch's and Sedgwick's interest in prison charities, there is a distinct possibility that the woman who received Fitch's gift was a former convict. A hymnbook would have been a natural choice for such a gift in the 1820s. In 1819, the Quaker reformer Ann Alexander in York, England, published *A Selection of Hymns, Designed Principally for the Use of Prisoners*, and a year later the New York Quaker publisher Mahlon Day reprinted the book. Day is most famous today as one of the first major children's publishers in the United States, and he seems to have found the jump from prisoners to children an easy one to make, for in 1824 he repackaged his Alexander book as *Hymns on Various Subjects*. The running head at the top of the pages continued to read "Hymns, for the Use of Prisoners," and of the two known copies of the 1824 title, the Library of Congress's copy bears an inscription to a prisoner, while the American Antiquarian Society's copy was given as a reward of merit to a Sunday school student. Alexander's original collection focused the first section of hymns for "juvenile delinquents," reprinting copiously from Watts's popular children's book, *Divine and Moral Songs*, so perhaps the distance between prisoners and children was not so great in the eyes of social reformers of the day (one initial goal of the Sunday school movement was to get delinquent children off the streets on the Sabbath). Certainly, children and prisoners shared an identity as objects of charity, and the hymnbook was the ideal "good book" to give both populations.

Another means of negotiating between the anonymities and intimacies of charity giving was the 4,000-copy print run—a huge one for the time—of Watts's *Divine and Moral Songs*, which was produced in keeping with the will of Samuel Phillips, a former lieutenant governor of Massachusetts and founder of the Phillips Academy in Andover. In his will, Phillips created an endowment for the printing and distribution of select devotional works to all the families in Andover.[7] This was meant to be a repeated, indeed perpetual, endeavor, but while it is not clear how long the holy papering of Andover continued, the Phillips Academy trustees did produce the Watts edition at least once in following their charge. The books were published as small pamphlets wrapped in wallpaper, and they used a remarkable trio of paratextual elements to perform and interpret the act of charity in each copy. First was a manuscript inscription to each recipient—whether to heads of household or to children is unclear—followed by the Phillips coat of arms, which literally stamped another ownership on the title page. If the inscription announced the move to a new owner, the coat of arms declared a provenance, symbolically keeping each pamphlet in Phillips's library even as the many copies circulated throughout the town. Finally, a preface explained the bequest and its intent to edify the children of the town, even if they could not attend the academy; this sought to negotiate the odd dual ownership already signaled by pen and print. The book's printer, William Hilliard, proprietor of Harvard's press, later prepared the edition for retail without the coat of arms and the preface, thus freeing the book for new routes of exchange, gift, and ownership. The Phillips edition displayed one of the great paradoxes of charity even after the supposed end of the age of patronage: the gift, as a bond between giver and receiver, is never wholly free.[8]

While giving hymnbooks grew to become big business, as in the case of Hilliard's contract with the Andover trustees, hymnbooks themselves had much to give. For one thing, they were codices, bound volumes that provided space to store (and hide) small objects, including other pieces of paper. Because of their value in home and church contexts, hymnbooks also gave the gift of mobility, more so than most other book genres, which tended to remain in the spaces where they were used (parlors, schools, closets). These gifts, which sociologists call "affordances," made hymnbooks particularly adaptable to many uses in and out of the gift economy.[9] Charles Ackworth, an AME minister in Worcester, Massachusetts, kept quarterly communion tickets in his 1861 copy of *The African Methodist Episcopal Church Hymn Book*; all congregants had to have a valid ticket to receive communion, and Ackworth was prepared to hand one out in an emergency. The tickets bore a verse from Isaiah and the first stanza of Charles Wesley's "And Wilt Thou Yet Be Found?"[10] When Ackworth's parishioners asked him, they

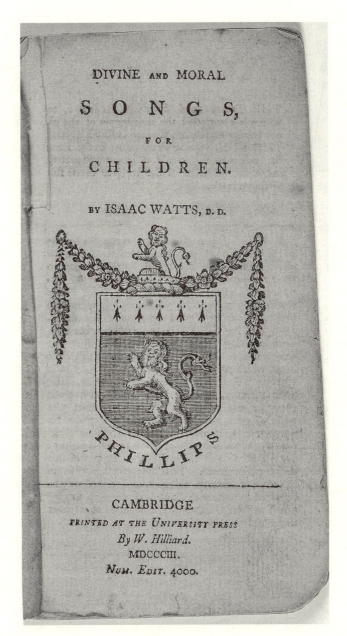

DIVINE and MORAL

S O N G S,

F O R

C H I L D R E N.

By ISAAC WATTS, D. D.

PHILLIPS

CAMBRIDGE
PRINTED AT THE UNIVERSITY PRESS
By W. Hilliard.
MDCCCIII.
NUM. EDIT. 4000.

Title page of Phillips Academy in Andover's edition of Isaac Watts, *Divine and Moral Songs for Children* (1803), displaying Samuel Phillips's coat-of-arms. *Courtesy of American Antiquarian Society.*

could be assured that his hymnbook-turned-wallet could give them access to the Lord's Supper. More romantic uses proliferated among hymnbook owners as well. A number of hymnbooks survive with clippings of
love poetry in them, presumably to hand to or show a prospective sweetheart
at an opportune moment. Most of these were innocent enough, though
they could be rather forward and comic. One left in an 1828 *Sunday School
Hymn Book* reads:

> What's sweeter than bees do sip,
> I 'spose as how you know that's honey,
> Ah! yes, one thing—from woman's lips
> A kiss is sweet—aint that funny?[11]

No evidence survives as to the success of such stealthy approaches to
courtship, but major life events of the love and marriage variety did leave
traces in a wide range of books. Hymnbooks were a standard gift between
spouses, particularly from husband to wife, and parent-child gifts are frequently noted on the flyleaves of books. In his copy of William Cowherd's
Manchester-produced *Select Hymns* (1823), "Master John Ogden" recorded
his children's births.[12] The marriage of Walter King and Elizabeth Moore is
recorded on the flyleaf of a finely bound copy of John Inglesby's *A Selection
of Free-Grace Hymns* (1807); while the year has been cut out of the page, a
wealth of detail remains, including the date, the officiant, the owner of the
house where the wedding took place, and even the hour, "7 Oclock Even."[13]
These books, so often carried in the hands of their owners, held memories
always ready for access.

Hymnbooks could also help to reinforce very precise notions of denominational identity, as in a large-format book belonging to Joseph Curtis
Platt of Scranton, Pennsylvania. Platt was one of the founders of First
Presbyterian, Scranton, and indeed one of the city's founders as a partner
in the Scranton brothers' ironworks. The church's elders of Session pushed
reform in congregational singing in the 1860s, going to the lengths of dis-
solving the choir and reorganizing it as a vehicle for training the congregation in song; the church adopted hymnals with music in the 1870s.[14] No
sign of conflict over these decisions appears in the Session minutes, but in
a blue envelope glued to the inside of his hymnbook's back cover Platt carried a newspaper clipping from the *Presbyterian*, a weekly newspaper pub-

lished by the denomination. The clipping discussed the 1869 case of a Philadelphia congregation in which the Session and the board of trustees went through two levels of church courts before turning to the state's Court of Common Pleas to settle the question of which group was authorized to hire the organist. The trustees had charge of the facilities, including the organ, and thus argued that they should choose the organist; the elders were responsible for the spiritual life of the church, including worship services, and thus argued that the organist was in their purview. The civil court made the same ruling that both church courts had: the elders of Session had authority over the organist. Platt had carefully underlined every statement in the article mentioning the session's authority, making the clipping a carefully prepared weapon against the threat of dissension in his church, and he apparently carried the clipping in his book until his death in 1887.[15]

More secular accumulations also built up in hymnbooks. James Floy, chair of the editing committee for the northern Methodists' 1849 *Hymns*, apparently traveled with a compact copy of the book, using the flyleaves for writing notes that have since been ripped out and leaving a railroad ticket agent's card, which remains in the book to this day. Other hymnbook owners stored insurance coupons, decorative bookmarks, ribbons, expense lists, ads for real estate auctions, embroidery offering Bible verses or words of encouragement, and the leaves and flowers more commonly associated with literary books. Robert Wilson used his Old School Presbyterian *Psalms and Hymns Adapted to Public Worship* (1841) to store snippets of business correspondence. Many of the short missives date from the 1860s, which, combined with the word "Choir" written on the edge of the page block, suggests that Wilson may have gotten his book secondhand, so as not to spend too much hard-earned cash on his hymnbook. As an inserted newspaper clipping said:

> Oh! this is a brave world that we live in,
> To lend, to spend, or to give in,
> But to beg, or to borrow, or to get a man's own,
> 'T is the worst world that ever was known!

The poem, titled "This World," faced a James Montgomery hymn that began:

O Thou, my light, my life, my joy,
My glory, and my all!
Unsent by thee no good can come,
No evil can befall.[16]

The portability as well as the storage capacity of the hymnbook as codex allowed for strange juxtapositions of sacred and secular devotion.

Mary Laurence Love's copy of *A Collection of Psalms, Hymns, Anthems . . . for Use in the Catholic Church* (1830) manifests devotion through accumulation. A lifelong resident of Washington, DC, Laurence had her name gilt-stamped on a red morocco binding, marking the book right away as a treasured keepsake. After her 1831 marriage to William Love, she wrote on a flyleaf: "Mary E. Love's Book March 16. 1832." Over time, she accumulated prayer cards and saint cards in her book, aids to devotion not normally connected with books but in Love's case creating a kind of holy portfolio.[17] This was somewhat typical of Catholic hymnbook use, but holy cards were not exclusive to Catholic books. A hand-colored woodcut holy card of St. Adelaide appears between the pages of a copy of the American Tract Society's *Family Hymns* (1838), an evangelical collection given to Jane Nichol as a New Year's present in 1839 by her teacher.[18] Whether the holy card has any connection to Nichol or not, her book's survival gives us a glimpse of the hymnbook's ability to share in practices and print cultures across denominational lines.

The hymnbook itself could become a powerful social conduit between loved ones, living and dead. A sonnet by the Anglican hymnist James Edmeston, "On Singing from the Hymnbook of a Departed Sister," imagined participating in the love and piety of the departed by holding and using her book.[19] To touch a book was to experience the echoes of loved ones and events held in memory; it was a material reminder of the communion of saints through whom the present moment touched eternity. One owner of a morocco-bound copy of *The Hartford Selection of Hymns* (1831) made an especially striking attempt to maintain access to a departed loved one through her book by attaching a framed photograph to the front cover. This alteration rendered the book virtually unreadable, transformed from a source of devotional text to a miniature shrine, one from which the countenance of an unidentified young woman stares out at the reader forever.[20]

A photograph of an unidentified woman is attached to the cover of Nathan Strong et al., comps., *The Hartford Selection of Hymns*, 8th ed. (1831). *Library Company of Philadelphia.*

While this photograph-bearing morocco cover is an extreme instance, a number of binding styles tended to discourage the reading, or at least frequent reading, of the books' contents while simultaneously celebrating and venerating the religious purposes the books were meant to serve. Black and red morocco covers often bore gilt ornamentation, including gilt page blocks; at times, the owner's name was gilt-stamped on the front cover as well. These binding styles echoed those of Bibles from the same era, but in the late eighteenth and early nineteenth centuries most of the small books that were bound in such fine forms were either hymnbooks or books of poetry—books meant to be held close as personal keepsakes, cradled in the hand, but also presented on end tables or shelves. These were books to be treasured, displayed, and enjoyed, whether through the reading of their printed words or otherwise. Bindings became even more sumptuous over time, including velvet covers, metal borders and clasps, and panel bindings that imitated the dramatic appearance of pulpit Bibles. One of the most extreme adornments I have found on a hymnbook is a fore-edge picture of a whaling scene on a copy of the 1847 Dutch Reformed (US) *Psalms and Hymns*.[21] Fore-edge painting was a luxury practice, most often done with large, fine books to enhance their aesthetic value for bibliophiles. To choose a hymnbook as the canvas for a fore-edge painting seems counterintuitive, though whether this was done by an owner or a professional painter (the picture is signed only with the letter *H*), it does make the book an object of contemplation in a new way, taking attention away from the text inside and placing it firmly on the physical surface of the object. Indeed, little attention seems to have been paid to the texts inside this book. Yet whatever importance whaling held as a visual subject for the book's owner, it is especially striking that this particular hymnbook should bear such a scene: the Dutch Reformed *Psalms and Hymns* was Herman Melville's source for the hymn sung in Father Mapple's chapel in *Moby-Dick*.[22]

An unusual binding technique for hymnbooks in the early nineteenth century was the strap or wallet binding, involving a leather cover that wrapped around the book and was closed by slipping a narrow tongue of leather through a strap. This style of binding was generally seen on diaries and pocket journals during this era, and it often had internal pockets and loops to hold small pens or pencils.[23] Some surviving hymnbooks have wallet bindings that include pen loops, but such books were rarely marked.

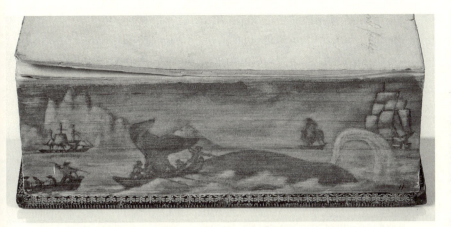

Fore-edge picture of whaling scene. Dutch Reformed Protestant Church, *The Psalms and Hymns* (1847). *Courtesy of American Antiquarian Society.*

The binding signaled not added utility for carrying small objects, as with the pocket diaries, but rather, a greater security in carrying the books; in addition, the aesthetics of the extended leather cover might have mattered more to purchasers and owners. At the heart of the choice of a wallet binding was the idea that hymnbooks were for living with across the various spaces of a person's life. Hymn texts were often recorded in diary entries of the period, testimony to the neighboring placement of two of the most lived-with print genres of the century.

The importance of hymnbooks for their owners' everyday lives and the ability to enhance or even transcend the everyday with a fine cover made the hymnbook an ideal carrier of memory. From the Sedgwick and *Hartford Selection* examples above, it is clear that hymnbooks had a way of standing in for their owners even after the books had survived them. I close this chapter with a description of a more multilayered action of preserving personal memory in a hymnbook. In the James Thin Collection at New College, Edinburgh University, is a hymnbook made for the Episcopal chapel in Dublin's Lower Gardiner Street. Hymn singing was apparently an early fixture in the congregation's practice: the first edition of *A Selection of Hymns Used in Trinity Church* appeared in 1841, less than two years after the chapel opened for Protestants on Dublin's north side. The book is a slim octodecimo (18mo), typical for a locally produced collection.

These books were apparently well used and needed replacement often; this copy is of the second edition from 1845, which was followed by a third edition eight years later. The first clue as to why this copy survives is its sumptuous cover of gilt-stamped blue morocco with a gilt page block. This book would have sold for a mere shilling, but an owner transformed it into a precious object.

On opening the book, another kind of value emerges. On the first front endpaper (which appears to have been pasted onto the binding when it was made) are two inscriptions. The first commends the book "To the beloved Elizabeth Brown, From her attached Elizth Macgregor," and it is dated "Drumcondra Dublin November 3d 1845." This already precious book has become a sign of love between dear friends, a favorite use of the hymnbook as gift. The location indicates a suburb of Dublin, some two miles northwest of the church—a surprising distance for a regular attender in Dublin at that time. Perhaps Elizabeth Brown was a member of the Trinity congregation, or perhaps this gift brought Elizabeth MacGregor's local spirituality to her more rural friend. This church-specific collection thus expanded its locality to mark and strengthen a friendship.

The book also celebrates another friendship, but only in memory. The second inscription is to "M. C. Wilson in remembrance of her friend Mrs Lundin Brown who entered into rest <u>February 12th 1868</u>." Below this inscription is a reference to Isaiah 35:10, which reads: "And the ransomed of the Lord shall return, and come to Zion with songs and everlasting joy upon their heads: they shall obtain joy and gladness, and sorrow and sighing shall flee away." This text, possibly from Elizabeth Brown's funeral, asserts hope in the midst of sorrowful memory. Whose hand wrote the inscription or whose decision it was to give this particular volume to M. C. Wilson is not known, though the formality combined with the heavier, more vertical pen strokes suggest that Lundin Brown may have written it. If this is the case, the page bears witness to a marriage as well as the widely accepted convention of using the book itself to record its relationships and relocations.

If the endpaper inscriptions attest to the intimate circles of friendship in which the book participated, the writing on the flyleaves points to the much larger circles of reading and allegiance that informed those friendships. On the next flyleaf, two texts have been transcribed. The second is a composite of Revelation 14:3 and 21:7, popular texts for funerals that speak of the saints'

new song in heaven and their inheriting all things. The first text deals with
similar ideas in verse:

> The men of peace have found
> Glory begun below,
> Celestial fruits on earthly ground
> From Faith and Hope doth grow,
> Then let our Songs abound

These lines, seemingly written from memory, are from an Isaac Watts hymn
that originally ran to ten stanzas. The hymn was adopted widely and indeed
appears in this very volume—though the quoted material does not. The
five-line quotation changes Watts's "men of grace" to "men of peace" and
ends with the first line of a stanza located two stanzas below the first in the
original version. It would have been rare that this text would be printed including the two quoted stanzas without the intervening one, and I have
yet to find a version that substitutes "peace" for "grace." In the context of
their transcription the substitution is understandable, since it shifts the
emphasis from the subjects' salvation to their repose, a more consoling association in what appear to be memorial texts for Elizabeth Brown.

The question remains where the inscriber would have found and memorized the Watts stanzas. Most reprintings of these stanzas in the nineteenth
century were in editions of "Watts entire," collections favored by more conservative Calvinist churches (such as Scottish Presbyterians) that retained
all the hymns and psalms in the original System of Praise. Another Presbyterian connection appears on the next page of Wilson's volume, where
a hand very similar to the one that wrote the memorial inscription to Wilson
has transcribed a description of the saints on earth learning to sing in the
heavenly choir; this was taken from an 1844 sermon by Rev. John Duncan,
the longtime pastor of the Free Presbyterian Church in Glasgow and a
professor at the Free Church College (now the New College, which houses
the James Thin Collection). The inscriber likely found the sermon reprinted
in a religious magazine, and this, taken together with the Watts text, suggests
that Elizabeth Brown was a Presbyterian with ties to the Free Church of
Scotland in addition to having an "attached" friend connected with the
Church of Ireland. This religious combination may seem surprising in
a world as fragmented along denominational lines as nineteenth-century

Dublin, but the fact that the book, dressed in a fine binding, was worth giving, worth keeping for more than twenty years, and worth giving again to preserve the owner's memory speaks to the hymnbook's ability to unite across several lines of affiliation, even when the book itself had been created to consolidate a precise, localized identity. The bonds of memory could make the hymnbook an instrument of peace even as it participated in ongoing debates about the nature of grace.

CHAPTER 5

Devotion and the Shape of the Hymnbook

In the preface to his *Church Psalmist*, New School Presbyterian minister Nathan Beman emphasized the importance of the book not only for the public life of the congregation but also for the private life of the minister: "A brief course of Lectures on Lyric Poetry, is hardly less necessary than a course on Sermonizing and Pastoral Theology; and a preacher of the gospel should read and study the best Psalms and Hymns, as an every-day-business, as he does his Bible, till he is acquainted with their sentiments, familiar with their structure and imagery, and deeply imbued with their spirit. . . . His volume of sacred poetry should be a Text-Book by the side of the Bible, and he should be equally familiar with both."[1] While seminaries never seemed to make a lecture series on poetry a standard element of liturgical training, the idea that the hymnbook should live next to the Bible in an individual's devotional life, whether clergy or laity, was broadly accepted in Beman's day. Devotional reading was by definition intensive, focused on rereading a few books rather than continually picking up and putting down new ones; people returned to favorite texts, memorizing and meditating on them, living for years with a single hymnbook until it was worn out or replaced by a different collection. In the vast majority of cases, the only trace left by this practice is the absence of the thousands of books that were read to death. The scarcity of copies of most pre-1820 editions is partly the result of this consuming reading, and the relative lack of clergy-owned hymnbooks in archives today compared to, say, Bibles, might owe something to this phenomenon as well. In surviving copies, the patterns of wear on covers, spines, sewn bindings, and pages suggest frequent use, habits of mind and body that Matthew Brown has called "hand piety."[2] Navigating a hymnbook involved tacit knowledge: the feel of a book in the hand, the design of the index, and the paratextual matter heading each text helped set the terms of devotional reading, and it is the interaction between book design and book use in devotional practice that is the subject of this chapter.

James Craft's copy of Watts, a 1788 *Psalms* bound together with a 1787 *Hymns* from the same Philadelphia printer, shows a particularly hands-on devotional reader at work. Who James Craft was or where he lived remains a mystery, but his hymnbook indicates that his devotional life combined rigorous organization, ecumenical reading, and an associative, playful dimension one might not expect.[3] Craft's copy of *Psalms* was a new revision by Connecticut poet Joel Barlow, who in 1785 brought out an Americanized version of Watts's System of Praise.[4] Watts's effort to make his psalm paraphrases relevant had included not only inserting New Testament theology but also updating references to the Israelite nation and its king to mentions of Britain and its monarch, details that proved embarrassing to Watts's American adherents after independence.[5] Barlow had included a first-line index to his version, but the 1788 Philadelphia reprint seems to have omitted that detail.[6] The solution, likely by Craft's request but possibly on the bookbinder's initiative, was to include several blank pages between the printed subject index and the first page of Psalm 1. On those pages Craft carefully wrote his own first-line index, with an imitation of a printed capital letter heading each sublist and the texts in page order under each letter rather than in strict alphabetical order. This index would have guided Craft's perusal of the book as he sought particular texts for singing or reflection, but in the remaining blank pages, Craft actually used his index as the starting point for a multistage recording of his reflections.

The last entry in the index is for "Ye sons of Adam join," a rendition of Psalm 148, and following the entry, Craft repeated the line, followed by a formula he would use several times in the subsequent pages: "These Words puts [*sic*] Me in mind of some Words, dropt by Paul [this name was retraced several times so that it appeared bold], some years ago," leading into a quotation of 1 Corinthians 15:22 concerning the resurrection. This was immediately followed by a quotation of another hymn, "Christ from the Dead is rais'd, & made / The first Fruits of the Tomb," taken from an appendix to Nahum Tate and Nicholas Brady's Anglican version of the book of Psalms, which Craft cited as "<u>Church</u> Prayer Book: Hymns," adding the "31st Article of <u>their</u> Creed"—which is actually another two stanzas from Watts's

Psalm 59.[7] Further quotations from Watts, from the popular Baptist *Selection of Hymns* edited by the English minister John Rippon, and from the book of Romans (in which Paul continued to "drop" his words "some years ago") fill the next several pages, ending only with the start of the printed psalms. Craft's version of Watts was a Presbyterian book, which had borrowed from Barlow's Congregational one, and Craft's use of Anglican and Baptist sources—the latter including a Wesley text—indicates that his spiritual outlook was not denominationally limited, even if he bristled at other churches' theology ("<u>their</u> Creed"). The treatment of Pauline excerpts as something like dinner conversation, the "dropt" words, exhibits a familiarity with the Bible in multiple senses, and the hymnbook's owner took a decidedly long view of sacred history—not only were Paul's words "dropt" "some years ago," but each of several instances of Craft's ownership signature in his book gives two dates: 1790 and 5790, the latter following the Jewish calendar. Such an odd combination of displayed learning and informal association is certainly an outlier in the history of reading hymnbooks, but Craft's choices point out how many books and motives could pile up in the use of a single book.

As it turns out, Watts had set the terms for Craft's interaction with his book, not only through his content (which Barlow had revised), but also through the innovations in book design he had introduced in his System of Praise. Dubbed the father of English hymnody, Watts defined an era in the history of British Dissenting Protestantism: an Independent minister who was born the year John Milton died and who lived to see the Great Awakening, he spanned the transition from seventeenth-century Puritanism to the later age of evangelical revivals. Watts was certainly not the first Englishman to write and publish original hymns, but no one occupied a more central place in the transition from psalmody to hymnody, or exerted more influence on the subsequent history of hymns in English. While the hymn, the psalm paraphrase, and the children's hymn all existed before Watts wrote in those genres, his approach made him the best-selling English verse writer in the eighteenth century—and possibly of all time. Explanations as to how Watts achieved such success tend to focus on his verse style, the freshness of his approach to the Psalms, his ability to write for the common person. Without discounting these arguments, I want here to look past the poetic genres Watts remade to the print genre he invented outright: the hymnbook. The design of *Hymns* (1707) and *Psalms* (1719) was as new as anything in the contents, and this design shaped an entire culture of devotional reading that extended more than a century beyond Watts's own time.

Watts's motives and aims in writing hymns have become the stuff of legend. Hymnody was apparently something of a rebellious youth movement for Isaac Watts and his brother Enoch, both of whom were so bored with the psalm texts at church that their father challenged a young Isaac to write something better. And he did. After more than a decade of composing hymns and other verse, Watts as a young minister brought out his poems in *Horae Lyricae* (1706), not long before *Hymns*. These were self-consciously experimental volumes; Watts led with *Horae Lyricae* ("sacred lyrics") to see whether he could manage a following as a poet before offering his more controversial project, and he revised and expanded both books in 1709 after soliciting feedback from readers. In a career that would produce dozens of publications, including sermons, catechisms, textbooks, philosophy, theology, and devotional guides, it is remarkable that Watts made poems and hymns his first books. No controversialist, Watts sought to bring denominations together through hymns, though he knew he was asking for a fight in attempting to introduce hymnody to church services. The hymns that Watts grew up with were devotional poems, used only rarely in liturgical settings. Thanks to Calvin's dictum that only the Word of God was fit for public worship, Anglicans, Congregationalists, Presbyterians, Independents, and Baptists could agree on at least one thing: psalms should be the primary content of congregational song. Successful hymnody before Watts was what worked on the page and in personal or family devotions. It was a literature of privacy that had accepted the enforcement of that privacy with few exceptions.

So why did Watts believe that a new practice, with an arguably new kind of hymn, was necessary? And why did anyone agree with him? As a pastor and an educator, Watts was deeply invested in the promotion of reading as a means of piety and inward authenticity. Watts did not invent genres so much as practices, ways of using and living with the texts he made, and these practices had to be taught both through instruction and through a careful use of print conventions to guide book users' behavior. Watts proved to be a master of the two techniques.[8] The prefaces to his volumes were a major part of Watts's instructional strategy; the preface to *Horae Lyricae* has been called one of the most important critical statements of the century and that to the *Psalms* is considered "revolutionary,"[9] but in *Hymns*, there are a few crucial innovations, subtle paratextual additions that tell a great deal about how Watts intended his books to be used.

In the most popular hymn collections of the late seventeenth century, a standard practice was to title each text by its main subject and then provide a numbered, alphabetically arranged table at the front or back of the book (or a section of it) to make the finding of a text easier. Both William Barton's *Century of Hymns* and John Mason's *Spiritual Songs* did this by the 1680s, and Barton's book even included engraved tunes by 1688.[10] In *Horae Lyricae*, Watts included a page-order table of contents; unlike in Barton's and Mason's hymnbooks, the texts in *Horae Lyricae* were only paginated, not numbered, keeping with Watts's intention to present them specifically as lyric poems rather than hymns. Something altogether new appeared in *Hymns*: an alphabetical first-line index followed the preface. For the first time in a hymn collection, a reader could find a text not only by its subject but by the words.[11] This indicated the kind of intensive reading Watts wished to cultivate among Dissenters; a first-line index is only useful to those at least cursorily familiar with a text, whether from previous reading or from hearing, and this type of index would come to be a defining mark of the hymnbook. The use of a first-line index or a table of contents often indicated whether an editor or publisher wished for readers to engage a book's contents as hymns or poems. Hymns were part of a deeply oral culture, even after printed hymnbooks were widely used, and Watts was keenly interested in giving his readers an easy return access to the hymn as it was "handed down" to the reader through memory and hearing as much as by lettered reading.[12] Another new feature appeared in the table of contents following the hymns: cross-references that would help a reader interested in hymns about Jesus, for example, look also under the headings "Lord" and "Christ." This forerunner to the subject indexes of later hymnbooks facilitated use by ministers looking for a suitable text and by lay readers interested in subject matter that might not normally be covered in the Psalms. The substantial essay on psalmody that closed Watts's volume made an impassioned argument for moving beyond literal psalm texts in worship to better reflect both the message of the gospel and the experience of the Christian.

The response to the 1707 *Hymns* was obviously positive and rapid; while Watts's essay sparked controversy, he brought out a second edition in 1709 (the last edition he altered) that not only included revisions but also incorporated around 150 new texts. In expanding the scope of the book's contents, Watts also added new apparatus to support the kinds of use he expected for his book. One such addition was the scripture index, identifying in biblical sequence which verses were the bases for which hymn texts. This again was a great aid to ministers who might be more interested in a hymn that used a sermon's text than one that emphasized a certain theme. This index also made an implicit argument for Watts's project: Watts dropped his major essay from the 1709 edition of *Hymns*, partly to save space (it would reappear in expanded form in the 1719 *Psalms*), and the new index invited readers to see how closely Watts was following the Bible—as well as how much more of it could be used by hymns beyond the book of Psalms.

If his new indexes directed readers into, through, and beyond his books in novel ways, another key addition to the 1709 edition went to the heart of what Watts thought his book was meant for. He added "crotchets" (brackets) around stanzas to indicate which could be dropped for corporate worship.[13] Watts realized that an eight- or twelve-verse hymn could be wearying to sing. Most churches in Watts's era still resorted to lining out congregational song, a practice Watts loathed but realized he would not be able to eliminate; communities and their customs still wielded great power in deciding how worship would be conducted, even in those progressive congregations that accepted Watts's approach to hymnody.

The crotchets demonstrated Watts's sensitivity to two realities: a sung collection of hymns would also continue to be a read collection of hymns, and the demands of reading and singing differ from each other. Watts's hymnbook would have to inhabit multiple spaces and practices and move between them if it was to be successful, and the crotchets provided guidance for navigating between those practices. In the first edition's preface, Watts had mentioned that while he hoped his book would be accepted for public worship, he wanted it to at least aid private devotion, and many congregations came to use Watts's book in services only after clergy and lay members had become familiar with the hymns as devotional texts. But the rapid appearance of the second edition indicated that the book was indeed finding a place in public worship, and Watts adjusted his apparatus to further meet the demand he was in part creating.

While the practice of bracketing verses did not become standard in later hymnbooks as first-line and scripture indexes did, the idea that hymns could be used as longer texts for reading and shorter texts for singing did take hold, although not universally. One of the frequent objections made in the last two centuries to considering hymns as poetry is that true poems cannot be excerpted. While the history of poetry anthologies is ready evidence against this claim, from Watts onward the hymn has in fact been excerptable, perhaps more so than any other genre, and that excerpting helped to fan Watts's popularity in more than one country.

Boston minister Cotton Mather became one of the most important excerpters of Watts's hymns, in effect introducing Watts to the American colonies by including Watts hymns in several of his sermon pamphlets. A December 1711 entry in Mather's diary records the arrival of a gift copy of *Hymns and Spiritual Songs* from Watts himself. Mather expresses his joy over the gift in terms so effusive they tended to ignore Watts: "I receive them [the hymns] as a Recruit and a Supply sent in from Heaven for the Devotions of my Family." The family setting was for Mather the natural place to "sing them, and endeavour to bring [his] Family in Love with them." It was for similar domestic purposes that Mather planned to encourage local booksellers to stock the volume and congregants to buy it, "and in this way promote Piety among them."[14] While the gift seemed to inspire new efforts by Mather, he in fact already owned the first edition of Watts's *Hymns* and had reprinted selections from it and from John Mason's 1685 *Spiritual Songs* in a 1709 work, *Family-Religion Urged*, a how-to guide for heads of household leading family prayer, which was published simultaneously in London and Boston. The hymns may indeed have been sung by families using Mather's book, as they almost certainly would have been by the musically inclined Mather family at some point. But in *Family-Religion Urged*, the point of the texts was that they were texts—printed matter that may be rendered into speech and thereby into shared devotion, prayer, and spiritual renewal. For Mather, Watts's hymns were powerful in large part because they worked so well as texts: they did not need to be sung to "promote Piety" among Mather's readers.

Mather's use of hymns as formal, spoken prayers followed earlier Dissenting practices exemplified by the influential Richard Baxter, who silently inserted one of his own hymns alongside several "psalms" as forms of prayer in *The Poor Man's Family Book*, a catechesis and prayer guide designed to condense all of practical divinity into a single volume for poor families.[15] Mather himself had a long, rich history with hymns as a reader and writer; the same month he celebrated his Watts gift, he recorded a hymn in his diary that he composed while suffering from a severe headache. His reaction to receiving the new, expanded *Hymns* speaks to the power of the personal use of hymns, as well as to their importance as printed material to be disseminated and marketed.

It was entirely appropriate that Mather would provide Watts's entry into American print. In addition to being perhaps the most-imported author in British America during the eighteenth century, Watts became the second most-printed author in America during that time—second only to Cotton Mather.[16] As correspondents, the two Congregational ministers exchanged news, printed and manuscript writings, and plans for mission efforts in the growing colonies. Watts provided one of the first gifts to the library of Yale College (characteristically, a set of his own works) and arranged for the first publication of Jonathan Edwards's *A Faithful Narrative of the Surprizing* [sic] *Work of God* (1737), the account that helped to internationalize the Great Awakening.[17] As a minister, theologian, and liturgical reformer, Watts saw America as a new space for building the Dissenting church, and among his most influential contributions to that effort were his System of Praise, his book of hymns, and his paraphrases of the book of Psalms, which from the 1740s onward would often appear bound together in Calvinistic churches on both sides of the Atlantic.

The System of Praise entered congregational worship in America in the 1740s, as Edwards joined revivalists such as George Whitefield and Samuel Buell in introducing the laity to Watts's works on a scale unknown before. Mather and his contemporaries were staunch psalm singers in church, but even before 1700 Mather had already begun to develop the hymn as a kind of paraliturgical vehicle for some of his sermons. One of the key elements of Mather's prodigious bibliography was sermon pamphlets, and as early as 1696, he included hymn texts in those pamphlets to reinforce his sermons.[18] Between 1696 and 1701, Mather silently inserted hymns of his own composition into three different sermon pamphlets.[19] Each of these pamphlets included at least one sermon given outside a typical Sunday or Thursday service, which may have made the author more at ease in adding a hymn text; as Mather had asserted in an earlier sermon, "There are savoury *Hymns*, of an Humane Composure, which no doubt we may praise God by singing of,"[20] despite the recognized preeminence of the Psalms in public worship. The hymns in the pamphlets give no explicit indication as to whether or not they were meant to be sung, but they amount to miniature, rhymed versions of the sermons, aids to memory as well as emotionally concentrated summaries of Mather's discourses. It might not be too far from the truth to imagine that Mather had in mind George Herbert's famous line, "A verse may find him who a sermon flies."[21] The hymn as a devotional text within the sermon pamphlets was even more removed from public liturgical space than the sermons were. Sermon pamphlets were reconstructions of oral performances that only became fully written documents after the decision to publish had been made, since most preaching was done from notes or memory.[22] If the sermon pamphlet transformed an oral event into a textual object, it rendered the hymn a textual ancillary to the sermon text, helping to make the sermon the main event in a context outside the worship service.

Mather's use of Watts proved influential among regional clergy. By 1740, no fewer than seven other Massachusetts pastors, some of them luminaries of their day, had published sermons that included Watts texts. When Jonathan Edwards's congregation began to show signs of unusual revival, Edwards published his 1734 sermon *A Divine and Supernatural Light* as a reminder to his people of the blessings they had received since the preaching of that sermon. On the final page of the pamphlet, Edwards included a hymn by "the Excellent Dr. *Watts*" that dealt with the same text the sermon had treated. Following Mather's lead, Edwards encouraged the use of hymns as devotional reading in concert with the reading of sermons, and this form of reading could reasonably be expected to be familiar to many of Edwards's readers as the movement that became the Great Awakening expanded.

Yet other forms of reading, more public and potentially more political, were emerging in Edwards's Northampton as well. Edwards found on returning from a guest preaching trip in 1742 that his congregation had decided (without his input) to sing from Watts in their services and "neglected the

Psalms wholly." The singing of hymns had been introduced in Edwards's absence by the young revivalist Samuel Buell, who not only impressed the Northampton congregation with the verve of his hymn singing but drove Edwards's wife, Sarah, to ecstasy while reading the hymns in her home. Edwards dryly commented, "When I came home I disliked not [the congregation's] making some use of the Hymns: but did not like their setting aside the Psalms."[23] Edwards negotiated to allow hymns in the Sunday afternoon services during the summer, while retaining the Psalms for Sunday mornings and other congregational exercises, but this was the first fault line to form between him and his congregation, a rift that would steadily widen until Edwards's dismissal in 1750. Clearly, there was power in the reading as well as in the singing of hymns, but that power could lead to tension and conflict.

It also led to solace, especially in the lives of individual hymn readers. More than a century after Watts had decisively entered American churches, Carrie Chippey recorded the gift of a hymnbook from her father on its front endpaper. Chippey's father, Rev. Edward H. Chippey, was Peter Spencer's successor as head of the African Union Church (formerly the Union Church of Africans) in Wilmington, Delaware, and one of the compilers of *The African Union First Colored Methodist Protestant Hymn Book* (1871), the first book made for the African Union after its merger with other local African Methodist churches and the book that Carrie Chippey received. The importance of the church's Methodist identity was clear in the book's preface and in the choice to place Wesley's "O for a Thousand Tongues to Sing" as the first hymn. Carrie seems to have spent a considerable amount of time with her book, the lone surviving copy of the edition: the covers are worn and detached, her name is written on the flyleaves, and two brief handwritten indexes point to her favorite hymns.[24] None of the favorites, it turns out, were of Wesleyan origin. In the first index, Augustus Toplady's "Rock of Ages" was listed (by number) above a Philip Doddridge text and a camp meeting song. In the back, Watts's "I Sing th'Almighty Power of God" and "Lord, Thou Hast Searched and Seen Me Through" topped the list. Chippey had asserted her ownership of the book on the facing flyleaf, writing: "Carrie Chippey's Book Feb. 24. 1889." Above the index, however, she wrote a more unusual inscription: "Carrie Chippey's peace." A product of her father's leadership in an African Methodist church, Chippey's book had become a companion, one in which her manuscript alterations took her back to the texts she had taken to heart and had likely memorized at least in part. Memories of singing, reading, and living were woven into the writing of those hymn numbers. Chippey's personalized index was an inscribed path to peace.

Philadelphia, 1844

In the early hours of Thursday, May 9, 1844, the aftermaths of three fires glowed in a sleepless Philadelphia. For the third straight night, violent riots had rocked the city, fed by months of growing tensions between nativist, anti-Catholic organizations and resentful young men of the burgeoning Catholic communities that supplied much of Philadelphia's new industrial labor force. On Monday, nativist mobs had broken into a convent and several homes; two nativists and one Irishman were killed in related gunfire. By Wednesday, the state militia had assumed positions around the city's Catholic churches, hoping that the crowds would stand down before further blood was shed. But that night, the previously attacked convent burned, along with St. Michael's Church in the Catholic-heavy Kensington neighborhood. This was shocking enough in a city that prided itself on a history of religious pluralism and patriotism. But around 10 p.m., St. Augustine's Church on the Old City's affluent North Fourth Street was set ablaze, while rioters broke into the neighboring rectory and threw that building's thousand-volume library into a bonfire, scorching the Methodist church across the street. The riots left Protestants and Catholics aghast.[1]

When it appeared later that Thursday morning, the weekly issue of Philadelphia's *Catholic Herald* gave breathless, one-line notices of the previous night's violence, hastily added as news came in while the paper went to press. The editor lamented, "Where these lawless acts are to end, cannot be told." On the back page, crowded with the usual advertisements, an item from Catholic bookseller and publisher John Cunningham offered a list of books, including *The Catholic Sunday School Hymn Book* for six and a quarter cents.[2] As it turns out, the book and the burning churches were connected by more than the pages of a newspaper.

Philadelphia in 1844 was a central hub for the massive world of hymn-book publishing and use. The birthplace of the African Methodist Episcopal Church and home to the AME Book Concern, the city also housed the headquarters of both branches of the Presbyterian Church in the United States of America, which produced a wide array of hymnbooks for congregations, families, and schools. The American Sunday School Union (ASSU), also based in Philadelphia, rivaled New York's American Bible Society and American Tract Society as the largest publisher in the United States, with hundreds of thousands of hymnbooks distributed to children and their teachers over the previous twenty years. But when Cunningham announced the publication of his cheap hymnbook in a February *Catholic Herald* advertisement and published it later that month, it was the first American hymnbook ever produced for Catholic children.[3] Competing books soon appeared on the *Catholic Herald*'s final page. In June, a Baltimore-produced hymnbook was for sale at the shop of M. Fithian, the newspaper's publisher; in July, Philadelphia's most prominent Catholic publisher, Eugene Cummiskey, announced *The Sacred Wreath*, designed for the Sodality of the Blessed Virgin, Philadelphia's first Catholic youth organization. The year 1844 proved to be a watershed for children's hymnbooks, offering a crucial new expression of minority identity and using design elements common to Protestant books, including text layout, suggestions for meter, and a first-line index. This double-edged assertion of Catholic distinctiveness through Protestant means had a very specific reason for appearing when it did, one that left the future of the city's Catholic youth in question.

Philadelphia's public school district had organized in the early 1830s, part of a statewide mandate that shared in a new interest in publicly provided common schools nationwide. These new schools were available to all classes, and they offered the children of laborers and immigrants access to a basic, nonsectarian education. Or so the policies stipulated. In practice, by 1838 the schools had adopted a routine of morning exercises that included Bible reading and the singing of hymns, practices borrowed from the ASSU and its predecessors that had provided basic literacy instruction in the decades before the common schools were established. These practices drew on texts, without comment, that spanned the range of Protestant denominations, and Presbyterians, Episcopalians, Baptists, Methodists, and (to some extent)

Quakers all saw these exercises as having less to do with churches and religion than with American public morality. For Catholics, however, reading from the King James Bible and singing hymns by Isaac Watts and Charles Wesley served to make them feel like religious others. After years of quiet frustration, tensions quickly mounted in 1842 when a Catholic teacher in a Kensington school was fired for refusing to conduct the opening exercises. Bishop Francis Patrick Kenrick intervened later that year, arguing in an open letter to the school board that forcing Catholic students to read a Bible translation that their church rejected and to sing hymns that often deviated from their church's teachings violated the Pennsylvania state constitution. The board seemed sympathetic at first, but when Bishop Kenrick's open letter drew the ire of Protestant clergy and leaders of the growing nativist movement, the board settled for an opt-out policy in January 1843: students could choose to leave during the exercises.

The *Catholic Herald* soon began receiving letters from readers describing the harassment students suffered, from both peers and teachers, for excusing themselves from the exercises. A preexisting problem of history textbooks including anti-Catholic accounts of colonial America, which Kenrick also had mentioned to the board, did nothing to help the situation. As frustrations mounted among Catholics over the next year, nativist organizations such as the American Protestant Association argued that the Bible was under siege in Philadelphia and that the very soul of the nation was at stake. Nativist groups had recently gained enough popular support to field a presidential candidate in 1844; the "Bible controversy" became a campaign issue, even as Bishop Kenrick and the editors of the *Catholic Herald* urged restraint and reconciliation. Up until this controversy, Philadelphia's Catholics had had more success integrating into local social institutions, such as public schools, than Catholics had in many other American cities. In New York, where nativist "b'hoy" culture and Irish gangs loomed larger and earlier, Bishop John Hughes had spearheaded parochial schools in his diocese in the 1830s, rejecting the public school system as inherently anti-Catholic. Philadelphia had a few elite Catholic academies, but those were too expensive for most families, and funds for parochial schools had not been forthcoming. The public schools had worked, and working-class Catholics needed them. Reconciliation was a necessity in the eyes of Kenrick's parishioners.

If many families lacked school choices, they had access to the Douay-Rheims Bible in the city's several Catholic bookshops, but the school controversy highlighted a lack of available children's hymnody to counter the influence of Protestant texts. The Bible controversy explains why the hymnbooks finally arrived in 1844, but a brief look at the history of Roman Catholic hymn traditions is necessary to understand why the books, so widely available to Protestants for more than 100 years, were not already in the Catholic community. Like the Orthodox, Lutherans, and Moravians, Catholics had always had hymns, but after the English Reformation Catholics in the British Isles tended to confine their hymn use to reading, usually silently. Especially in Ireland, where the Mass was forced underground, secrecy meant that singing was kept to a minimum. In places where the Mass could be celebrated more openly, choirs took charge of the hymns. The texts, Latin and translated, were widely available in missals (which gave readings for the Mass), breviaries (which contained the daily prayers of the Divine Office), and a range of lay devotional books, but there was little need for a designated Catholic hymnbook as Protestants would have understood that term. This changed in the United States at the turn of the nineteenth century as clergy in Boston, Baltimore, and elsewhere began to compile Protestant-style collections of hymn texts. This was partly to meet demands among continental European Catholic immigrants, many of whom had traditions of congregational singing in their countries of origin, but partly also to make Catholics look more American—that is, more Protestant. Since Protestants increasingly lived with their hymnbooks, carrying them between home, church, and school, Catholics sought equivalent textual support for their religious identity.

It is clear how much community leaders perceived was at stake in having Catholic hymnbooks available. The *Catholic Herald*'s brief notice of Cunningham's *Sunday School Hymn Book* summarized this view: "It is of great importance to accustom children to the recital of pious canticles, which may fill their minds with holy thoughts, and preserve them from the contaminating influence of corrupt songs."[4] While "corrupt songs" was traditional shorthand for secular street ballads, a longtime target of American clergy of all persuasions, recent events also implied that Protestant hymns could corrupt the purity of Catholic piety; Cunningham's book was an antidote to that threat. Yet the design similarities between this new book and the Protestant books it resisted told another story—about integration with the Protestant mainstream. The book made a Catholic spiritual tradition available to a rising generation in the community, but in a way that also made it legible to Protestants. Like the earlier hymnbooks in Boston and Baltimore, the *Sunday School Hymn Book* defined a subculture by appropriating the conventions of the mainstream. Cummiskey's book was even more a creature of a subculture, since the sodality his book served had organized in 1841 to give the city's Catholic youth a social space for learning to grow up Catholic. Catholics had their own Bibles, their own schoolbooks (a Cummiskey specialty), their own newspaper, their own devotional works, and now their own hymnbooks. That all these print genres were mirrored in the dominant Protestant culture was not lost on neighboring Protestants—one of two surviving copies of Cunningham's first edition is in the ASSU's library, now held at the Free Library of Philadelphia—and they helped Catholics, both citizens and recent immigrants, have a media environment of their own.

Yet this environment enabled appropriation even in the choice of texts. The earliest American Catholic collections included not only Protestant design elements but also Protestant texts alongside new and ancient Catholic hymns. Watts's "Before Jehovah's Awful Throne" was a favorite; Charles Wesley's "Jesus, lover of my soul, / Let me to thy bosom fly" also appeared widely, even before many Protestant communities could bring themselves to sing of lovers and bosoms at church. Despite fears of "corrupt songs," the 1844 Catholic hymnbooks included several Protestant texts, and a remarkable hybrid appeared in all three of these books, a communion meditation with an opening stanza largely by Watts:

> My God, my life, my love,
> To thee, to thee I call;
> O come to me from heaven above,
> And be my God, my all.

Watts's original would remain popular among Protestants throughout the nineteenth century, eventually becoming a standard in southern shape-note traditions. From the Catholic version's first appearance in *Hymns for the Use of the Catholic Church in the United States of America* (1807), it gained such popularity that a tune supplement to the 1844 books, produced by Cunningham's successor, John McGrath, in 1850, gave six different settings for the hymn, the most of any in the entire collection. Indeed, the text circulated so widely that the renowned Presbyterian hymnologist Edwin Hatfield included it alongside Watts's original version in his 1873 *Chapel Hymn Book*, giving "Anon., 1849" as the attribution.[5] While the author of the Catholic version may never be known, the presence of Watts's lines, the addressing of Christ in the third stanza as "Sweet lover of my soul," and other allusions and reworkings indicate that the author was well read in popular Protestant hymnody—and had a keen sense for what imagery and cadences in those hymns would find a ready audience among Catholics.

Thus the hymnbook became a nexus of cultural exchange as well as a marker of denominational identity, a carrier of tradition and a site for innovation. It was a source of prayer, of poetry, of community, and of conflict. By the time *The Sacred Wreath* was published, a second wave of the Bible riots convinced Philadelphia's Catholics that the time for parochial schools had come. The hymnbooks would move from the pluralism of public schools to these new bastions of Catholic youth identity, and these books would grow more popular in the coming decades. The events of 1844 could also have been called the "hymnbook riots," since hymnbooks had been part of the conflict's source and part of the Catholic community's response to discrimination and fear for the future of their children. Yet amid all the conflict, Protestants and Catholics both agreed through the rest of the nineteenth century that hymnbooks, and books drawing from those hymnbooks for pedagogical content, belonged in schools.

PART II

SCHOOL

CHAPTER 6

Hymnbooks and Literacy Learning

A longtime favorite Watts hymn begins:

> When I can read my title clear
> To mansions in the skies,
> I bid farewell to every fear,
> And wipe my weeping eyes.[1]

The image of seeing one's title, or deed, to a heavenly mansion and thus finding release from earthly troubles struck a chord with hymn readers of all denominations. The assurance of salvation, symbolized in the tangible, visible body of a legal document, took an experience from the increasingly important property law of the British Empire and made it cosmic. Yet simply seeing and holding a document, even symbolically, is not enough in Watts's hymn—the action that sets the speaker free from trouble is *reading*. The document is not merely visible, but legible; it holds not just good news, but good news for *me*. In her study of slave literacy, which took the opening line of the Watts hymn for its title, Janet Duitsman Cornelius recounted the testimony of Belle Myers, a formerly enslaved ninety-year-old woman, who had painstakingly taught herself to decode words and syllables using her master's children's letter blocks and a copy of Noah Webster's famous speller. As Cornelius pointed out, decoding did not amount to reading until looking at an actual text could provide a "click of comprehension," and Myers retained a vivid memory of just such a moment: "I found a Hymn book . . . and spelled out, 'When I Can Read My Title Clear.' I was so happy when I saw that I could really read, that I ran around telling all the other slaves."[2] Watts did not likely have knowledge of the politics and circumstances of enslaved people's literacy, but no text could better epitomize the euphoria and empowerment of Myers finding she could read than the words of his popular hymn.

"When I Can Read My Title Clear" is the most famous of many hymns of the eighteenth and nineteenth centuries that celebrated the power of reading, and many of those were produced for children. Combining accessible language, wide availability, and moral and religious instruction, hymns quickly became a standard literacy resource as reading instruction became more widespread across the eighteenth century in particular. As I show in this chapter, the hymnbook was often a schoolbook, even before most children attended formal schools. Whether at home or elsewhere, children and their parents turned to hymns, most frequently those of Watts, to help them read.

Watts's prominence in the blending of hymnody and literacy was no accident. He was, among other things, an educational authority, writing popular textbooks on subjects ranging from astronomy to logic to reading. As the product of a particularly rigorous Dissenting education, marked by close bonds with his teachers and classmates, Watts worked as a tutor before he was called to Mark Lane Church as assistant pastor. One of his first projects at Mark Lane was the organizing of what we would now call a Sunday school for members' children.[3] When he moved to Thomas Abney's estate to recover his health, Watts repaid his host by tutoring Abney's three daughters, and his work with the Abney girls resulted in his *Divine and Moral Songs for Children* (1715) and *The Art of Reading* (1721), both of which he dedicated to his pupils. The former title was the most-printed children's book of the eighteenth and nineteenth centuries; the latter is something of a companion piece with *Divine Songs*, since they formed a speller-reader combination some twenty years before such pairings were standard among literacy books. Such a curricular combination was a new concept in the early eighteenth century, and understanding how Watts specifically, and the hymnbook more generally, fit into Anglophone literacy education requires a brief look at the norms Watts inherited from his society.

While being able to read the Bible was more clearly the goal of literacy in the New England colonies than it was in England, Watts's fellow Dissenters shared with their American counterparts the conviction that their children, girls as well as boys, should all learn to read the Word of God for themselves, and thus Dissent largely drove the culture of learning to read in the English-speaking world of the seventeenth and eighteenth centuries. (This is a key reason that literacy rates were so much higher in nearly all-Dissenting Massachusetts than it was in largely Anglican England.) Dissenters and Anglicans alike followed a similar approach when teaching reading, which was generally done at home by mothers or female relatives. One source of income for women at this time was to open their parlors as "dame schools" for basic literacy instruction to neighborhood children.[4] Whether at a dame school or by their mother's side, children could expect a standard sequence of textbooks, what John Locke in his educational writings would call the "ordinary Road." After learning the alphabet from a single, reinforced sheet called a hornbook, a student would turn to the primer, the core of which was a syllabary, a series of tables of syllables, starting at two letters each and gradually lengthening, with brief, catechism-style readings to offer practice in decoding. Students who completed their primer would move on to readings, all holy writ, organized by increasing difficulty: the psalter, which was essentially the King James translation of the book of Psalms; the testament, meaning the New Testament; and, finally, the Bible, which marked the end of this basic course in reading.[5] From the primer onward, the main method for teaching students to decode text was "spelling," sometimes called the ABC method, in which a student would speak the letters of a syllable, speak the syllable, repeat with subsequent syllables, then speak the whole word. To read the word "able," for instance, would involve the following speech: "a, b, ab, l, e, le, able." Little time was spent on issues of grammar, such as verb tenses, which were only taught to those learning to write—considered an independent skill and generally taught separately and by men. All students needed to do to be considered literate was to decode words to the point where they could follow the train of a whole sentence, especially a sentence of scripture.

This method, while effective enough to remain in place for at least two centuries, was admittedly joyless. One of Watts's aims in writing *Divine Songs* was to make children's learning to read, as well as doctrine and morality, "a Diversion" by using the pleasures of rhyme and image to motivate children to not only read but memorize his texts; memorization was a central part of most people's reading practices with secular as well as sacred texts. In his preface to *Divine Songs*, Watts called on parents and educators to "turn their [children's] very Duty into a Reward, by giving them the

Privilege of learning one of these *Songs* every Week, if they fulfil[l] the Business of the Week well, and promising them the Book it self when they have learnt ten or twenty Songs out of it."[6] Confronted with lists of syllables, catechism questions, and other dry material, children (as Watts expected) found his "How Doth the Little Busy Bee" and "Let Dogs Delight to Bark and Bite" much more entertaining, and the adults that cared for them found the songs' content good enough to buy copies of *Divine Songs* early and often. The latter part of Watts's advice quoted above points to another factor driving demand for the book. While hornbooks, primers, and other schoolbooks tended to be handed down from child to child until they literally disintegrated, Watts encouraged adults to make *Divine Songs* the beginning of a child's own private collection. If learning from the book was a treat, having the book for one's own was even more desirable. Patricia Crain offers the compelling argument that the rise of children's literature and children's literacy in the eighteenth and nineteenth centuries was fueled by a new ideal of ownership: children learned to read and to own books at the same time.[7] Watts was the greatest single influence on this new equation of literacy and property. A century before the gift book industry was launched, Watts had created a book that was made to be given away, and *Divine Songs* as well as his *Hymns* and *Psalms* would be gifted in the tens of thousands before the eighteenth century ended.

One of the largest distributors of Watts's texts by the close of the eighteenth century was the Sunday school. These schools began as a movement in Britain in the 1780s and quickly expanded to the United States, initially as a solution to a decidedly urban, working-class problem: a record percentage of the population was now under the age of twenty, and while many urban children found work in factories at the start of the Industrial Revolution, orphanhood, homelessness, and general poverty left many of these young people on the streets, particularly on Sundays, when the factories were closed. Sunday school was a way of reducing crime as well as offering basic education in literacy and hygiene with the goal of evangelism, and the offer of a free meal was an effective early recruitment device. In the first years of the movement, in the absence of official curricula and formal teacher training, a common practice was to divide a school into two classes. Teachers would devote most of their time to the lower class, who would work through primers to learn the alphabet and basic syllabic decoding. The upper class, those who could already decode, were assigned passages to read and memorize for recitation at the end of the day. The passages came from either catechisms or hymnbooks, both being cheap sources of religious material and, for the first schools' purposes, virtually interchangeable; assignments were based not on preference or a set sequence but on the availability of books. Since the attendees of the early Sunday schools were among the poorest in their city, the schools (usually organized by parachurch associations) would frequently give their students food, clothes, and books— Bibles, hymnbooks, and catechisms for the most part—as gifts.[8]

Among the first volumes produced by and for Sunday schools were hymnbooks intended for literacy instruction as well as shared worship at school. Watts's *Divine Songs* was a popular reprint, and more eclectic collections generally incorporated Watts texts (children's and adults' selections) along with a mix of congregational favorites and new children's material, including Ann Taylor and Jane Taylor's *Hymns for Infant Minds* (1810) and original pieces contributed by school supporters. Hymnbooks thus inhabited the core of both the duties and the rewards of Sunday schools from their very beginning, and as Sunday schools became more organized, more professional, and more cross-class in their outreach, the reprinting and compilation of hymnbooks remained one of the major elements of print output in Britain and the United States.

An intriguing American variant on these hymnbooks was the supplement for adult learners. Often convened as evening schools, the adult classes were most prevalent in large cities such as Boston, New York, and Philadelphia, and most of the students in urban areas were black, both free and slave.[9] A board member of the New York Sunday School Union Society prepared what is almost certainly the first such supplement in 1818, explaining that he conceived of the collection after the disturbing experience of hearing an elderly black woman recite Watts for her lesson. The text was from *Divine Songs* and the speaker was a little child, which the board member thought insulting for a woman with grandchildren to have to imitate.[10] Many of the texts in the supplement reflected much older speakers looking back on their lives, and they also included several identifiably black speakers. While stereotypes of "the African" appear in these texts, the absence of dialect speech—already a popular marker of racial difference in American print—signals the respect that the author-compiler wanted to show to adult nonwhite students. One of the African-voiced texts, "On Afric's Land Our Fathers Roamed," traced a narrative from heathen innocence to the tragedy of slavery to the redemption of Christianity, and it struck enough of a chord among members of the Union Church of Africans discussed in chapter 1 that it appeared in the first two editions of their hymnbook.[11]

The adult Sunday schools would fade after the mid-1820s as the American Sunday School Union absorbed the older local unions and took a more middle-class, Bible-based approach that left literacy education to the cities' emerging public school systems. But the creation of adult- and African American–specific reading materials, which lived on through appropriation in African American hymnody, was the culmination of a decades-long effort to teach black literacy through hymns. As early as 1745, Joseph Hildreth reported to his patrons that his New York Charity School had attracted a group of black adults (whether they were enslaved is not known) who asked Hildreth to teach them psalm singing. Hildreth obliged by organizing a separate night class for them, and years later the class continued, with modest increases in the number of students and Bible reading added to the psalm-singing instruction.[12] In 1755, the Presbyterian missionary Samuel Davies made an even more extraordinary connection with enslaved black people through the blend of literacy, music, and property that the hymnbook enabled.

Davies was a New Light from Delaware, inspired by the Great Awakening, and a devotee of the writings of Watts and Jonathan Edwards. Trying to build a ministry in Virginia from nothing, Davies discovered that poor whites were resistant to his dual message of salvation and literacy, in part because they were not interested in spending money on even the discounted books that Davies's sponsor, the London-based Society for Promoting Religious Knowledge among the Poor (SPRKP), provided. The SPRKP's logic in expecting sales was that book owners would be more invested in their books if they paid for them. In Tidewater Virginia, this logic did not hold for white residents—but the enslaved people who made up half of colonial Virginia's population seemed remarkably eager to read, to learn about God, and to consume the books slighted by their white neighbors. Writing to his sponsors in 1755, Davies argued that a new distribution model could finally bring success to his evangelistic efforts, since "the poor neglected negroes . . . are so far from having money to purchase books, that they themselves are the property of others." In other words, the people with the most spiritual and intellectual hunger in Virginia were also those most economically and politically impoverished. Davies identified his most fertile mission field as one barred from the very possession of money. "These poor unhappy Africans are objects of my compassion," he explained, "and I think the most proper objects of the Society's charity."[13]

A key reason Davies gave for this charity was the demonstrated will to make good use of the books. He recounted the slaves' strenuous efforts to learn to read, such that a number of Davies's congregants "can intelligibly read a plain author, and particularly the Bible." Davies had distributed "*Bibles, Testaments, Watts's Songs for Children*, &c." to those who had learned to read, and "I never did a charitable action in all my life, that met with *so much Gratitude* from the receivers." Yet his small stock was now long gone, enslaved people kept coming from miles around to seek a gift of a book, and Davies begged his sponsors to help replenish his supply of free books— especially "Watts' Psalms and Hymns, and Bibles."[14] The latter text was an obvious choice, since the goal of literacy in much Protestant mission education was to give lost souls direct access to God's Word. But the Watts books weren't on the society's list of books available to distribute in 1755, and Davies understood that a special collection by individual members would be required to provide him with the hymnbooks he desired. Davies explained his request by relating his observation that "the *Negroes* above all the human species I ever knew, have an ear for music, and a kind of extatic [*sic*] delight in Psalmody; and there are no books they learn so soon, or take so much pleasure in, as those used in that heavenly part of divine Worship." The hymn seemed to be the door into the minds and hearts of the enslaved people, and in his ethnological wonderment at their interest in music, he realized that "nothing would be a stronger inducement to them to learn to read, than the expectation of such a present [of a hymnbook]; which they would consider as a *help* and a *reward* at once."[15] Thus Watts possessed a double power for Davies's literacy campaign among the enslaved people: the musical connection made the books ideal literacy aids, and the object status of the book as gift provided a concrete, attractive reward for the trouble of learning to read.

Davies's argument, combined with the shock that thousands of enslaved Africans would make such a ready field for evangelism, won over his

London correspondents, and less than a year later, a large shipment of books, including a specially procured lot of Watts's *Psalms* and *Hymns* arrived in Virginia, which Davies told his benefactors was "the most agreeable surprize, that ever I met with in my whole life." Having received what he wanted, Davies was careful to give his London correspondents what they wanted: a vivid account of the efficacy of their generosity: "The books were all *very acceptable*; but none more so than the *Psalms* and *Hymns*, which enabled [the enslaved people] to gratify their peculiar taste for *Psalmody*. Sundry of them have lodged all night in my kitchen; and, sometimes, when I have awaked about two or three a-clock [*sic*] in the morning, a torrent of sacred harmony poured into my chamber, and carried my mind away to Heaven. In this seraphic exercise, some of them spend almost the whole night."[16]

Davies's literacy campaign here seemed to be working almost too well. His own house had become a scene of literacy to such an extent that he lost sleep over it. Davies's work revolutionized the SPRKP's distribution strategy; earlier, the society had distributed Watts's *Catechisms and Prayers for Children* (1730) and *Divine Songs*, and the total of those works combined with the *Psalms, Hymns,* and other titles made Watts's writings as a whole more popular than the Bible in the SPRKP's records by 1795.[17] In the lives of the black learners who responded to Davies, the effects were even more profound and lasting. An eyewitness report of seeing a descendant of one of Davies's students still in possession of his hymnbook was published in 1843, nearly ninety years after Davies had distributed the books. The irony of this account was that it was given in a review of Charles Colcock Jones's *The Religious Instruction of Negroes in the United States*, a work advocating the use of hymn singing to teach slaves religion—without giving them access to books.[18] Davies had taught enslaved people to read legally, but by the time Jones's ideas were circulating, Virginia had banned slave literacy, making the Davies books even more radical interventions into the plantations than they had been before.[19]

The status of the Watts books as objects within enslaved communities would have called for multiple forms of reading: the interpretation of objects and property as well as words. The books came to represent ownership itself, recognition itself; they were both gifts bestowed to help their recipients and prized possessions that lent status to their owners. They became heirlooms. They became primers, used to teach other black people to read despite laws and threats against such practices. They became cornerstones of some of the first black-led worship services in the South, evolving into a lined-out singing tradition still extant today in the rural southeastern interior and known in communities still practicing it as "Wattsing" or "Dr. Watts singing"—even if the text may be Newton's "Amazing Grace," Wesley's "Father, I Stretch My Hands to Thee," or the Scottish minister Horatius Bonar's "A Few More Years Shall Roll."[20] Watts's name came to stand for an entire tradition, a singing technique, and a style of hymnody that has defined the worship of rural black and white congregations from the Great Awakening to the present day. Watts—in book form—could serve as both a defining characteristic of Calvinist benevolence and a rally- ing cry for black slaves and white sharecroppers. The textual transmission and consumption of hymns had a power far beyond what we typically think of as the workings of print culture in modern society, and allowed for practices of identity formation more complex than mere assimilation or appropriation. Watts was a key catalyst for the growth of black identity in America, just as he helped to fuse the evangelical movement as an inter- national community built by text, not geographic borders.

For all the difficulties faced by advocates of slave literacy, one point of consensus they shared with their opponents was that the language of liter- acy would be English. For missionaries elsewhere in North America, the linguistic situation was often more complicated and contested. While later efforts, such as the Carlisle Indian School in Pennsylvania, started from an English-only assumption, many missions before 1850, even ones committed to English-language education, sought to harness the power of communi- cating in the Native nations' languages. Most of these languages did not use alphabetic writing at the time of contact, and while some missionaries learned the local Native languages, many did not; the project of taking a religion of the book into new linguistic territory thus involved challenges of media as well as content. Hymns proved to be ideal starting points to face these challenges, since First Nations people generally had long-standing practices of singing, and the brief, accessible texts were easier to translate, teach, and memorize, especially in oral delivery, than were catechisms or scripture passages. As missionaries developed orthographic systems for writ- ing and printing Native languages, hymnbooks were frequently among the first productions. These books were the constant companions of itinerant missionaries, ready for use in prayer services, counseling, and other settings. But what if the missionary couldn't read the language? What if Native readers couldn't parse the orthography? Hymnbook compilers tried a range of solutions, and their strategies and assumptions shed light on the standard uses of these books and the politics of literacy in various missions.

Some books were clearly experimental. British Canadian missionary James Evans produced such a book while working with Cree-speaking nations in northwestern Canada in 1841. Evans devised a syllabary instead of transliterating the Cree language into the roman alphabet, based on a system he had developed for Mississaugas in Ontario but had never been permitted to use. He then designed and cast his own type using lead from melted bells and bullets, printing his small books using a modified fur press. It was the first book printed in western Canada, but the syllabary proved too difficult to teach for the book to have much influence.[21] More successful were the books made for the Mississaugas, but the history of those volumes shows how fraught the politics of missionary hymnbooks could be. White missionaries could rarely succeed without translators and cultural ambassadors from the Native populations; while Evans was a gifted linguist, his Cree translations were riddled with grammatical errors, and when he had been recruited in the mid-1830s to revise and expand a book of hymns in Ojibwe (the Mississaugas' language), he enlisted the help of George Henry, a Christian Mississauga.

Leaders of the Methodist missions in Ontario had become convinced that the earlier translation's orthography needed correcting, but this was as much a clash of personalities as it was a matter of linguistic authenticity. The earlier work had been done by Peter Jones, a Mississauga who converted as a young man in 1825 and quickly rose to prominence as a translator and exhorter unique in his ability to both write fluent English and preach well in Ojibwe. By 1830, he had become both a Methodist minister and a Mississauga chief; he had developed a written, alphabetic form of Ojibwe and had translated enough Methodist hymns to fill a book. The hymnbooks were printed in Toronto and were reprinted in New York and Boston, all with English and Ojibwe texts on facing pages.[22] Jones went on speaking tours in the United States and Britain, and a children's choir he organized drew large crowds in New York.[23]

Jones's story reflects those of the Mohegan minister Samson Occom and the Pequot minister William Apess, both of whom found themselves marginalized by white supervisors who nevertheless relied on them for fundraising and evangelism. Evans's rapid acquisition of Ojibwe made him an ideal means for his directors to limit Jones's role in the Ontario mission field. Evans's arrival coincided with the merging of Canadian and British Methodist missions in Canada, and the new leadership had little experience in the region or knowledge of the language. Part of Evans's task was thus to help English-speaking missionaries learn enough Ojibwe to function, and a speller he produced in 1837, despite what its title page implied, was primarily for white adults to learn basic Ojibwe.[24] His and George Henry's hymnbook appeared the same year, funded by the American Tract Society and published in New York.[25] It was twice the length of Jones's book, despite not having side-by-side texts. The book amounted to a new version of the British Methodist book, not an adapted selection like Jones's, and while the texts were all in Ojibwe, the intended users were missionaries. Each text was headed by its English first line, and an Ojibwe first-line index in the back accompanied an English first-line index, an English subject index (not given in Ojibwe), and a bilingual list of theological vocabulary, which facilitated missionaries' ability to locate texts relevant to their preaching. A pronunciation guide accompanied the preface.

Jones was shocked to learn of the new translation; the fact that Evans's assistant, Henry, was Jones's half brother added insult to injury. The communities Jones had served as minister were also incensed at the new book. Accustomed as they were to Jones's orthography, they declared Evans's book unreadable, even with the pronunciation guide, and voted to demand a new revision of Jones's book in the original orthography. The mission's leadership quickly realized that their efforts to aid their missionaries threatened to lose them their audience, and they published Jones's revision in 1840 in Toronto while sending Evans west into Cree territory. Jones's book would be reprinted in Toronto and New York by the respective national mission societies as late as the 1960s. While even Jones admitted his orthography was flawed, his people found only his renderings of the Methodist hymns to be legible.[26]

The question of what counted as legible could be a matter of debate among white and Native adults; for Native children, legibility had other rules and stakes. While missionaries made great efforts to put hymns in the hands of adult Native Americans in their first languages, books that included sections for children often took different approaches. The American Methodist Episcopal Church sponsored a mission to the Mohawks that produced *A Collection of Hymns for the Use of Native Christians of the Mohawk Language, to Which Are Added a Number of Hymns for Sabbath Schools* (1832). The main body of the book was produced in a side-by-side format similar to Jones's Ojibwe books, but the "hymns for Sabbath schools" were given only in English. Those texts included standard congregational hymns and numerous selections from Watts's *Divine Songs* and the Taylors' *Hymns for Infant Minds*, among other children's hymn sources. If the missionaries' goal for adult Mohawks was conversion, they saw acculturation as having greater importance for Mohawk children. This signaled a crucial step toward the Carlisle Indian School–style, English-only instruction that would gain favor among missionaries on reservations as the century continued. In making a book that missionaries, Native adults, and Native children could all use, the rules of engagement were clearly set for each group, and the category of "child" increasingly erased the category "Native" for the youngest cohort. The child was taking over the missionaries' imaginations, and that conception of the child had been built over a century, to a considerable extent, by hymns.

CHAPTER 7

How Hymnbooks Made Children's Literature

Isaac Watts's *Divine and Moral Songs for Children* (1715) was, as I showed in the previous chapter, one of the most influential books in building deep connections between hymnody and early literacy. Yet despite its influence and ubiquity, it has been disqualified as a monument of children's literature since critical writing in that field began in the late nineteenth century. Or has it? Remember the copy of *Divine Songs* I discussed in this book's introduction, the book Eliza Anne Walker received on her fifth birthday from her uncle Charlie. The gift inscription, large format, sumptuous illustrations, and large type all visually signaled that this was, in fact, children's literature, in all its Victorian glory. How did Watts's humble little book gain the dress of Victorian children's literature? Why was it still popular enough for that treatment well over a century after its first publication? And why, if it warranted such treatment from publishers and readers of children's literature, does the book not count as children's literature today? To get at these questions, I begin with a brief account of the standard history of children's literature, one that has largely rejected hymnbooks out of hand, before taking up a thought experiment: What if we thought of hymns as children's literature? How would that change our emphases in talking about that field?

For virtually all readers today, the category of children's literature seems natural enough. Books written, illustrated, and packaged for children have their own publishers, their own space in bookstores and libraries, and their own style that makes it easy at a glance for most readers to spot a modern children's book. Yet the equation of illustration with children's literature is less than a century old; the high-end literary magazine *Scribner's* still produced illustrations for short stories by the likes of F. Scott Fitzgerald as late as the 1920s. And the massive crossover appeal of the *Harry Potter* series—complete with parallel cover designs for the adult and children's editions—indicates that the visual and marketing borders of children's literature are still permeable. Children's literature, like any concept that carries social power, has a history to it, and that history is bound up, literally, in the world of publishing.

The traditional starting point for modern children's literature is John Newbery's publication of *Goody Two-Shoes* and other "pretty books" for children in London in the 1740s. Scholars of children's literature have generally pointed to these books as the crucial turning point from what children *had* to read—didactic, religious, dry—to what they *got* to read, with fantasy, adventure, and entertainment moving to the fore.[1] Newbery's pretty books were indeed designed for leisure reading, but their moral teachings were still frequent and explicit. The world of Newbery's books was decidedly secular, however, coupling morality to financial success rather than religion. Newbery connected everything to money, it turns out, and his foundational place in children's literature is not so much a matter of literary breakthroughs as of branding. By packaging a product line of leisure reading for children, Newbery laid the groundwork for what today is arguably the healthiest segment of the publishing industry, and his firm's slogan wed fun and finance: "Commerce and plumb-cake forever, huzzah!" Children's literature is the only major literary field whose point of origin is traced not to an author or a text but to a publisher. Relying on a stable of write-for-hire, uncredited authors and maintaining a strong editorial hand, Newbery published books whose authors are still unknown today. The birth of children's literature, its liberation from earlier strictures to the freedom of leisure, is at one level a story of commodities and marketing.

In a way, this was inevitable. Some dimension of persuasion, particularly of adults, has always been necessary in children's literature. Adults are generally the purchasers or the sources of purchase money, and thus what they conceive would be desirable to a child is a major element in determining what is sellable from the standpoint of authors and publishers. On another level, the Newbery narrative traces back to the field-defining *Children's Books in England*, published in 1932 by F. J. Harvey Darton, the scion of a major children's publishing house in Britain whose own history goes back far enough to make it a competitor of Newbery's—and a beneficiary of the sales of reprinted Newbery titles. Darton's publishing acumen gave him great appreciation for Newbery's accomplishments, but by emphasizing *A

Little Pretty Pocket-Book (1744) and *Goody Two-Shoes* (1765) as the true start of children's literature, he ignored a fact that would have been highly relevant to his publishing forebears: Watts's *Divine Songs* outsold all of Newbery's titles across the eighteenth century.[2] So did Anna Letitia Barbauld's *Hymns in Prose for Children* (1781). So did the works of Ann Taylor and Jane Taylor, including their *Hymns for Infant Minds*, an immensely popular work first published in 1810 by Darton and Harvey of London, an early iteration of the Darton family firm. Watts, Barbauld, and the Taylors sold thousands of books, whether as gifts, schoolbooks, or leisure reading—often in some combination. Parents, teachers, and benevolent institutions certainly enhanced the demand for these works, and they would certainly have been forced on many reluctant children.[3] Yet many children loved the Watts and Barbauld works especially, and the cheapness of many reprints made book ownership available to a wide range of children; this held a particular glamor in an era when adults' personal libraries rarely went beyond ten or twenty titles.

This alternative story begins like many stories in this part of my volume, with Isaac Watts. In his bibliography of Watts's *Divine and Moral Songs* (1715), Wilbur Macey Stone explained Watts's importance to the history of children's reading: "If the New England Primer was the 'little Bible' of New England, Dr. Watts' Divine and Moral Songs has a worthy place beside it as the 'little Hymnbook,' not only of New England but of Old England as well."[4] Part of the success was reflected in Watts's preface: he was keenly aware that children were not the book's only readers. In addressing the parents and teachers whose money would likely purchase the book, Watts recognized the social structures that underwrote children's literacy and acted on those structures by defining children's use of the book as fundamentally social: the adult reads to the child, the child reads and then recites to the adult, and in time the adult rewards and memorializes the shared work of the child by giving the book to them. Book ownership and literacy were intimately entwined for Watts, but this was not so much a matter of building the Lockean individual as of situating a responsible person within a visible network to which that person could be responsible. The book carried the memory of spending time with the donor, with Watts serving as an intermediary—sometimes visualized in the portraits that some later editions included, but often invisible and abstract.

Watts's positioning of the children's hymnbook as a socially powerful gift was a source of its cultural as well as economic power. It also likely contributed to Darton's privileging of Newbery's approach over Watts's. Newbery's books were certainly frequent gifts as well, but his business strategy emphasized children's participation in a market economy as active consumers (commerce goes with plum cake) rather than in a gift economy that left the pleasures of shopping and buying to adults. Many children's booksellers followed Newbery's lead, even as some, like Mahlon Day in nineteenth-century New York City, created advertising for parents and for their children, operating from the insight that the gift economy was also good for business. Indeed, a book made to be given could potentially claim greater popularity than otherwise, and that is precisely what happened to hymn-books. Benevolent societies, Sunday school unions, and even schools such as Samuel Phillips's Andover Academy published hundreds of thousands of copies. These books were given away as tracts, rewards of merit, and gifts marking birthdays or graduations or church milestones. These volumes also stocked the parish and Sunday school libraries that proliferated in the mid-nineteenth century, by which time publishers in London, New York, Hartford, Sheffield, and many other cities had harnessed the selling power of illustration and produced versions of *Divine Songs*, whole or abridged, in formats ranging from Samuel Wood's "toy books," printed on a single sheet of paper and priced as low as three cents, to leather-bound volumes packed with engraved plates and selling for several dollars or pounds. The latter imitated the visually busy style of the annual gift books that became a significant sector of the publishing world and the exploding Christmas gift market beginning around 1830. Watts's gift to children had become big business indeed.[5]

And that business was not limited to works explicitly designed for children alone. Watts's *Psalms* and *Hymns* were also popular with children and their caretakers for quite some time and were frequently given as school rewards or gifts. In 1715, the year *Divine Songs* appeared in London, an anonymous Boston compiler (possibly Cotton Mather) seems to have anticipated Watts's project, bringing out a small collection from *Hymns* titled *Honey Flowing Out of the Rock to Young Children*. Apparently, the availability of *Divine Songs* obviated the need to reprint *Honey*. Memoir accounts, including James Raine learning Watts hymns by heart from his blind grandmother's recitations, William Cullen Bryant's childhood habit of standing on a chair to recite Watts at full voice, and Lucy Larcom following her mother around the house reading "Watts and select" to her, attest to how memorable, and social, the experience of Watts in any form was for many children.[6]

This should raise skepticism about the claim that good children's literature must be purely for entertainment. That perspective, originating from a publisher intent on selling such entertainment, renders invisible the real aural, literary, social, and spiritual pleasures of reading Watts's works, as well as the pleasures associated with a decidedly female cadre of authors, convened as a group by Charles Lamb in an often-quoted tirade resulting from the most famously bad children's book shopping trip in history. After Lamb's sister, Mary, struggled to locate a copy of *Goody Two-Shoes* in the Newbery store, he exploded in a letter to Samuel Taylor Coleridge: "Goody Two Shoes is almost out of print. Mrs Barbauld's stuff has banished all the old classics of the nursery; and the Shopman at Newbery's hardly deign'd to reach them off an old exploded corner of a shelf, when Mary ask'd for them. Mrs B's & Mrs Trimmer's nonsense lay in piles about. . . . Damn them! I mean the cursed Barbauld Crew, those Blights and Blasts of all that is human in man and child."[7] Scholars have long taken this quotation as the testimony of a clear-eyed, if worked-up, witness to the decline of children's literature between its first flowering through John Newbery's efforts and its Victorian "golden age" exemplified by Lewis Carroll (to whom I return below). Increasingly, however, scholars who have rediscovered Anna Letitia Barbauld and her literary heirs have questioned Lamb's eloquent invective.[8] While Barbauld is returning to the canon of British poetry, her achievement as a children's author has yet to receive wide recognition, and I argue that this is in large part because her greatest work for children was in hymns.

That Barbauld would have an interest in hymnody is hardly surprising: she was something of an intellectual great-granddaughter of Watts.[9] Her father studied under Watts's protégé Philip Doddridge at his influential Dissenting academy in Northampton, England; Barbauld spent her childhood there while her father was on the academy's faculty. The Calvinist Doddridge's penchant for teaching both sides of the great theological debates of his day had led his students to take a decidedly Unitarian turn once they inherited the academy, and Barbauld had long-standing friendships with liberal intellectuals like the sometime Northampton instructor Joseph

Priestley. She married a Northampton graduate and directed a boys' school with her husband. Barbauld was proud to have learned to read at age two from her mother, and when she adopted her nephew Charles Aiken, she set about creating a literacy curriculum. Using everyday scenarios and a mother-child dialogue format to catch his interest, Barbauld enjoyed success in teaching Charles and published a version of her curriculum as *Lessons for Young Children* (1778–1779), which had graded parts from age two to four. *Lessons*, sold collected or separately by age level, quickly went through multiple reprintings on both sides of the Atlantic, and Barbauld's follow-up project proved even more popular: *Hymns in Prose for Children* (1781). A series of twelve monologues took the maternal voice of *Lessons* and gave it the rhetorical grandeur of the Psalms, using natural imagery to guide reflections on God, morality, death, and immortality. The voice performed both authority and imitation, audacious but approachable in beckoning the young reader, "Come, let us sing praise to God, for he is exceeding great; let us bless God, for he is very good"; "Come, let us go into the shade, for it is the noon of the day."[10] Nothing quite like it had ever been done before, or would be again; Walt Whitman's *Leaves of Grass* might be the closest relative, and given the ubiquity of *Hymns in Prose* for nearly a century, it is not difficult to imagine the boy Whitman absorbing Barbauld's cadences or drawing from that reading as he wrote, "A child said, 'What is the grass?' "[11] The simplicity, vivid imagery, and nonsectarian spirituality of *Hymns in Prose* made them equally welcome in Sunday schools, public schools, and even Harvard's early Italian courses, for which Professor Pietro Bachi had a translation of Barbauld's *Hymns* printed.[12]

Barbauld's *Hymns* had unquestioned pedagogical utility, and that, combined with her involvement in a wave of new female authorities on education in Britain, likely sparked Lamb's ire. Newbery represented for Lamb a childhood ideal that blended entertainment with commercial and Anglican values, and Barbauld's Nonconformist insistence on taking a child's powers of reason seriously through a motherly persona threatened that ideal. The choice of *Goody Two-Shoes* as the embodiment of Lamb's (and many scholars') ideal is a curious one, however, given that the story is not about children having fun but about an impoverished orphan girl who earns herself a fortune as an itinerant teacher, armed only with what amounts to a font of type in her basket and a roving band of friendly animals. It was a kind of female Horatio Alger story with fanciful creatures. And the business model that brought out the book resembled nothing so much as the corporate write-for-hire systems that today produce the continuing adventures of Curious George and Disney characters. While Newbery published works by named authors for adults, he built his children's brand by hiring writers, some as noteworthy as Oliver Goldsmith, to write books anonymously, likely with the publisher exercising a great deal of creative control over the manuscripts. Thus *Goody Two-Shoes* is associated with his name alone; we don't know who wrote it.[13] A member of the generation of British writers associated with the rise of the romantic author as genius, Lamb ignored both the content and the creation of Newbery's books for the sake of his declension narrative, which focused on a certain kind of quality that he could gender as masculine in the face of an increasing number of successful women (and men) writing for children in new ways.

At this time two sisters were just emerging as children's authors who would reassert the importance of hymnody for young readers: Ann and Jane Taylor. As with Watts and Barbauld, it is difficult today to appreciate the sheer ubiquity of the Taylors' works in the nineteenth-century English-speaking world. Their best-known text today is Jane's "Twinkle, Twinkle, Little Star" (originally titled simply "The Star"), a poem whose widespread use has left its author's name far behind.[14] Yet in their own time, when most children's authors had their names removed from their books, the Taylor name was a valuable commodity alongside Watts and Barbauld. The two sisters, along with their brother Isaac, were voracious readers, and their writing to a magazine led to their "discovery" by the editor, who asked them to submit further poems. *Original Poems for Children* first appeared in 1804, quickly becoming a best seller and creating a market for more Taylor material. *Hymns for Infant Minds* (1810) was roughly as successful as *Original Poems*, at least in terms of reprinting. In their preface, the Taylors acknowledged their affection for and debt to Watts, and they saw their work as continuing and updating his *Divine and Moral Songs*. Some of that updating involved returning to Watts's favorite topics for children; two of their most popular hymns, "Great God! and Wilt Thou Condescend" and "This Is a Precious Book Indeed," reflected on the child's respected standing before God and on the value of the Bible and Bible reading, respectively. But other updates moved into new territory, expanding on Barbauld's nature-as-conduit-to-God approach. Indeed, as the Taylors' volumes of poetry and hymns proliferated and were continually mined for material in other books for children, the line between hymn and poem became quite blurred. The Taylors were willing to dub their own texts "hymns" whether or not they could thematically or formally fit congregational use, and later editors such as Samuel Wood saw little reason not to call the other poems hymns if a collection with "hymns" in the title could sell.

It is worth pausing a moment here to look across the century from *Divine Songs* to *Hymns for Infant Minds*. Watts never called his works for children hymns, but few of his readers and publishers seem to have questioned if "How Doth the Little Busy Bee" and "I Sing th'Almighty Power of God" were indeed hymns. Barbauld openly claimed the label for her works, which from a formal standpoint (works in prose) were not nearly so obviously part of the hymn tradition, though their themes and rhetorical aims were certainly related. By the time the Taylors were actively publishing hymns, they could use the term as a synonym for devotional or even moral verse marked by brevity and regular meter but not necessarily explicating a theological point or analyzing a passage of scripture. Decades before the barrier between hymn and poem was effectively blurred among poets for adult audiences—as I discuss in this book's final part, that line was fairly fixed in adult readers' minds until the 1820s at the earliest—children's hymns enabled and enjoyed a genre fluidity between hymn, religious poem, and secular poem that had been latent in Watts's work and had become a firm expectation by the time the Taylors were writing. The Taylors were literary pioneers who clearly saw the trajectory of the older tradition they followed in their work: one that took children seriously as readers, thinkers, and souls, and that created poetry especially for them in ways that would eventually lead their elders to wonder what it was precisely that made a hymn a hymn, and a poem a poem—and to wonder why they couldn't be the same thing.

By the early nineteenth century, one of the ways hymns could be quickly identified as poetry, at least children's poetry, was the presentation of a hymn-book as children's literature. The American Tract Society's 1840s reprints of the Taylors' *Hymns for Infant Minds*, for example, used a profusion of engraved illustrations—many depicting children and mothers reading together—to signal that the book belonged in the world of children's literature. Indeed, one way of understanding John Newbery as an originary figure in children's literature is not so much the textual content of his books as the fact that they were heavily illustrated, creating a relatively lavish visual style that would be imitated so extensively that the *look* of a Newbery book became the norm. And this ties Newbery even more strongly to Watts, whose *Divine Songs* has been claimed as the first work for children to be frequently illustrated, in the sense of including pictures that commented on the text rather than merely including pictures at random.[15]

The lasting popularity of Watts's *Divine Songs* and the success of Barbauld and the Taylors in an era generally considered to be a time of the secularization of children's literature and the move from didactic to imaginative writing should lead to a reconsideration of the premises of what counts as children's literature and what shape that literature has taken over time. As a further revision to this old story, I finish this chapter with Lewis Carroll, often considered the greatest of children's authors, whose parodies of Watts's *Divine Songs* in *Alice's Adventures in Wonderland* (1865) have frequently been cast as a sign of the old regime's overthrow and the arrival of a new golden age of children's literature. A closer look at Carroll's parodies, however, shows that the Oxford don, a devout Christian who took for granted Watts's place in early literacy and school culture, was not as ready to slight Watts as later readers have assumed.

The first parody appears as a diagnostic, which the increasingly anxious Alice uses to demonstrate to herself, through her memory of information acquired at school, that she is Alice and not one of her lower-performing school friends. She first attempts the multiplication table, mixes it up hopelessly, and then insists hastily that "the Multiplication Table doesn't signify." She turns next to geography, but she can no longer separate cities from countries, and last of all she turns to recitation for reassurance of her intellect:

"I'll try and say 'How doth the little—'" and she crossed her hands on her lap as if she were saying lessons, and began to repeat it, but her voice sounded hoarse and strange, and the words did not come the same as they used to do:—

"How doth the little crocodile
Improve his shining tail,

HYMNS

FOR

INFANT MINDS.

BY JANE TAYLOR.

PUBLISHED BY THE
AMERICAN TRACT SOCIETY,
28 Cornhill, Boston.

And pour the waters of the Nile
On every golden scale!

"How cheerfully he seems to grin,
How neatly spread his claws,
And welcome little fishes in
With gently smiling jaws!"

"I'm sure those are not the right words," said poor Alice.[16]

This rewriting of Watts's "Against Idleness," or "How Doth the Little Busy Bee," is hilarious for its exotic transforming of the English bee's work into the Egyptian crocodile's leisure and appetite. But it's not funny to Alice. She breaks down in tears, convinced that she has lost her identity and that she will have to return to the normal world as a dullard. Watts is so much a part of her that not being able to recall his words accurately is a shock to her system.

The next attempt at recitation does not improve. After a series of further disorienting adventures, Alice meets the Gryphon and the Mock Turtle by the seashore. After they regale her with a nonsensical song they call "The Lobster Quadrille" and she recounts her adventures to them, the Gryphon commands her to recite " 'Tis the Voice of the Sluggard," another favorite recitation piece by Watts. Indeed, Alice feels herself placed in school with this command performance, but she finds her memory is still impaired, and her recent experiences morph the voice of the sluggard into that of "the Lobster," who now cries not "You have waked me too soon! I must slumber again," but "You have baked me too brown! I must sugar my hair." Again, the results are hilarious, as are nearly all the real-world things that get mixed up in Wonderland, but Alice's performance induces not glee but confusion and criticism: " 'That's different from what I used to say in school,' said the Gryphon. 'Well, I never heard it before,' said the Mock Turtle; 'but it sounds uncommon nonsense.' "[17] The parody follows the original as if the sequence of the words, but not the words themselves, are remembered, and the result

Opposite, Frontispiece and title page, [Ann Taylor and] Jane Taylor, *Hymns for Infant Minds*, published by the American Tract Society after 1840. *Courtesy of American Antiquarian Society.*

is "uncommon nonsense." This is a game that could be played with any well-known text, and the fact that Watts's poems were so famous a century and a half after they were first published that Carroll could assume universal recognition of them is worth noticing. Indeed, not the least hilarious part of this scene is the fact that the Gryphon has recited Watts in a Wonderland school and can ask for a recitation text that Alice (as well as her readers) immediately recognizes.

It is important to understand why Carroll could assume such universal knowledge of the Watts texts. Alice has been trained in the British elementary school practice of poetry recitation, and she strikes a pose when reciting that was taught to thousands of children in Carroll's time. Twenty-first-century scholarship has emphasized the importance of school recitation exercises in popularizing certain poems, such as Watts's, and in ensuring that poetry as a literary form would be, to modify Angela Sorby's phrase, read through the body.[18] Both of Carroll's Watts parodies are highly embodied against oceanic backdrops: Alice's dismay at her loss of identity leads her to weep "a pool of tears . . . nine feet high,"[19] while a beach is the setting for her encounter with the Gryphon and the Mock Turtle. Perhaps Britain was nearing its saturation point with the hymns of Watts, Barbauld, and the Taylors (though they would all stay in print into the twentieth century), but the larger point that Carroll implied is this: Watts was the atmosphere, the foundation, the surrounding margins of children's early reading before 1900. Carroll knew in 1865 that any fresh effort in children's literature would need to be launched upon a sea of Watts.

CHAPTER 8

How Hymns Remade Schoolbooks

In the Library Company of Philadelphia's main reading room, if you request the title *Picture Hymns*, you receive a small archival box. Open it, and you see what looks like a deck of large playing cards. Each of the twenty-six thick cards includes an intricate engraving, a decorative colored border, and two hymn texts, one on each side. A complete set, these cards are in pristine condition, as is the only other known set, held about a mile away at the Free Library of Philadelphia. These cards are striking, but what is most distinctive about them is that they have survived. The *Picture Hymns* set is one of the fancier examples of cards produced in the hundreds of thousands by the American Sunday School Union (*Picture Hymns*'s publisher) and other organizations as study aids and rewards of merit for their students, and many of these included hymn excerpts. For excellent attendance, appropriate behavior, progress in learning, or special accomplishments, students received such cards from their teachers, both reinforcing good behavior and further cementing the bond between teacher and pupil. As precious keepsakes for students, many of these rewards would have gone into the private collections of children, eventually deteriorating from handling or cramped storage, or simply disappearing with other childhood ephemera. Many rewards of merit were inscribed by teachers, often using blank spaces designed for just such a purpose. The cards could be precious artworks to the recipients as well as handwritten votes of confidence, even as they introduced students to the growing adult world of printed forms through what one scholar has called "the ephemera of childhood."[1]

One striking example, held at the American Antiquarian Society, squeezes two hymn stanzas below a large engraved scene of a farming family preparing to walk to the church in the background. The hymn quoted is a variant of "Lord, Dismiss Us with Thy Blessing," a popular closing hymn

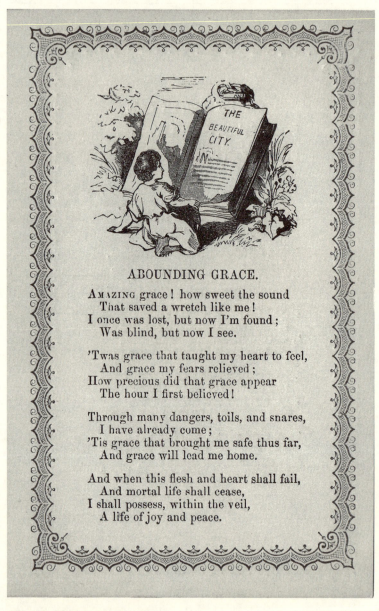

ABOUNDING GRACE.

AMAZING grace! how sweet the sound
   That saved a wretch like me!
I once was lost, but now I'm found;
   Was blind, but now I see.

'Twas grace that taught my heart to feel,
   And grace my fears relieved;
How precious did that grace appear
   The hour I first believed!

Through many dangers, toils, and snares,
   I have already come;
'Tis grace that brought me safe thus far,
   And grace will lead me home.

And when this flesh and heart shall fail,
   And mortal life shall cease,
I shall possess, within the veil,
   A life of joy and peace.

Reward card with text of "Abounding Grace" (now known as "Amazing Grace"). American Sunday School Union, *Picture Hymns* (1857). *Library Company of Philadelphia.*

that circulated widely in a number of versions; the hymn's authorship is still in some doubt. There is no doubt of the recipient of this card, however: "Master Julius Smith" received this reward from "his teacher Cordelia E Hildreth." Hildreth's inscription left no space for further writing on the recto of the card, so her parting message to young Julius appears on the verso: "Will you Learn the Hymn[?]"[2] For his good behavior, Julius Smith was given an award that came with homework. Yet this was a kind of homework that Watts had said that many children enjoy, and thousands of teachers, publishers, and parents agreed that the learning of hymns was one of the best things that successful students could do. In this chapter I trace the learning of hymns beyond the formal space of the hymnbook to another print genre, the schoolbook. The rise of modern schoolbooks, beginning with the primers and spellers of the eighteenth century, owed a great deal not only to the content provided by hymnbooks but also to the catechetical goals shared between the genres. The previous chapters showed the intertwining practices of children's hymnody and literacy; this chapter turns specifically to books, tracing the circulation and editing of hymns to shed new light on the truism that the path from the *New-England Primer* to the *McGuffey Readers* was one of secularization.

The practice of using hymn texts in secular (nonscriptural) schoolbooks began, as it turns out, with Isaac Watts. His work as the Abney daughters' tutor, which produced his *Divine Songs* (1715), also produced his *Art of Reading* (1721), a text that assumed the ability to spell or decode and continued to the practice of reading aloud, a skill crucial for the sharing of texts in a time before mass literacy and one that formed the foundation of oratorical skills, both for content and delivery. Until the early nineteenth century, the term "reading" in an educational setting referred specifically to reading aloud, a skill generally taught only at elite grammar schools, where boys alone would be trained in the classical canons of rhetoric; the boys also learned grammar in a circuitous path that started with Latin and Greek and then circled back to English (if formal instruction in English grammar was offered at all). Watts explained in his preface that he wished for a vernacular approach to reading that relied on, and taught, knowledge of English alone—both for ease of learning and to acknowledge the humbler literacy needs of the poor.[3] It is no coincidence that the first use of the full version of *Art of Reading* was at a charity school the Abneys sponsored in Cheshunt.[4]

Yet while Watts's effort is recognizably democratic to readers today, it would be difficult to call his book a secular one. *Art of Reading* used a catechetical question-and-answer format to explain rules of pronunciation and delivery (Watts was also a widely reprinted catechist), and this fusing of sacred and secular pedagogies paved the way for a guide to the book as print object.[5] Watts showed concern that students learn to navigate not only the sentence but the page and the codex as well. Later chapters in *Art of Reading* explained forms of punctuation, including an entire chapter devoted to special marks used in Bible printing. Other chapters explained how to recognize and read non-roman typefaces, pointed out the differing conventions between written and printed English, and provided writing exercises (a controversial skill among charity schools well into the nineteenth century). Particularly important for my argument in this book, Watts also provided an introduction to the basic genres of English literature, including a chapter on poetic meters in which he used examples from his own "'Tis the Voice of the Sluggard" to illustrate anapests, the first time a hymn was used as an example in a language textbook. Watts wanted his students equipped for the worlds of language, of script, of print, and of books—four realms that overlapped but differed in important respects.

Watts had good reasons to want to teach new readers how to navigate the designs of various books since print genres were proliferating in the first third of the eighteenth century, not least in a rapid expansion of material intended specifically for young readers. The spelling book (or speller) became prominent in the 1730s as a sequel to the primer, guiding students from basic decoding skills to the reading of connected texts; by the late eighteenth century, the reader joined the speller as the next genre for students learning the art of reading aloud, a skill gradually expanding beyond grammar schools to parochial and newly established common schools. Scholars of education have generally seen the rise of the speller and the reader as secularizing literacy education, replacing the earlier "ordinary Road" of primer to psalter to testament to Bible with a selection of excerpts, placing scriptural texts alongside sermons, speeches, essays, stories, and poems in the spirit of the literary miscellanies that distilled and delivered "good reading" to an increasingly sophisticated audience.[6] What the secularization narrative ignores is that the 1730s also saw the first waves of the transatlantic revivals now known as the Great Awakening, a phenomenon that introduced hymn singing to a much wider public than before and that made hymn-books ubiquitous even in communities that resisted singing hymns in church. One index of how popular these hymns were by the mid-eighteenth century is their use in schoolbooks of the time.

In British North America, *The New-England Primer* was the preeminent schoolbook, with an estimated six million produced and sold from its first appearance in the late seventeenth century to the early nineteenth century (it stayed in print nearly up to the Civil War). Long considered a holdover from grim Puritan fire-and-brimstone discourses, this primer actually proved nearly as flexible in incorporating regional and generational changes as it was enduring.[7] While the earliest editions and many thereafter came from Boston and other New England printing centers, many editions were produced in New York and Philadelphia, and some northern editions were prepared specifically for distribution to southern booksellers. Multiple editions also appeared in Britain, both for domestic use and for export back to the colonies. Thus what appeared on the pages of *The New-England Primer*, eclectic and varying as the content was, provided something like a shared cultural baseline for generations of American and, indeed, British readers.

The rhymed alphabet of *The New-England Primer*, with its evolving spiritual and secular subjects and eye-catching woodcut illustrations, has been the focus of most analyses of the book's content. Some attention has been given as well to the included catechisms, usually either the Shorter Catechism (a compromise document among English Dissenters) or the New England–produced *Milk for Babes*. The most consistently included reading across the decades of *New-England Primer* editions was a poetic farewell by the Protestant martyr John Rogers to his family as he prepared for execution during Bloody Mary's persecution in the mid-sixteenth century. This stern, dense call to stay true to Protestant orthodoxy, accompanied by a dramatic woodcut of Rogers burning at the stake in sight of his wife and children, is exhibit A for scholars who see this primer as a nightmare-inducing book. What those scholars generally overlook is that, even as the alphabet became more biblical in the 1740s and 1750s, new texts were added to editions from Boston and New York in 1750 that would appear in nearly all subsequent editions of *The New-England Primer*: morning and evening hymns and "Cradle Hymn" from Watts's *Divine Songs*. The latter text was often juxtaposed with the Rogers poem, soothing the young reader with the story of Christ's love for his people. While the morning and evening hymns are in the voice of the child reader, allowing students to make the text their own, "Cradle Hymn" is voiced by a mother rocking her baby to sleep, a remarkably comforting and homely scene in a book reputed for its cerebral severity. Even as the primer was gradually secularized, including selections celebrating the financial benefits of literacy borrowed from John Newbery's competing *Royal Primer,* "Cradle Hymn" remained as an expression of Christian salvation that spoke equally to the revival era of Jonathan Edwards and to the growing commercialization of the early republic. Watts's texts provided a common-denominator Christianity that both participated in and checked the secularization of education.

A similar role for Watts appeared in Newbery's *Royal Primer.* While no first edition survives (as is also the case with *The New-England Primer*) and the date of its initial publication is unknown, scholars agree that the book first appeared no later than 1750, the year that Watts entered *The New-England Primer.*[8] The Newbery book was popular on both sides of the Atlantic, serving as *The New-England Primer*'s main competition until Noah Webster's books appeared in the 1780s; in histories of education it has generally been held up as "the more liberal Anglican" alternative to "the rigid Puritanical" *New-England Primer.*[9] Indeed, with excerpts from the Book of Common Prayer outnumbering those from the Bible, and the royal seal appearing opposite the title page of early British editions, the *Royal Primer* exhibited its mainstream Englishness at least as adamantly as the John Rogers poem announced its Protestant difference. And yet, from the earliest known editions, the Dissenting Watts's hymns were a fixture in Newbery's supposedly Anglican book. Nearly a century before most Anglicans were prepared to sing the words of Watts or Wesley in church, the morning and evening hymns from *Divine Songs*—rather than, say, those by the Anglican bishop Thomas Ken—were part of the reading curriculum assembled by the man considered to be the father of children's literature. Even as enterprising a publisher as John Newbery could not easily get by without Watts. Hymns had become such an expected part of early reading curricula by the mid-eighteenth century that the earliest surviving American reprint of the *Royal Primer,* a 1753 Philadelphia edition, added a series of woodcuts depicting different types of ships that would have been seen in the city's port, and running below the images was a Joseph Addison hymn, "How Are Thy Servants Blest, O Lord."[10] A selection from Watts's *Divine Songs* closed the volume. The book's publisher, James Chattin, clearly expected that his readers would want hymns as what at the time was called "useful entertainment," whether as closing prayers or accompanying seemingly secular illustrations.

Thus part of what drove what scholars have considered the secularization of literacy was the hymn, deemed to have a more accessible and adaptable aesthetic than the King James Bible. The hymn had the dual advantage of being able to distill scriptural content and to range into other subject matter, often in the same text. While the Bible remained as a source, it now had relatively equal status with the secular sources that surrounded it—and with the hymns that continued to be included. Anna Letitia Barbauld's efforts to imitate the Bible in her *Hymns in Prose*, together with her elegant writing style, made her a favorite choice for "secularizing" educators who revered the Bible but sought to diversify their students' readings. From Noah Webster's *Grammatical Institute* (1785) to Lindley Murray's *Introduction to the English Reader* (1801), Barbauld filled pages alongside Watts, and sometimes even more than him. For Murray in particular, who sought to balance the prose and poetry selections in each of his readers, Barbauld and Watts represented two complementary sources of religious material that would also prepare students to absorb the kind of taste that Murray emphasized.

Murray was something of an unlikely educator. A New York Quaker (Murray Hill in Manhattan is named for his family), Murray attended elite schools in Philadelphia and New Jersey, a mediocre student who found himself fascinated by his own personal reading in a wide range of subjects but bored with the Greek and Latin drills that were the standard curriculum of the time. The onset of the American Revolution led him to relocate to Yorkshire in England, where his Quaker Loyalism could have safe haven. He never returned to America, but his schoolbooks would be imported, and then reprinted, by the thousands. Murray began his career in textbooks around the age of fifty, following the suggestion of some Yorkshire Friends. Sensing a gap in the early readers' curriculum, where grammar instruction was reserved for those studying the classics, Murray first published his *English Grammar* in 1795. The book's immediate success led him to consider new approaches to rhetoric. Rather than teaching from principles, Murray chose to compile readings for students to learn to perform aloud—the eighteenth-century art of reading.

Guided by the writings of Edinburgh professor Hugh Blair, Murray taught techniques of pronunciation, inflection, and pacing as means of conveying the deeper intellectual and emotional content of a text. As Murray put it in one introduction, "It is essential to a complete reader, that he minutely perceive the ideas, and enter into the feelings, of the author whose sentiments he professes to repeat."[11] In other words, Murray's idea of a successful reader was someone who could read closely enough to fully understand what an author was saying as well as the tone with which the author conveyed it—to such an extent that the reader could temporarily take on the text as their own, in effect reauthoring the text for the reader's audience. This ideal reading built on the ancient rhetorical practice of *imitatio*, the effort of writing or speaking in the style of a specific text or author as a way of internalizing the values and ideas of the source. It also bore more than a passing resemblance to the work of an actor performing a play, a form of work rarely considered virtuous in Murray's day (though it was quite popular).[12] In order to avoid the pitfalls of hypocrisy and sophistry that adopting another's text as one's own could lead to, Murray stressed the care he took in selecting texts marked by their "purity, propriety, perspicuity, and . . . elegance."[13] He admitted that these standards were especially difficult to maintain in poetry, and he had to excerpt and adapt his passages to avoid any corrupting tendencies they might have. Murray selected only British texts, including portions of the King James Bible, which he held up as a literary as well as a spiritual paragon for his readers.

Scripture passages appeared throughout the *English Reader* and his *Sequel to the English Reader* (1800), a more advanced version that was published soon after the original volume. While much of the poetry also had religious dimensions to it—particularly works by John Milton, James Thomson, and Edward Young—he did include a few hymns: two by Joseph Addison in the *English Reader* and one by Barbauld in the *Sequel*. The next book Murray compiled, *Introduction to the English Reader* (1801), was for students not quite advanced enough to rise to the challenge of his previous volumes. Murray found that his stylistic and moral standards were even more difficult to maintain while seeking a greater simplicity of expression, and this led to a

remarkable departure from the highly varied, elite miscellany of his selections in the earlier books. Four of the prose works were taken from
Barbauld's *Hymns in Prose*, while a full third of the poetry selections were
hymns. Eleven of these were from Watts's *Divine Songs*; the other eight were
largely congregational hymns by Watts, his associate Philip Doddridge, and
Barbauld. With limited materials of sufficient quality at hand, Murray
turned to hymnody—notably, Dissenting hymnody—to serve his youngest
readers, introducing them to poetry by using hymns as a fundamental
benchmark of aesthetic and moral excellence. In so doing, Murray realized
a dream Watts had expressed in *Art of Reading* of a graduated reader focused
on the cultivation of piety and of good English style.[14] Murray was Watts's
pedagogical heir as well as the beneficiary of Watts's hymns.

Murray's *English Grammar* and his *Readers* were the top-selling books of
their kind on both sides of the Atlantic during the first third of the nineteenth century, with only Noah Webster's books offering what might be
considered stiff competition in the United States. Yet even Webster, who led
a chorus of American educators in criticizing the popularity of a British-only
line of readings, incorporated Watts and Barbauld into some of his editions,
if not on the same scale as Murray did. For educators who wanted students
to learn poetry while strengthening rather than compromising traditional
morals, hymns simply were the most obvious choice for their anthologies.
Indeed, the choice was so obvious that one distinctive aspect of Barbauld's
and Watts's appearances in the spellers and readers of the eighteenth and
early nineteenth centuries is the rarity of attribution. Since both *Divine
Songs* and *Hymns in Prose* were extremely popular, the texts likely did not
need identification as much as other choices did. Yet these authors' names
were selling points for publishers of their books as individual volumes,
and their anonymity in Murray's schoolbooks made them nearly the only
exceptions to his practice of including authors' names at the end of readings. This helped to contribute to the notion that hymns might not be true
poetry, an issue to which I return in this book's final part. The inclusion of
hymns in schoolbooks (and their authors' anonymity in those books) continued for another century in the United States especially, thanks to Murray's
greatest American follower: William Holmes McGuffey.

Remembered today as the quintessential American schoolbook, Mc-
Guffey's *Eclectic Readers*, later known simply as *McGuffey Readers*, were a

self-conscious product of the West, offered by Cincinnati publisher Truman and Smith as competition for the northeastern books edited by Webster, Samuel Worcester, and other minister-educators. Winthrop Smith had envisioned the reader series before beginning his partnership with William Truman in 1834, and the early history of the *McGuffey Readers* stems from the arrival of the Beecher family in Cincinnati in 1832, when Lyman Beecher became the inaugural president of Lane Theological Seminary. Smith approached Catharine Beecher, Lyman's eldest daughter and already a famous educator from her girls' academy in Connecticut, to edit the readers, but Beecher declined and recommended McGuffey instead.[15] McGuffey had become acquainted with the Beechers and their circle, including future Lincoln cabinet member Salmon P. Chase and the future husband of Harriet Beecher, Calvin Stowe, through a reading group called the Western Literary Institute, where abolitionism, religious commitment, and moral uplift were the bedrock of their conversations.[16] A professor of classics at Miami University at the time, McGuffey was perhaps a surprising choice for producing the best-selling books for teaching young children to read in the nineteenth-century United States, but McGuffey's upbringing as a Scottish Presbyterian in western Pennsylvania and his affinities with the moral suasion that the Beechers advocated for creating a postdenominational American Christianity gave him the right ingredients to make a more democratic version of Murray's books.

When McGuffey's *Eclectic Readers* began appearing in 1836, he continued many of Murray's practices. He included biblical excerpts alongside prose and poetry with moral messages; he relied especially heavily on Barbauld's *Hymns in Prose* in the earlier books, including selections from three prose hymns in the *Second Reader* alone. Like Murray, McGuffey did not generally attribute Barbauld's texts, even when he did so with neighboring ones. He also omitted Watts's name in the *Third Reader* when he included the then-famous hymn "How Beauteous Are Their Feet." People were likely puzzled by this at the time, and in the book's first revision in the 1840s that hymn disappeared, while a new hymn by John Bowring was added—with the author's name attached.

While modern reprints of the *McGuffey Readers* give the impression that the books were fixed expressions of antebellum American culture, they were actually revised several times. After some initial minor changes, McGuffey undertook more substantial revisions in the 1840s following a copyright law-suit from Samuel Worcester's publisher, who felt McGuffey's books resembled those of New England a bit too closely. McGuffey ended his personal involvement with the series in 1845 upon accepting a faculty position at the University of Virginia, but Smith and his publishing partners continued to update the books, from the primer and speller through the *Sixth Reader*, for decades. The first major overhaul was in the 1850s, undertaken by Obed J. Wilson and his wife, Amanda Mariah Wilson, both Cincinnati school-teachers whose work on the books (now titled *McGuffey Readers* as a brand) resulted in Obed's elevation to editor in chief and later to partner at the publisher following Smith's retirement.[17] Unknown editors performed a new round of editing between 1879 and 1885, when the books assumed their near-final form, now pitched lower than McGuffey's original books had been. The *Sixth Reader*, for example, was now intended for sixth-graders, students around eleven years old; the original *Sixth Reader*, edited by McGuffey's brother Alexander, was essentially an advanced high school book that few students would have achieved sufficient proficiency to study.

According to McGuffey's biographer John H. Westerhoff, the revisions "severely secularized" the readers, based on his count of biblical passages and the number of mentions of God across the books.[18] What this index of secularization misses is the remarkable persistence, even the increase, of hymn texts over the editions. The respective place of hymns in the *McGuffey Readers* changed somewhat over time, but the pattern held from the early editions to the last. The *Second Reader* emphasized Barbauld's *Hymns in Prose* as well as popular Sunday school hymns about God as Creator, such as "Remember, child, remember, / That God is in the sky"; Lydia Sigourney's "The Sun Hath Gone to Rest"; and Sarah Josepha Hale's versification of the Lord's Prayer, "Our Father in Heaven." The *Third Reader* focused more on hymns that tended to cross over between Sunday school hymnbooks and collections of poetry, particularly selections from Felicia Hemans's *Hymns on the Works of Nature*, an 1827 collection written for children using the model of Barbauld's technique in *Hymns in Prose*: starting with descriptions of nature and moving to moral and theological reflections on them. One of the Wilsons' additions to the *Second Reader* was a prose piece titled "Puss and Her Kittens." This too followed Barbauld's lead, beginning: "Let us go and look at puss and her kittens." To arrive at a moral, the speaker says at the end, "There is a pretty hymn, which tells us how we should feel. It says, 'Let love through all your actions run, / And all your words be mild.' This is a very pretty hymn. We hope you will learn it. Let love run through every thought and look."[19] The lines, taken from Watts's "Let Dogs Delight to Bark and Bite," exhibit how quotable and ubiquitous Watts had become at this point, and the idea that this detached couplet should be recognized as coming from a hymn also suggests the equation of hymnody with early childhood reading for the Wilsons and their audience.

In the 1870s–1880s editions, hymns still held their own. In the new *Second Reader* Barbauld's three prose hymns were reduced to one, and Hale's versified Lord's Prayer was replaced by her more secular "Mary Had a Little Lamb." Yet two new hymns by the Virginian composer Aldine Kieffer were added, as were an altered version of William Cutter's "Fear Not, Fear Not, Dear Little Ones" and, remarkably, Watts's "Whatever Brawls Disturb the Street." The "Puss and Her Kittens" piece stayed intact, including the similarly themed Watts quotation. The new *Third Reader* included no fewer than twelve texts that had appeared in Sunday school hymnbooks earlier in the century, ranging from David Bates's didactic "Speak Gently, It Is Better Far" to Ann Taylor's iconic "Great God! and Wilt Thou Condescend." Hale's versified Lord's Prayer appeared again, as did a selection entitled "The Sluggard," which consisted of excerpts from the book of Proverbs about the fate of the lazy man, followed immediately by Watts's "'Tis the Voice of the Sluggard," which comments on those biblical passages. In another feat of blending the Bible with hymnody, an excerpt from Barbauld's prose hymn number 1 concluded with verses directly from Psalm 95. Hymns had not previously been a major element in the *Fourth Reader* and beyond, presumably because they were not challenging enough as readings for students at those levels, but in the later edition another excerpt from Barbauld's *Hymns in Prose* and several hymns of nature by Sigourney and Hemans were added. Hymns for children evolved considerably across the nineteenth century and had already blended praise and a didactic function as early as Watts's *Divine Songs*. Their ability to serve changing cultural purposes kept them in the *McGuffey Readers* for a century, both contributing to and tempering the process of secularization that early scholars of the books perceived.

The advanced *McGuffey Readers* never included many hymns, following Murray's readers before them. As textbooks continued to diversify throughout the nineteenth century, hymns became increasingly identified as fit mostly for early literacy or preliteracy curricula. Their predictable form and their association with children's "first book" experiences increasingly relegated them as reading texts for nurseries, infant schools, and beginners' schoolbooks. One common method for infant schools—where learning obedience and the alphabet took priority over reading instruction—was for the teacher to read a hymn, lead the children in singing it, and then ask a series of questions to be answered from the text, not unlike a traditional catechistic format. The strong oral presence of hymns made them available to the preliterate, yet they were far from absent from schoolrooms even at much more advanced levels.

Singing became increasingly prominent as music education expanded in the new public schools through the middle third of the nineteenth century. By the 1850s, publishers began providing hymnbooks and songbooks with hymn sections specifically for public school use; while drawing heavily on the Sunday school and congregational repertoires, these books also aided the gradual blending of devotional, moral, and entertaining texts. The *Public School Singing Book*, first published in Philadelphia in 1848, was a prime example of this new type of book; alongside Watts hymns, such as "When I Can Read My Title Clear," and texts by Addison and Heber appeared sentimental songs, such as "Flow Gently, Sweet Schuylkill" (a localized imitation of Robert Burns's "Sweet Afton"). Charles Dexter Cleveland, the headmaster of a girls' academy in Philadelphia, edited his own collection in 1850, *Hymns for Schools*, which included tunes as well as texts. He intended the book for devotional exercises at his own school, and copies survive that he inscribed to his students.[20] A few enterprising editors attempted to combine new innovations in music education and children's publishing by producing books that included hymn texts, printed music, and engraved illustrations. Lilla Linden's *The Linden Harp* (1855) did so with striking, visually chaotic results.

As it turns out, new directions in music education were as much part of Truman and Smith's 1830s publishing scheme as books like the *McGuffey Readers* were. Smith's vision to build a western version of the vibrant New England intellectual culture to which the Beecher family had contributed led him, even before the first *Eclectic Reader* appeared, to publish *The Sacred Harp; or, Eclectic Harmony* (1834), jointly edited by the brothers

146 WHAT IS HEAVEN?

DIALOGUE BETWEEN GERTRUDE AND HERBERT.

German Melody.

GERTRUDE.
O, what is heav'n? I want to know: And what is passing

HERBERT.
Yes, there are flow'rs which never fade, And streams that never

there? Do gen - tle riv - ers bright - ly flow, And
dry; And there is known no eve - ning shade, To

flow'rs per - fume the air?
din the glo - rious sky.

GERTRUDE.
3. O, what is heav'n? I want to know, Are children playing there? And do they thirst and hunger now, And feel a parent's care?

HERBERT.
4. No, never do they hunger there, Nor precious moments waste; But beauteous as the angels are, With Christ's own image graced.

GERTRUDE.
5. But where is heaven? O, is it far Above the ground I tread? Or is it fix'd in yonder star, Whose beams shine mildly red?

HERBERT.
6. No! No! Saviour's smiling face, That makes the heaven above; And would we reach that happy place, We here his bairns must love.

7. T is in his word that we are told Of bliss beyond the sky, And how to obtain a crown of gold, All glorious, when we die.

GERTRUDE.
8. Dear Jesus, may I now be thine, And have my sins forgiv'n: Along with saints and angels shine With thee—for that is heav'n.

LINDEN HARP. 147

WHAT IS DEATH?

DIALOGUE BETWEEN ELIZA AND HER MOTHER.

ELIZA.
1. "Mother, how still the baby lies, I cannot hear his breath; I cannot see his laughing eyes; They tell me this is death.

2. "My little work I thought to bring, And sit down by his bed; And pleasantly I tried to sing— They hush'd me—He is dead!

3. "They say that he again will rise, More beautiful than now; That God will bless him in the skies, O, mother, tell me how.

MOTHER.
4. "Daughter, do you remember, dear, The cold, dark thing you brought And hid upon the casement here? A wither'd worm you thought.

5. "I told you, that almighty power Could break that wither'd shell, And show you, in a future hour, Something would please you well.

6. "Look at that chrysalis, my love; An empty shell it lies; Now raise your wond'ring glance To where yon insect flies.

ELIZA.
7. "O, yes, mamma, how very gay Its wings of starry gold— And see it lightly flies away, Beyond my gentle hold.

8. "O, mother, now I know full well, If God that worm can change, And draw it from this broken shell, On golden wings to range;

9. "How beautiful will brother be, When God shall give him wings Above this dying world to flee, And live with heav'nly things."

Lowell and Timothy Mason. Lowell Mason had helped to build the nation's first public school music program in Boston in the 1820s, and Timothy had recently arrived in Cincinnati to teach music at the new Eclectic Academy and to serve as the organist of Second Presbyterian Church, where Lyman Beecher was the pastor. *The Sacred Harp* was the first western volume of the "better music" the Masons and their eastern collaborators urged the churches to adopt over the older folk-based repertoires. Other books were specifically designed for children in schools, but books like *The Sacred Harp* took the Masons' educational campaign to adult choirs in the churches. In doing so, they locked horns with those devoted to more traditional music styles, particularly in the South and West, even as they participated in an ever-widening culture of hymn reading. The singing of hymns was itself a form of reading, and that practice and the Masons' involvement in it forms the subject of the next chapter.

Opposite, Sample pages from Lilla Linden, comp., *The Linden Harp: A Rare Collection of Popular Melodies, Adapted to Sacred and Moral Songs, Original and Selected* (1855). *Courtesy of American Antiquarian Society.*

Singing as Reading; or, A Tale of Two Sacred Harps

In 1844, the first edition of Benjamin Franklin White and Elisha J. King's *The Sacred Harp* appeared in Philadelphia. This was a tunebook with formatting typical of the genre: a horizontally oriented page (often called oblong) filled primarily with multipart staff music and a stanza or two of text for each tune. An introduction offered a basic course in singing and reading music, and an index to the tunes (but not the texts) was in the back. Dozens of similar books had appeared in the United States in the previous century, far more than in Britain, where music education was still largely an elite activity. The tunebooks had initially provided music imported from Britain, but by the 1760s American compositions began to share space with the British tunes, and White and King's book boasted old and new American tunes alongside several adapted from Europe.

But even as the music became more locally produced, the texts provided with the music were still largely British. In fact, there was little ground between the venerable names of Watts, Wesley, Doddridge, and Newton and the largely anonymous texts developed at American revival meetings. As distinctive as the music became, the words drew on a very conservative canon, and parallel practices among African American churches would become known as "Dr. Watts singing" or simply "Wattsing." The father of English hymnody was now the name as well as the vehicle for American musical practices that would inspire genres such as gospel and R&B but that were also consciously backward-looking.

What then was the way forward in the nineteenth century? That path was exemplified by another *Sacred Harp*, which developed out of a partnership between the brothers Timothy and Lowell Mason, straddling Boston and Cincinnati. The Masons had grown up in a Massachusetts shopkeeper's home, where Congregational worship was the default. The Mason children were musically gifted, Lowell most of all, but the only music professionals in the United States had emigrated from Europe (where they had been trained).[1] Lacking the opportunity for European study, business seemed a much more realistic career choice for the Masons. Lowell took up shop-keeping in Savannah, Georgia, before settling into life as a bank clerk there. In his teenage years, he had been mentored by a German-trained musician, and Mason had developed considerable skill on a range of instruments, allowing him to find part-time employment as the organist for a Presbyterian church in Savannah. Mason became deeply involved in the Sunday school then developing at the church, and his lifelong interests in music education and congregational singing grew from his Georgia years. Mason had kept ties with music societies in Boston that emphasized bringing European music—Haydn, Mozart, and Beethoven especially—to public attention through widely advertised concerts. He assembled a choral book for one of those societies that sought to bridge the gap between church and concert hall. *The Boston Handel and Haydn Society Collection of Church Music* (1822) proved so popular that Mason's Boston associates urged him to return north and focus professionally on music. Over the next decade Lowell Mason became the most famous promoter of music education in the country, serving as the Boston Academy of Music's first professor of music and persuading the city's school superintendent, Horace Mann, to make Boston the first American city to offer music instruction (mainly choral singing) in public schools.

Lowell's youngest brother, Timothy, became an ideal partner for the enterprise of music education. Following a stint teaching at the Boston Academy, Timothy moved to Cincinnati to become the first professor of music at the Eclectic Academy. This appointment came likely through the influence of Lyman Beecher, president of Cincinnati's Lane Theological Seminary and a longtime friend of the Masons, who shared their passion for congregational singing (as did Beecher's son Henry Ward Beecher). Timothy Mason had learned from his brother a Pestalozzian philosophy of music education—teach by doing, not by rote memorization of concepts—and they both believed that the best way to win popular support for music in schools and churches was to combine dynamic teaching with attractive published collections of tunes. Timothy collaborated with Lowell to bring out *The Sacred Harp; or, Eclectic Harmony* in 1834 with the Cincinnati publisher

Truman and Smith, a firm just embarking on the *Eclectic Reader* series with William McGuffey. The Masons' *Sacred Harp* was stereotyped and quickly went through several reprintings, eventually amassing tens of thousands of sales, and the success led to something of a *Sacred Harp* series.[2] Lowell seems to have led the creation of *The Sacred Harp; or, Beauties of Church Music* (1838) in Boston, while Timothy appears alone on the title page for a new volume called simply *Beauties of Church Music* (1840).[3] All of the books listed publishing partners in Cincinnati and Boston and often other locations as well. Yet the books displayed certain regional distinctions, and these differences illustrate the rivalry that scholars like George Pullen Jackson have posited between the Masons' urban, Eurocentric approach and White and King's *Sacred Harp* folk idiom. The gap between Cincinnati and Boston in the Masons' experience also highlights the complexities of that rivalry as regional cultures continued to evolve in the 1840s.

The most dramatic difference was the use of patent notes (shape notes) in the *Eclectic Harmony* sold in Cincinnati. Shape-note tunebooks originated in 1801 in Philadelphia, reorganizing the eight-tone scale into two linked sequences of four tones, each tone represented by a distinctive shape. This innovation made the learning of scales and the relationships between tones faster and easier, and it appeared when American singing schools, which had become popular during the Great Awakening as a way of empowering the congregation's worship and social bonds, were still widespread. The Mason children had attended one of these schools in the early nineteenth century, but Lowell had by 1820 rejected the musical tradition the school fostered for the more "scientific" music favored in Europe, especially Germany. Timothy shared his brother's views, and the annoyance at the felt necessity to bring out shape-note tunebooks in the West is clear in the editorial comments: "The whole work is now stereotyped, so that successive editions can be used together. The publishers would further remark, that the 'Sacred Harp' is printed in patent notes (contrary to the wishes of the Authors) under the belief that it will prove much more acceptable to a majority of singers in the West and South."[4] This typographical choice meant that while the tunes and harmonies of *Eclectic Harmony* may have fit northeastern standards better than those in White and King's book (which was printed and published in Philadelphia, where the best shape-note type was available), the look of the page was remarkably similar across the two projects.

While scholars since George Pullen Jackson have continued to see the Masons' approach and White and King's approach as exemplifying two increasingly divergent traditions of American vocal and sacred music, scant attention has been paid to the repertoire of texts used in those traditions. While the range of available hymnody had grown exponentially since the early tunebooks of the 1720s, and both the Masons and White and King encouraged the production of new textual as well as musical material, a popular conservatism marks all the *Sacred Harp* books at the level of the text. And the heart of the old canons they drew from, unsurprisingly, was Watts.

To say that Isaac Watts was a central figure in the *Sacred Harp* books would be an understatement. By my count, out of nearly 1,400 printed works, Watts accounted for 189 different texts (not counting variants). Of those 189, 77 appeared in the 1844 *Sacred Harp*, and 146 appeared in the Mason books—a similar proportion, since the three Mason books included just over twice the number of overall texts compared to the later book. These numbers dwarfed the individual contributions of all other known authors, and even the number of anonymous texts—including improvised camp songs, traditional texts like the Te Deum and the Lord's Prayer, and relatively unedited scripture passages for anthems and chants—paled in comparison to Watts's works. This corroborates the preponderance of Watts in leading hymnbooks at the time; Lowell Mason's 1831 *Church Psalmody*, a words-only book popular among Presbyterians, Baptists, and Congregationalists, was in many ways a "Watts and select" volume.

Beyond recognizing Watts's continued dominance, however, there is the question: Which Watts actually appeared in these books? Even 189 texts was a far cry from "Watts entire," and each individual *Sacred Harp* volume included a smaller slice of Watts's works than the one before it. There are some surprises as to what appears where; "Joy to the World," despite the fact that we today sing the tune Lowell Mason paired with it in some of his later collections, does not appear in the Masons' *Sacred Harp* books—but does in the White and King book. Of greater significance is the degree to which the various books shared Watts texts, 34 texts in all. This number was close to a quarter of the Watts texts used in the Mason books, but it was a full 44 percent of White and King's use of Watts. Multidenominational favorites, such as "There Is a Land of Pure Delight" and "My God, My Life, My Love," made this shared list, as did a large number of texts calling people to praise God's power and transcendence. The more personal, Christ-centered hymns—"Alas! And Did My Savior Bleed," "He Dies! The Friend of Sinners Dies," and "When I Survey the Wondrous Cross"—were absent from the Masons' books, suggesting that atonement theology may have been fading as a preferred hymn topic among their mainline audiences. Tellingly, few of Watts's most-sung texts today were part of the shared canon, and that modern list is distributed between the two *Sacred Harps* (only the Masons included "I Sing the Mighty Power of God," for instance). An intriguing detail of the shared canon, however, was that 23 of the 34 shared texts appeared in multiple Mason books. One of the few shared texts the Masons used only in the initial *Eclectic Harmony* was "When I Can Read My Title Clear." While there was considerable diversity in Watts selections across the books, there was too much overlap for the musical traditions to be said to emerge from distinct reading cultures.

The shared canons of hymnody across the two *Sacred Harps* went well beyond Watts. Among the more popular authors in both projects were John Newton, William Cowper, Reginald Heber, Joseph Stennett, Charles Wesley, and Joseph Hart. Some authors had distinctly different assortments in each project; Charles Wesley, a distant second to Watts with 47 texts (which appeared a total of 68 times), had only 3 shared texts, while Timothy Dwight, Samuel Francis Smith, and Anne Steele were in both *Sacred Harps* with no shared texts between them. Some authors were only represented by a single text that was shared in both, such as John Bowring's "Watchman, Tell Us of the Night," Edward Perronet's "All Hail the Power of Jesus' Name," and Robert Robinson's "Come Thou Fount of Every Blessing." From Watts's protégé Philip Doddridge to the Masons' contemporary Thomas Hastings, the shared texts covered the span of evangelical hymnody, reaching even into the Moravian tradition with John Cennick and James Montgomery and into Catholicism with Alexander Pope. The authors not shared between the *Sacred Harps* give some indication of the contours of the hymn canon. The colonial Congregationalist William Billings and the Methodist revivalist John A. Granade both appeared in White and King's book but not in the Masons'—the brothers' project was in many ways defined against the self-taught fuguing style of Billings and the emotional appeals of Granade. On the other side, the Masons included a number of Anglican or Episcopalian authors, from Joseph Addison to William Blacklock to American bishops George Washington Doane and William Muhlenberg, whose works were not part of White and King's repertoire, though all those authors were known to southern churches. Nahum Tate and Nicholas Brady's version of the book of Psalms, long considered the fashionable choice for Anglicans over the time-honored *Whole Book of Psalms* (1562) by Thomas Sternhold and John Hopkins, rivaled Wesley in the Masons' books, but only three of their texts were in the White and King book. New authors with a decidedly literary approach to hymnody, such as Harriet Auber, Phoebe Brown, and Ray Palmer, featured prominently in the Masons' books without appearing in White and King's collection. As with the Watts texts, a few canonical texts that failed to overlap might leave us wondering today. Newton was well represented in Mason, but "Amazing Grace" appeared only in White and King (as did the now-famous final stanza, which begins "When we've been there ten thousand years," of unknown authorship and given as a stand-alone chorus separate from Newton's hymn). While little from Tate and Brady is in the southern collection, "While Shepherds Watched Their Flocks by Night" appeared there but not in the Masons' books. And Cowper's "Sometimes a Light Surprises," a song about the ecstasy of singing in congregational worship, would seem a perfect choice for the Masons, but it only appeared in the rival book.

One shared text highlights the dynamics of this canon as well as the mutability of hymn texts. In the first *Beauties of Church Music* volume, the Masons included Reginald Heber's Epiphany hymn "Brightest and Best of the Sons of the Morning." The text had been one of Heber's most popular since he first published it in the *Christian Observer* in 1811, but the meter made it difficult to set to music, at least older music. This was just the sort of text the Masons found and created music for, and in *Beauties* the tune is named Folsom, an arrangement Lowell Mason first made in his *Carmina Sacra* (1838) and attributed to Mozart.[5] This was quite a pedigree to claim for the tune, but what was especially curious about the Masons' Folsom was that the text changed depending on the collection containing it. The Masons used the Folsom-Heber pairing in several of their books, but the shape-note *Eclectic Harmony* gave a variant found nowhere else in their works: "Brightest and best" was the start of the second stanza, while the hymn began:

> Hail! thou blessed morn, when the Great Mediator,
> Down from the regions of glory descends!
> Shepherds, go worship the babe in the manger;
> Lo! for his guard the bright angels attend.[6]

This new stanza was added to Heber's text as early as 1823,[7] and it was generally favored in more revival-friendly parts of the United States, especially the South and West. The original hymn, with its Epiphany calendar context and its focus on the magi and the star they followed, places the speaker in the position of the magi; the new stanza speaks to the shepherds, making the hymn more of a Christmas text, and it was often classified as such in books using the variant. By the time *Southern Harmony* (a major source for White and King's *Sacred Harp*) appeared in 1835, three more stanzas had appeared at the end, celebrating the consolations of worshiping the (adult, risen, glorified) Savior and looking forward to saints' rise to heaven.[8] That new text was also in White and King's first appendix, set to a minor-key tune called "Star in the East," the first instance of which may have been in Joshua Leavitt's *Christian Lyre* (1830).

Taken together, these texts illustrate two key points: Heber's text was popular enough to share across traditions (as was his missionary hymn "From Greenland's Icy Mountains"), and the fluid nature of revival hymns influenced the Masons as well as White and King. For the latter, revival hymns were a familiar tradition, but the Masons supposedly defined their work against the revival aesthetic of homegrown tunes and improvised texts. The publisher of *Eclectic Harmony* had insisted that the book could not be sold in Cincinnati and the surrounding region unless it was published in shape notes, and apparently part of what came with this revival-friendly style of notation was a textual canon whose force was felt even by Timothy Mason. The Masons were not shy about revising texts; in the *Sacred Harp* books alone, Wesley's "Jesus, Lover of My Soul" became "Jesus, Savior of My Soul," Perronet's "All Hail the Power of Jesus' Name" became "All Hail the Great Immanuel's Name," and even the Heber variant "Hail the Blest Morn" became "Hail! Thou Blest Morn." But the fact that the Masons felt the need to change their hymn text to a revival variant while keeping the same tune (Folsom) indicates that what words people sang could make as material a difference as what tunes they sang—and the wrong words, like the wrong notation, could hurt sales. The Masons' European approach to tunes eventually won nationwide support, and within several years of *The Sacred Harp*'s initial publication, round-note versions were available in the Ohio valley. But the shared core of hymn texts, variants and quirks included, remained vital and stable through the reformation of sacred music.

As it turns out, the Masons' success was built on a regimen of wide reading in hymnody, and one unique source lends unparalleled insight into just what kind of hymn reading the Mason family themselves did. Johnson Mason preceded Timothy to Cincinnati, leaving his family in 1831 to help construct a factory. Through long months of cold, illness, work frustrations, catastrophic flooding, and prayer meetings good, bad, and indifferent, Johnson Mason kept a diary of his time in the West.[9] Each entry included references to morning and evening prayers and concluded with a hymn stanza. For the first several months, all the hymns were by Watts except for Helen Maria Williams's "While Thee I Seek, Protecting Power" (a shared *Sacred Harp* text); later entries included texts by Anne Steele, George Washington Doane, and Charles Wesley. Many selections show evidence that Mason was using his brother Lowell's 1831 hymnbook, *Church Psalmody*, and that his general practice was to jump around in the text rather than follow a strict sequence or adhere to a thematic section. At the same time, he mentioned Wesleyan texts like "Jesus, Lover of My Soul," as well as Baptist favorites like "Jesus My All to Heaven Is Gone," which were not in that collection, suggesting that the small bookshelf Mason described building for himself included more than one hymnbook. Mason was certainly exposed to a wide range of hymnody in Cincinnati, as his diary recorded his attendance at meetings in Methodist and Baptist societies and at Sixth and Second Presbyterian. He was a member of the latter and stayed in town just long enough to shake Lyman Beecher's hand after Second Presbyterian's new pastor had preached his first sermon in Cincinnati. The overwhelming importance of Watts, the turning to texts old and new to guide spiritual seeking, and the search for consolation in distress all show Johnson Mason to be both a representative reader of his time and a representative of the Mason family, drawing heavily on his New England Congregational heritage for hymnody while availing himself of resources beyond his denominational home. If each church had a distinctive canon by this point, a larger, more ecumenical canon behind the canon, anchored by Watts, shaped church collections of hymns, popular tunebooks, and the devotional exercises of a New Englander far from home. Whether in singing or reading, American hymnbook users continually found themselves on the same pages.

Henry Ward Beecher Takes Note

Henry Ward Beecher had a flair for impossible missions. Since filling the pulpit in Brooklyn's new Plymouth Church in 1847, he had made his congregation an unofficial headquarters for abolitionism in his adopted city. Raised by leading Connecticut Congregationalist Lyman Beecher and having experienced the intense political tensions in Ohio's Presbyterian community, Beecher advocated for a united evangelical movement that would put gospel-driven reform above partisan loyalties. And he wanted his congregation to sing in church.[1]

This last goal, like the others, required a novel solution. Organizing and political advocacy could be done through his charismatic preaching and private persuasion, enhanced by access to mass media, such as the Brooklyn *Independent*, a weekly newspaper owned by Henry Chandler Bowen, a founding member of Plymouth Church who had personally worked to recruit Beecher as the pastor. But none of that would help Beecher overcome his congregation's habit of sitting with their hymnbooks and quietly enduring the choir's self-indulgent renditions of the hymns he'd chosen for Sunday worship. Beecher was a firm believer in the importance of the emotional engagement of the faithful in worship and in the power of music to shape lives. He was keenly aware that music was a missed opportunity in his church. And he was sure that there was a media solution: get the music literally in the hands of the congregation, and they would sing.

Yet that was not as simple as contracting with the nearest printer and carpeting the church with tunes. There were economic, technical, and above all cultural reasons that members of his church didn't have music already. For one thing, music was expensive. True, sheet music was exploding as an industry, in part thanks to the cheapness and quality of lithographic printing—but that mainly worked for a few pages at a time, a song or two.

Assembling a collection of 100, 200, or more tunes would require music type, which meant specialized printers with huge sets of type, specially trained compositors, and fees to match.[2]

But there was an even larger problem. There were plenty of books with printed hymn tunes available, but none of them were designed for congregational use. Since the 1720s, tunebooks had circulated as texts to aid singing schools and, later, the new church choirs that grew from those schools. Before the choirs, churches had relied on an orally taught, memorized set of tunes, which varied greatly between congregations and often were limited to as few as six tunes in a single church. The tunebooks offered music that was fresh, interesting—and beyond the capacity of the uninitiated. Whether they were intimidated, confused, or indignant, congregants chose to read their hymnbooks (which included only words) in silence rather than attempt to follow those intended to lead them in song. An entire culture of reading hymnbooks—elements of which were older than the choirs and tunebooks—was so firmly entrenched by the mid-nineteenth century that the printed tunes Beecher wanted would likely drive people away; they might prove more an obstacle to congregational singing than a path to it.

Yet Beecher had seen for himself that it could be different. While the old tunebooks filled their pages with music and rarely gave more than a stanza of text, more recent collections, such as Joshua Leavitt's *Christian Lyre* (1830) and Thomas Hastings's *Spiritual Songs* (1832), used a side-by-side format that made singing and reading a small, targeted set of texts viable in less formal worship settings, such as revivals and prayer meetings. Why, Beecher wondered, could a larger collection suited to the decorum and topical needs of a Sunday service not succeed? Working with Darius Jones, Plymouth Church's music director, Beecher made a trial run with a book on the scale of *Christian Lyre* called *Temple Melodies* (1851). Limited to 200 tunes and using the side-by-side format of the social worship books he admired, Beecher's book attracted enough interest for him to attempt a full-scale production. Over the next years, he compiled and edited more than 1,300 hymn texts, shaping them to his ecumenical ideal. With the Calvinists' favorite, Isaac Watts, and the Methodist poet laureate Charles Wesley as his top contributors, Beecher included texts from Baptist, Lutheran, and even Moravian and Roman Catholic sources in addition to more revival-oriented, evangelical songs. With tunes to match gathered by Plymouth organist John

Zundel and the pastor's brother Charles Beecher, the book promised to be a robust embodiment of Beecher's vision of the church at worship.

But who was going to publish such a huge, expensive book? It would need to be made from stereotype plates cast from combined music and letter type; not only did the high cost of setting the music type mean that a publisher would want plates so that any reprintings wouldn't involve paying the typesetters again, but also the actual music type was generally too delicate to print anything but small editions directly. This double cost up front, even before concerns of binding, distribution, and promotion entered the equation, was a real problem. Beecher had provided much of the starting expenses for the original *Temple Melodies* himself, in a typical arrangement to buy the plates from his publisher, Mason Brothers of New York. The firm was run by two sons of Lowell Mason, a great champion of congregational singing and music education in schools, but Beecher never considered offering his big book to them. Earlier, Beecher had found that the Masons left his name off *Temple Melodies* and asked them for an explanation. They replied (according to Beecher's account) that they "would not have the name of a d—d abolitionist in their book."[3] No one else seemed interested in taking on such a massive, untried publication, despite the fact that Beecher's celebrity status would guarantee at least some public interest. Beecher finally convinced Alfred Barnes to take the book.

Barnes had never published a music book before, though his flagship series of educational books had involved a fair amount of technical illustrations and he had new printing and stereotyping firms handling those complex books well. Like the Masons, though, Barnes insisted that Beecher pay for the plates up front before production started. This new book's cost was dramatically higher than that of *Temple Melodies*, not just because of its size but also because Barnes made this book his first foray into electrotyping, a new process being offered by his usual stereotyper, Thomas B. Smith. Electrotyping involved placing the set type in a chemical bath to grow a copper "skin" for the plates rather than casting metal in a mold. Electrotype plates reproduced graphic material more clearly than stereotype plates did, and they were lighter and more durable, capable of producing tens of thousands more printings per set of plates—good reasons for Barnes to consider the new process.[4] It was also slower and more expensive to create the plates using electrotyping, and it may have been that Barnes meant to

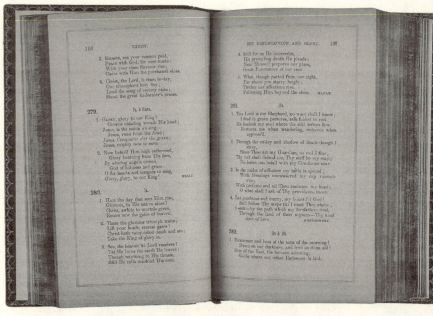

Sample pages from Henry Ward Beecher, comp.: top, *The Plymouth Collection of Hymns* (1855); bottom, *The Plymouth Collection of Hymns and Tunes* (1855). *Courtesy of American Antiquarian Society.*

scare off Beecher with a higher price—or else he recognized a customer who would pay enough to fund a printing experiment. In any case, two wealthy Plymouth Church congregants provided the funds, and the 1855 publication of *The Plymouth Collection of Hymns and Tunes* was confirmed with a handshake.

The book was designed for Plymouth Church, but it was quickly adopted by congregations in several different denominations; a supplement of nearly 100 more texts was produced for Baptist churches. Another version was also available, possibly even before the main book. *The Plymouth Collection of Hymns* had the same preface, the same texts, and the same indexes for subjects and first lines as the *Hymns and Tunes* book—just not the tunes. Remarkably, this volume was physically larger than the version with music. While the latter used double-column printing and small type to squeeze the texts into every available inch of space, the words-only book used large, clear type surrounded by generous white space and a simple decorative border on each page. At more than 900 pages, it looked like a gift book, meant to provide a luxurious reading experience in a parlor chair. Only a book so massive and ostentatiously elegant could make its 500-page musical counterpart seem small. It was almost as if Beecher were trying to make the words-only version so large and expensive that it would dissuade people from buying it—unless possibly as a home copy. But Beecher and Barnes both understood that even within Plymouth Church a number of congregants would not want the music.

If having separate hymnbooks and tunebooks had served to silence the congregations in many churches, the situation had also fostered a number of practices of reading and use, some highly individualized, some remarkably consistent. Inserting music alongside the texts that before had appeared like selections in a poetry anthology would disrupt many of those practices— and for the many adults who could not read staff music, there was little to be gained from the new books.

Plymouth Church would become famous as one of the great singing churches of its day,[5] but the survival of words-only copies of *The Plymouth Collection* marked with pew numbers from Beecher's own church shows how complicated the reform's success would be and how tenacious earlier cultures of reading and living with hymnbooks were. It would take a generation for the modern style of hymnal to become established as the norm in church worship. Collections that followed on *The Plymouth Collec-tion*'s success, including the Boston *Sabbath Hymn and Tune Book* (1859) and the London *Hymns Ancient and Modern* (1861), also had words-only versions to attract wider adoption and sales. When the renowned English Baptist preacher Charles Haddon Spurgeon compiled *Our Own Hymn Book* for his Metropolitan Tabernacle congregation in London in 1866, it had only words. Only ten years later would an edition with tunes appear.

Beecher's large repertoire of hymns stemmed not only from his wide ecumenical net but also from his interest in the use of lyric poetry as hym-nody. In addition to some of the classic English poets, including Herbert, Milton, and Henry Vaughan, he used texts by some of the most popular contemporary writers of the day: William Cullen Bryant, Henry Wadsworth Longfellow, William Wordsworth, Lydia Sigourney, Felicia Hemans, James Russell Lowell, John Greenleaf Whittier, and Caroline Norton. Beecher used poetry alongside traditional hymnody to get his congregation singing, and in doing so, he brought cultures of hymn reading, hymn singing, and poetry reading colliding together. By the time his *Plymouth Collection* appeared, the line between hymn and poem had become much more ten-uous, both in churches and in libraries and parlors, than it had been a century before. I would argue that the rich culture of hymn reading not only complicated Beecher's efforts at congregational song but also deeply informed cultures of reading poetry on both sides of the Atlantic. The next part of this book traces the process by which hymn and poem came to-gether, particularly in the realm of sacred reading at home.

PART III

HOME

CHAPTER 10

Did Poets Write Hymns?

It is not far-fetched to say that hymns, as a core element of early music education in and beyond the public schools, had a major role in the history of modern music. Some readers may be quite ready to accept my claim in chapter 7 that hymns had tremendous influence in the growth of children's literature. But what relationship did hymns have to what we now think of as literary poems? Wrapped up in this question is the issue of what we think the hymn–poem relationship *should* be. Scholars have never contested that hymns swirled in the air of previous centuries by the thousands, and nearly all have been content to leave it at that. Yes, hymns were ubiquitous, but they are not seen as literary.

The chapters in this part of my volume tell a series of stories to aid in the reconsideration of the place of hymnody in the forming of literary taste; I focus primarily on the editors of hymnbooks and poetic collections who have proven to be the most influential of hymn readers among consumers of literature. One aspect of these stories involves coming to terms with the fact that across two centuries that are generally assumed to be marked by a decline in religious practice and consensus, hymns constantly rose in number, diffusion, and influence in literary culture. In other words, to think that literary history in the eighteenth and nineteenth centuries is a matter of inevitable secularization ignores the role of the hymn in literary history—and that neglect has created a distorted picture of canonical poets like William Cowper and Emily Dickinson, while consigning influential poets such as Felicia Hemans, Reginald Heber, and, indeed, Isaac Watts to oblivion.

At the same time, the divide between hymns and poems has often been very real, particularly as it has been policed by critics and anthologists. Curiously enough, the first English writer to make a firm hymn–poem

distinction was Watts. Recall that he began work toward his System of
Praise with a book of poems, *Horae Lyricae* ("sacred lyrics"). This was freer
and wider-ranging than his *Hymns*, both in form and in subject matter—elegies
and odes, including experiments in free verse in the tradition of the Greek
poet Pindar's great odes, shared space with more regular devotional pieces.
Watts never intended the texts in *Horae Lyricae* to be used as public hymns,
but admirers of Watts appropriated his lyrics as hymns before they were a
decade old. This introduced an ambiguity into Watts's work that had
marked the reception of Elizabethan psalm paraphrases,[1] one that would
become an increasingly challenging issue as hymnbooks proliferated and di-
versified. Can a poem be a hymn, and vice versa?

Dr. Samuel Johnson did more than any other English writer to establish something of a wall between hymn and poem. In his *Lives of the
English Poets* (1779–1781), Johnson used the examples of several earlier
writers, including Watts, to make a case for the mutual exclusivity of
devotion or worship and poetry. In his account of the seventeenth-century
court poet Edmund Waller, who turned to religious verse in his retirement,
Johnson offered his first extended opinion on the problem of the devotional poem:

> Contemplative piety, or the intercourse between God and the human
> soul, cannot be poetical. . . .
>
> The essence of poetry is invention; such invention as, by producing
> something unexpected, surprises and delights. The topicks [*sic*] of devo-
> tion are few, and being few are universally known; but few as they are,
> they can be made no more; they can receive no grace from novelty of
> sentiment, and very little from novelty of expression.
>
> Poetry pleases by exhibiting an idea more grateful to the mind than
> things themselves afford. This effect proceeds from the display of those
> parts of nature which attract, and the concealment of those which repel
> the imagination; but religion must be shown as it is; suppression and ad-
> dition equally corrupt it; and such as it is, it is known already.
>
> From poetry the reader justly expects, and from good poetry always
> obtains, the enlargement of his comprehension and elevation of his fancy;
> but this is rarely to be hoped by Christians from metrical devotion.
> Whatever is great, desireable, or tremendous, is comprised in the name

of the Supreme Being. Omnipotence cannot be exalted; Infinity cannot be amplified; Perfection cannot be improved.[2]

Sharing Alexander Pope's assumption that good poetry is "nature to advantage drest," Johnson here argued that the sublimity and perfection of religion, and particularly the God it worshiped, could only defeat attempts to dress it. Milton was wise, in Johnson's view, to take on elements of salvation history that the biblical record left to the imagination; a direct devotional versifying of God would be doomed from the start.

This concern with "devotion," however, does not necessarily mean that the modern hymn, as Watts practiced it, should be excluded. Johnson took up this issue more pointedly in his account of Watts. He praised Watts's "purity of character" and "laborious piety," recommending Watts's textbooks and approving that his Dissenting persuasion did not lead him to take any polemical stances that the churchman Johnson would by necessity disdain. He even noted Watts's considerable talents as a poet, but these talents amounted to misdirected potential in Johnson's mind:

> As a poet, had he been only a poet, he would probably have stood high among the authors with whom he is now associated. For his judgement was exact, and he noted beauties and faults with very nice discernment; his imagination . . . was vigorous and active, and the stores of knowledge were large by which his fancy was to be supplied. His ear was well-tuned, and his diction was elegant and copious. But his devotional poetry is, like that of others, unsatisfactory. The paucity of its topics enforces perpetual repetition, and the sanctity of the matter rejects the ornaments of figurative diction. It is sufficient for Watts to have done better than others what no man has done well.[3]

Johnson clearly included *Horae Lyricae* here as well as the System of Praise, but Watts's prime association by the 1770s was with hymnody, and later critics and editors took Johnson's critiques as justification for keeping hymns separate from other kinds of poems. Yet even as Johnson developed his views in his lives of Waller and Watts, a new poet was emerging whose work would challenge Johnson's assumptions: William Cowper.

A London barrister by profession, Cowper had written little poetry and published none by the time he met John Newton. Given to bouts of severe depression that would drive him to several suicide attempts, Cowper left his work to convalesce in the rural Buckinghamshire parish of Olney, where the already-famous Newton was curate. The slaver-turned-priest quickly formed a close friendship with Cowper, counseling him through the aftermath of a nervous breakdown and discovering a poetic gift in his ailing parishioner. Newton had for some time been composing hymns as meditations on scripture to accompany his sermons; his church was a poor one, and many of his parishioners could not read, so the hymns gave them something to take home, reinforcing his weekly messages. He proposed that Cowper join him in producing a collection of hymns for the use of the parish, though Newton's considerable fame owing to his popular memoirs made it likely that the collection would gain a wider audience. Cowper agreed. While the original plan was for both men to contribute an equal number of hymns, Cowper suffered another breakdown, limiting his contribution to sixty-seven texts compared to Newton's 219 in *Olney Hymns* (1779).[4] The collection included Newton's "Amazing Grace" and texts such as "Glorious Things of Thee Are Spoken," which was much more popular than "Amazing Grace" in the nineteenth century. Cowper's texts were interspersed throughout, marked simply with a *C* to indicate his authorship.

As James Montgomery asserted in an introduction first published in an 1829 reprint of *Olney Hymns*, hymnody produced Cowper the poet.[5] Hymn writing was initially Cowper's means to psychological recovery. Following the depression that disrupted his hymn writing at Olney, Cowper again turned to poetry at the suggestion of his friend Lady Austen to aid his recovery. The results of this new wave of writing amounted to a literary sensation. Cowper's two-volume *Poems* appeared in handsomely printed London octavos in 1782 and 1785, the first mainly consisting of rhapsodic odes, the second nearly filled by his multicanto poem, *The Task*, still considered his most important work. New editions of Cowper's works were frequent, especially after his death in 1800, and continued for decades, yet by far his most-read works were not *The Task* or his odes, but rather his hymns. "God Moves in a Mysterious Way," "O for a Closer Walk with God," "There Is a Fountain Filled with Blood"—these hymns anticipated the individuality of the Romantic lyric as much as poems like Cowper's "The Castaway," but their directness and relevance to Christian spirituality made them favorites in Anglican churches and Baptist revival meetings alike. For the first time, a writer at the poetic forefront of his day was also contributing substantially to churches' sung repertoire across the Anglophone Atlantic.

This remarkable crossover caused problems for Cowper's editors, however. When he and Newton assembled the *Olney Hymns* for publication in 1779—the year Johnson began publishing his *Lives*—Newton clearly had Watts on his mind, choosing a three-part structure for the book and including a first-line index on the model of Watts's *Hymns*. In his preface, Newton also showed Watts's influence as he drew a line between the work of a poet and that of a hymn writer: "There is a style and manner suited to the composition of hymns, which may be more successfully, or at least more easily, attained by a versifier than a poet. They should be *Hymns*, not *Odes*, if designed for public worship, and the use of plain people."[6] Were the hymns, in fact, poems? Newton, like Watts, cast serious doubt on the question, and because Johnson's wall separating hymn and poem influenced later editorial practice, the massive circulation of *Olney Hymns* and its association with evangelicalism were two reasons for editors to resist including Cowper's hymns in elegant editions of his poems.

Montgomery's engagement with Cowper's hymns is instructive here. Already famous as an abolitionist, journalist, and narrative poet, Montgomery in the 1820s developed his critical ideas of Cowper, Newton, and the genres of hymnody and religious poetry in a series of volumes commissioned by the Glasgow Presbyterian publisher William Collins (forerunner of the present-day HarperCollins firm).[7] Montgomery first noted the excellence of Cowper's hymns and their role in the poet's career in his introductory essay to Collins's 1824 reprint of Cowper's *Poems*; the volume nevertheless included only the texts in the 1782 and 1785 London books. Montgomery included Cowper's hymns in his pathbreaking hymn collection *The Christian Psalmist* (1825) and Cowper's religious verse in *The Christian Poet* (1827), and in his introduction to the 1829 Collins edition of *Olney Hymns* Montgomery took issue with Newton's hymn–poem distinction, saying that "hymnwriting, like every other kind of poetry, has a style suitable to itself." He praised Cowper's hymns as "miniature poems, regularly planned, brilliantly adorned, and felicitously executed."[8] But he never, across these four volumes, included Cowper's hymns alongside his poems. Among editors of the early nineteenth century, this was typical of the treatment of Cowper's works.

Later editions gradually collected Cowper's fugitive writings, including a hymn that he composed for the Sunday school at Olney, but the *Olney Hymns* material remained absent as a general rule until after 1830, and appeared only then within the context of gathering as much Cowper material as possible.[9] John Smythe Memes claimed that his three-volume edition of Cowper's *Miscellaneous Works* (1834) was the first to include Cowper's contributions to *Olney Hymns*. Biography was Memes's main emphasis, with the first two volumes consisting of a collection of Cowper's letters and a lengthy memoir by Memes. The third volume contained all the major poems usually included in previous editions as well as translations and collected lyrics. Cowper's work from *Olney Hymns* here appeared as a monolithic section in the table of contents, with numbers (and no titles) distinguishing the individual texts in the body of the book. To Memes, these texts were more valuable as a group than as individual poems. He wrote a headnote for the section arguing for the hymns' worth as poems and their consistency within Cowper's career, echoing Montgomery's arguments in his Collins essays. Yet Memes could not quite bring himself to treat Cowper's hymns as poems. Lamenting that they were scattered throughout Newton's arrangement and the lack of dating information that prohibited a chronological ordering of the texts—which would have assimilated them to the logic of the collected edition framed by the author's life—Memes used an arrangement designed to "impress" the "practical or exegetical nature" of the hymns. The sixty-eight texts (one newly collected poem was added to those from Newton's collection) were sorted "into three heads, of PRAISE, PRAYER, and DOCTRINE, forming an admirable manual of personal devotion."[10] Recognizing, as Montgomery had, the decades-long use of *Olney Hymns* for devotional reading, Memes sought to highlight the utility of Cowper's work by creating a "manual of devotion" out of them—in the middle of an expensive, belletristic, multivolume collection of the author's writings. Needless to say, later collections did not adopt Memes's editorial approach, but their choices reflected a shared ambivalence over how (or whether) to represent the hymns as poems.

The major Cowper editions of the 1830s were T. S. Grimshawe's eight-volume *Life and Works* (1835) and poet laureate Robert Southey's fifteen-volume *Works* (1833–1837), which shared an editorial approach to the hymns: they restored Newton's titles to the texts, numbered them according to the order they appeared in the original volume, and listed the individual titles in the table of contents. One thing united all the Cowper collections, from Montgomery's to Memes's to Grimshawe's and Southey's, however. None of them used a first-line index to point readers to the texts, despite this being Newton's primary help to readers of his *Olney Hymns*. If Cowper's hymns were to join the body of his poetic output, the reading protocols of the hymnbook had to be set aside, but editors and readers still seemed ambivalent about the alternatives. Most Cowper collections of one or two volumes through the first half of the nineteenth century kept things simple, and simply excluded the hymns entirely.

Not surprisingly, the collected editions of James Montgomery's writings showed similar ambivalence. As mentioned before, comparisons between Cowper and Montgomery were common in the latter's lifetime, and in addition to his further association with Cowper via the Collins books, Montgomery had also turned to poetry in the face of personal adversity.[11] The son of a Moravian minister and a radical journalist, Montgomery in Sheffield in the 1790s was imprisoned twice for libel. He began to write poetry in prison, and works such as *The West Indies* (1809) merged his literary and political interests, while a range of religious lyrics and psalm paraphrases channeled his spiritual energies while advocating for relief and mission work. After taking over the ownership of the *Sheffield Iris*, Montgomery amassed a fortune that allowed him to write full time. Some of his short lyrics had already been adopted as hymns when he compiled *The Christian Psalmist* for William Collins in 1825. That book was Montgomery's intervention into debates over the quality of modern hymnody: part manifesto for the hymn as poem and part sourcebook for hymnbook compilers interested in high literary quality. In the final section of the book, Montgomery included his own works as a group, having filled earlier, broadly thematic sections with the works of Watts, Wesley, Newton, Cowper, and other notable hymnists. But as much as he defended the literary merits of hymns and advocated for a more poetic hymnody, he kept his own writings separate in his mind and in his books. His next Collins anthology, *The Christian Poet* (1827), focused on religious poetry beyond the hymn, and, tellingly, he arranged it chronologically by author, giving the poems' titles in a table of contents with no first-line index; the first-line index had been the only finding aid for individual texts in *The Christian Psalmist*. Montgomery organized these two different kinds of poetry into distinct schemes of reading, despite the fact that many of the *Christian Poet* entries were just as famous and recognizable by their opening lines—Anna Letitia Barbauld's "God of my life, and author of my days," for example. As much as his essays railed against Samuel Johnson's prejudice against religious verse, Montgomery still assumed a difference between the poetic genres.

This distinction manifested in Montgomery's several editions of his collected poems. He was highly attentive to his self-presentation as a poet and acted as his own editor several times, with a final edition running to four volumes in 1841. Long narrative poems like *The Wanderer of Switzerland* held pride of place, and in the miscellaneous sections everything was assiduously presented as lyric poems; even a few popular hymn texts were included under poetic, usually occasional, titles such as "The Christian Soldier," the title for one of Emily Dickinson's favorite hymns, "Servant of God, Well Done." The volumes' tables of contents gave the titles, and no first-line index appeared.

But Montgomery's hymnic output only grew over time, and the wide popularity of his hymns and the frequent changes in text that went with the popularity led him to assemble what he considered to be the authoritative edition of his hymns in the last years of his life. *Original Hymns, for Public, Private, and Social Devotion* (1853) combined Montgomery's acceptance of his texts as hymns with an authorial insistence on textual integrity that was increasingly common among hymnists by the mid-nineteenth century. In his preface to the volume, Montgomery, while recognizing that the changing of hymn texts was "*the cross,* by which every author of a hymn who hopes to be useful in his generation, may expect to be tested," pointed out to his enthusiastic editors that "if good people . . . cannot conscientiously adopt [the hymnist's] diction and doctrine, it is a little questionable in them to impose upon him *theirs,* which he may as honestly hesitate to receive."[12] Montgomery felt the need to set the record straight by giving his texts in the form that expressed his own beliefs, whatever others may wish to do with them. At the same time, he fully considered these texts to be hymns, and the book's design indicated as much: for the first time since *The Christian Psalmist* nearly three decades earlier, Montgomery produced a book with a first-line index and no table of contents.

The difference this made in signaling the kind and use of text in that volume became especially apparent in Little, Brown, and Company's 1858 posthumous edition of Montgomery's poetical works. This five-volume edition was part of the Boston publisher's British Poets series, edited by Harvard professor Francis Child. As with other writers' works, Child's editing of Montgomery amounted largely to reprinting; the first four volumes followed Montgomery's 1841 edition, while the final volume reproduced *Original Hymns*, with the first four using Montgomery's tables of contents and the fifth his first-line index. Child did gather a small group of fugitive poems in the back of volume 5—headed by a table of contents listing their titles, making a sharp paratextual distinction between the lyrics in the back and the hymns that made up the bulk of the volume. Eighty years after the appearance of *Olney Hymns* and a century and a half since Watts's books, editors still found it difficult to place hymns and poems in the same volume on the same terms. A major reason for the ongoing difficulty was the issue of intended use. Both Cowper and Montgomery, in following Watts's example, wrote nearly all of their hymns as patently devotional and liturgical works, not lyrics.

One of Montgomery's contemporaries took a decidedly different approach to the hymn, one that let her hymns move much more easily between literary and liturgical collections. Felicia Hemans, a poet even more popular than either Cowper or Montgomery, was in a way the quintessential woman poet of her time. Her themes focused on domestic and family life, even as her learned reaches into history gave her a larger scope for writing about women's lives than the confines of the contemporary home would allow. From her breakthrough volume, *The Domestic Affections* (1812), to works on travel and nature to her ambitious portraits of historical women in *Records of Woman* (1828), Hemans found mostly female audiences across denominations and classes. Her large following in the United States only grew with poems like her 1825 "Landing of the Pilgrim Fathers," a celebration of the religious ideals of the *Mayflower* Pilgrims that enjoyed pride of place in gift books, schoolbooks, and hymnbooks alike.

Hemans wrote one book that was initially published in the United States, a volume for children that took advantage of the blurred boundary between genres in children's literature to offer a hybrid poetry that could speak to children and adults as poems or hymns—or both. *Hymns on the Works of Nature* (1827) followed Barbauld's example in directing the child reader to God through the beauty of nature. A lifelong Anglican, Hemans showed the influence of what Isobel Armstrong has called Unitarian poetics, a nonsectarian Christian mode developed by Dissenting writers like Barbauld, William Blake, and James Martineau.[13] Hemans's *Hymns on the Works of Nature* did indeed prove popular with Unitarian hymnbook compilers, as I discuss in the next chapter, and it confirmed her place as one of the premier children's writers of her time. While the patriotic "Casabianca" (1826) would be her most widely read poem in the century following her death,[14] Hemans was one of only a few literary celebrities of the nineteenth century who was widely trusted to teach child readers religious truths. Hemans's statement in the preface to *Hymns* that she had originally written the hymn-poems for her own children made her book a domestic space writ large;[15] in a classic blending of biographical detail and personal reading experience, Hemans's readers could imagine themselves at home with the poet, even as her hymn texts found their way into homes with or without church attachments.

A later Hemans volume, *Scenes and Hymns of Life* (1834), demonstrated a much more striking and radical experimentation with form than her earlier crossover book did. In her preface to the volume, Hemans explained that she found that hymnody generally ignored the spiritual richness of everyday domestic life, and she wanted to offer a way to fill that gap. "It has been my wish to portray the religious spirit, not alone in its meditative joys and solitary aspirations," Hemans wrote, "but likewise in those active influences upon human life, so often called into victorious energy by trial and conflict."[16] Hemans had recently made an unsuccessful foray into playwriting, and many of her new hymns were embedded in dramatic poems of one or two scenes each. The opening poem, "The English Martyrs," portrays a young Protestant couple in prison during the reign of Mary I. The couple, initially separated, are presented with the same choice between freedom via Catholic conversion or execution. They both choose death, and as they are brought together before their execution, the heroine, Edith, improvises a hymn. This scenario is clearly far from the everyday nineteenth century, and it provides a striking counterpoint to the quiet scene that follows: a girl comforting her anxious mother and ailing sister with a hymn—another song by a woman in the face of death, but with a very different setting.

Several texts in the volume used only a descriptive title to set the scene in what we might term the "dramatic hymn," a blend of devotional hymn and dramatic monologue. The dramatic hymn featured regularly in the gift books and periodicals of the mid-nineteenth century, and the subgenre opened new possibilities for poets, including Emily Dickinson (see chapter 13). For Hemans, it made her hymnody into poetry in a way that encouraged hymnbook compilers to use more of her texts, even beyond those she had marked as hymns. Often, a dramatic hymn, with a more general title or no title, could simply be a hymn.

Hemans's crossover hymn-poems were able to fit into poetic collections more easily than the hymns of Cowper and Montgomery. One of the most telling examples of this was Rufus Griswold's *Sacred Poets of England and America* (1849), an anthology designed as a high-end gift book that provided an expansive survey of religious verse in English, beginning with sixteenth-century writers, such as George Gascoigne and Edmund Spenser, and drawing on the growing body of scholarship on earlier English writers. Griswold was one of the most prolific American anthologists of the nineteenth century, with works ranging from *Poets and Poetry of America* (1842) and *Prose Writers of America* (1846) to *The Illustrated Book of Christian Ballads and Other Poems* (1844), the latter a precursor to *Sacred Poets*. For his new volume, Griswold generally avoided hymn texts; even as he included authors such as Isaac Watts and Charles Wesley, he drew exclusively from their lyric poems, as he did for more recent writers, such as William Cullen Bryant and John Greenleaf Whittier. The main exceptions were women; Hemans was represented by several hymns, and Anne Steele and Anna Letitia Barbauld each had at least one hymn under their name. Griswold had nothing but praise for the two earlier writers, identifying Steele as "distinguished as a devotional lyrist," adding that "many of her hymns are now in the collections of most of the churches," and commenting on Barbauld: "Of her devotional poems too much cannot be said in commendation; they entitle her to the esteem of every Christian."[17] On Hemans, Griswold was more ambivalent. He identified her poetry's "most remarkable characteristics" as "a religious purity and a womanly delicacy of feeling, never exaggerated, rarely forgotten," noting that "devotion to God, and quenchless affection for kindred, for friends, for the suffering, glow through all her writings" and that "as the poet of home, a painter of the affections, she was perhaps the most touching and beautiful writer of her age." Yet, he complained, "her sympathies were not universal," by which he meant too British, elitist, and historically oriented, while "the tone of her poetry is indeed monotonous," being "pervaded by the tender sadness which forever preyed upon her spirit."[18] Griswold's judgments are telling here. Hemans met his standard of "purity" and "delicacy" as a religious poet, but her proper subject to him is the home, not the pages of history—despite the reliance of *Scenes and Hymns of Life* on historical sources as much as domestic spaces. Griswold expressed his surprise at how much tenderness Hemans could express, given how little she wrote about love (which Griswold considered the foremost topic for women poets), but this tenderness was also her greatest liability for him. Griswold has developed quite a reputation among literary scholars for his dismissive views of women authors, and his assessment of Hemans sounds like a condescending wish that she, despite her loveless marriage and frequent illnesses, would have smiled more.[19]

Griswold's thinly veiled contempt for women poets, particularly those as commercially successful as Hemans, may be linked to his choice to include hymns by women whose non-hymn religious verse (Hemans's and Barbauld's especially) could have served his collection just as well. The hymn's contested status as poetry became paired with women authors' treatment as poetesses instead of poets, writers of less genius and thus less praiseworthy than their male contemporaries. A few men had hymns included in the collection, but they were generally the exceptions that proved the rule. Like Steele, whose surviving works largely consist of hymns, Augustus Toplady and Reginald Heber both published most of their verse in hymn form. Toplady, most famous today for "Rock of Ages, Cleft for Me," was represented only by another text, titled simply "Hymn." Heber's several entries were nearly all hymns, including his popular missionary hymn "From Greenland's Icy Mountains" and his Epiphany hymn "Brightest and Best of the Sons of the Morning." This did not count against those men, however. Heber, indeed, comes across as something of a hero for Griswold, who called the Anglican bishop "one of the sweetest of the poets who have sung of religion. His hymns are for the Christian what the unchaste songs of Moore are for the sensualist."[20] The pairing with the popular Irish poet Thomas Moore is remarkable, since Moore was, like John Donne, a practitioner of devotional poetry as well as racy romantic lyrics. In fact, Moore was one of the most-collected poets in a pair of Unitarian hymnbooks from the same era as Griswold's book, which marked a decisive shift in the inclusion of literary texts in liturgical collections. Those books are the subject of the next chapter, and they help to show from a different angle how the changing relations of hymnody and poetry took those forms into new territory—and ran up against old barriers.

CHAPTER 11

How Poems Entered the Hymnbook

In a formal, plain, leather-bound volume with "Pliny Merrick / No. 80" stamped on the front cover, a curious blend of hymns and poems appears. The first text to meet the eye on opening the volume is not part of the printed book but a small, yellowed clipping placed between the front end-papers. Judging by the acid stains left by the clipping, the addition significantly postdates the book and possibly even its association with Merrick; we cannot know who left the clipping in the book.[1] We might guess at the intent, however, with a look at the text: it is William Wordsworth's "London, 1802," one of the British poet's most famous sonnets, which opens with the ringing invocation: "Milton! thou shouldst be living at this hour; / England hath need of thee."[2] It is a secular poem calling for the moral and spiritual renewal of a "stagnant" nation, a reform that the genius of England's greatest religious poet could produce. Such a call to spiritual revival would not seem too out of place in a church, although the form of the Petrarchan sonnet does not fit easily into the typical hymnbook. But this is not a typical hymnbook.

Despite its mundane title, *A Book of Hymns for Public and Private Devotion*, this book caused a sensation, as well as some controversy, when the Church of the Unity in Worcester, Massachusetts, placed the first order for it in 1846. Edward Everett Hale, entering his first pastorate at the start of an illustrious career as a Unitarian minister and author, chose the book for his newly formed congregation, a progressive offshoot of Worcester's First (Unitarian) Church, where Pliny Merrick was a founding member.[3] More than any previous hymnbook, *A Book of Hymns* pushed the boundary between hymns and poems in a congregational collection; it was the product of two of Hale's fellow Harvard Divinity students: Samuel Longfellow, younger brother of Henry Wadsworth Longfellow, and Samuel Johnson. If the latter's famous namesake had driven a wedge between hymn and poem in the eighteenth century, *A Book of Hymns* would place American Unitarians at the forefront of a new spirituality that recognized the devotional potential of poems not previously considered hymns. In this chapter I use Longfellow and Johnson's project as a window into the reading that editors, publishers, and reviewers brought to bear in creating a new concept of a modern hymnbook, one that would shape editorial practice for later generations of hymnal compilers as well as poets and anthologists.

Longfellow and Johnson began their collaboration while attending Harvard Divinity School in 1845. It was a heady time for the school; the higher criticism had recently arrived from Germany to revolutionize biblical studies, while the transcendentalist philosophy of Ralph Waldo Emerson, Theodore Parker, and William Ellery Channing introduced a new spirituality of private communion with God, the power of created beauty, and the otherworldly potential of the individual. This idealism blended with social activism over slavery, and by 1846 the Mexican War and the careers of classmates Edward Everett Hale, Thomas Wentworth Higginson, and William Henry Channing (nephew of Ellery Channing) helped move these sensibilities into the elite cultural mainstream. Longfellow borrowed something of his famous brother's literary approach—and some of his poems—as he moved to modernize Unitarian hymnody alongside its theology.

The seed for Longfellow and Johnson's hymnbook project was planted when their Harvard Divinity friend Frank Appleton took a congregation in South Danvers (now Peabody), Massachusetts, in 1845 and complained of the outdated hymnbook the church was using.[4] The students insisted they could assemble a better one for him, and they arranged with the Cambridge printer Metcalf and Co. to bring out the book, which appeared in July 1846.[5] The surviving correspondence between Longfellow and Johnson indicates a wide range of hymn research, or "hymnbooking,"[6] as Longfellow would later call it. While previous Unitarian collections provided the bulk of the material, Methodist and Moravian collections and even the Roman Catholic breviary were part of Longfellow's reading for the work, as were Sunday school books and poetry collections. Longfellow also urged Johnson to "look over all religious newspapers, where lurk many good hymns."[7] The collection clearly relied on a wide variety of religious print material, the product of a culture in which hymns had become ubiquitous by the 1840s.

Henry Longfellow's Craigie House, the colonial mansion on Cambridge's Brattle Street where Sam lived with his brother's family while completing his Harvard studies, was the friends' main site for gathering and editing their materials.[8] Johnson never seems to have grown close to the Longfellow family despite his deep friendship with Sam, but if Johnson was not strongly influenced by the proximity of a famous poet and professor, Sam Longfellow certainly was. Twelve years younger than Henry, Sam lived consciously in his brother's shadow. He was a Harvard undergraduate while his brother held the Smith Chair in Modern Languages on Harvard's faculty. As a divinity student, Sam did secretarial work in lieu of rent at Craigie House, copying Henry's manuscripts and spending an hour before breakfast every day taking dictation to help his brother manage his massive correspondence.[9] (Sam's hand was generally clearer than Henry's, so the letters' recipients likely benefited as well.) Sharing the family's taste for fine reading and music and possessing considerable skill as a visual artist, Sam had a well-honed aesthetic sensibility that shaped his selection of hymn texts. His immersion in transatlantic poetics through his own reading and that of Henry and Henry's wife, Fanny, helped Sam to see a place for poetry in his hymnbook. Modern poets from Hemans to Whittier to Wordsworth to (of course) Henry Longfellow featured largely. Poems celebrating nature and the might and goodness of God were especially amenable to the project.

Yet as Longfellow and Johnson moved Unitarian hymnody closer to literary poetry, they ran into the basic problem of how to sell a hymnbook. Their project had begun as part thought experiment and part favor to a friend, but in order to make the book available in the hundreds of copies for Appleton's church, a publisher was needed. It is not clear why or how Longfellow and Johnson settled on Metcalf and Co., though familiarity and convenience were likely factors. Based in Cambridge, the Metcalf firm was the official printer for Harvard, so it would not be unheard-of for the firm to make a small print run for a pair of Harvard students. The initial run was not exactly small, though at 500 it was modest for a hymnbook. Longfellow and Johnson assumed they were agreeing to royalty publishing, in which the publisher assumed the costs and risks of production and paid the authors a set rate per sold volume. This system had become the norm among literary professionals in the United States by the 1840s, and as his brother's secretary Longfellow had witnessed the workings of this system firsthand. Yet Metcalf and Co. was more a printer than a publisher, and the young compilers began scrambling for book buyers after receiving a bill for part of the production cost.

The ideal customers for hymnbooks were churches and their pastors, each congregation's adoption of a book typically amounting to a bulk order of at least 100 copies at a time. Longfellow and Johnson had an advantage in reaching these buyers: a crop of classmates just embarking on their first pastorates and ready to introduce reforms in the liturgy. Edward Everett Hale placed the first order for his Worcester church; Thomas Wentworth Higginson used it in at least one of his churches; and one celebrity preacher, the Unitarian-turned-transcendentalist Theodore Parker, adopted the book for his Music Hall congregation in Boston (he affectionately called the volume "the Book of Sams").[10] All three of those ministers had contributed texts to the book at the compilers' request, so the importance of Longfellow and Johnson's circle of influence for the book's financial success was great indeed. Most of the book's promotion was the compilers' doing, out of necessity.

The combination of the unexpected bill from the printer, anemic marketing, unexplained supply issues, and the generally cold business manner of the Metcalf firm quickly convinced the compilers to look elsewhere for a publisher for the second edition to meet the growing demand for the book. Yet they needed the initial edition to sell out first to clear their debt with Metcalf. Since only about 450 copies of the planned 500 materialized and 300 had been shipped to Worcester, there were only 150 books available for the Danvers church for which the book was made, although it had ordered 200.[11] Appleton opted to wait for the second edition rather than deal with a partial order, leaving the 150 books temporarily unclaimed. Longfellow managed to convince James Fields to take the remaining stock to retail at his Old Corner Bookstore, the bookselling and social center of Ticknor and Fields's multifaceted operation. Both Fields and Longfellow had their doubts that so many hymnbooks could be sold individually at retail (the latter joked to Johnson about the "eager cravings of the Hymnical public"),[12] but thanks to good reviews and word of mouth, the books sold out in a few months. Ticknor and Fields offered to publish the second edition on the royalty system.[13] Longfellow and Johnson had prepared a revised book with a supplement and updated indexes to avoid confusion with the first edition (to which Metcalf held the copyright), and the new edition went to press in June 1848. Ticknor and Fields would keep the book in print for more than twenty years, bringing out a seventeenth edition in 1871. And yet, as much as *A Book of Hymns* proved a steady seller for its publisher, the long history of its printings tells a story of a literary publisher unsure of how to value a book that resembled its poetry books and yet stood apart from them.

James Fields, William Ticknor's junior partner, had the reputation of being the firm's promotional talent, and he ensured that periodicals like the *Literary World* reviewed *A Book of Hymns* well, but neither he nor Ticknor had experience with church sales. The firm's new role as Henry Longfellow's publisher in 1847 and the great success it was enjoying with *Evangeline* at that time likely made Ticknor receptive to working with the poet's younger brother. Yet while the firm was one of the nation's most prestigious literary publishers by the late 1840s, it relied on Longfellow and Johnson's salesmanship nearly as much as Metcalf had. Without a clear sense of how they would sell the book, Ticknor and Fields were very conservative in their print runs—most were 500 copies, and none were more than 1,000, even when sales were so rapid that the third edition (500 copies) followed the second (also 500) by only weeks, perhaps days.[14] By contrast, the week before the third edition was ordered, Ticknor and Fields sent reprint editions of Henry Longfellow's earlier books of poetry to press in runs of 1,200 or more each; the first printing of his *Evangeline* (1847) was 2,100.[15] *Thalatta* (1853), an anthology of secular poetry Sam Longfellow coedited with his Harvard classmate Higginson, had only one printing of 1,500 copies.[16] When Ticknor and Fields published Henry David Thoreau's *Walden* in 1854, Fields gushed that it was "no common book & is sure to succeed."[17] The firm brought out an initial edition of 2,000 copies and attempted to secure a London publisher for it. Demand, however, proved so slow that it took eight years to sell out, and the London edition would not materialize until 1886. Meanwhile, *A Book of Hymns* continued to sell, 500 copies at a time. The publishers were apparently more comfortable taking a risk on a patently literary work than on a hymnbook, not quite sure how to gauge demand for a book outside their usual market.

The value of Longfellow and Johnson's authorship as hymnbook compilers was also doubtful to Ticknor and Fields. They were paid only five cents a copy: a mere twenty-five dollars in royalties for every 500 copies sold, which was shared between them. Longfellow and Johnson lamented the paltry payments, eventually turning them into a running joke. While the royalties on *Thalatta* were not princely either, Longfellow at least got half of the seven and a half cents per copy the firm paid; Henry Longfellow, meanwhile, routinely earned twenty cents per copy, and Thoreau received fifteen cents per copy sold of *Walden*. As Johnson quipped: "Who talks of Pike's Peak? Let him make Hymn Books and be wise."[18] The market for hymnbooks was booming, but that boom was hardly felt in the midst of literary Boston.

If Ticknor and Fields were unsure how to understand the nature of Longfellow and Johnson's project, reviewers raised similar questions. Early reviews of *A Book of Hymns* came in the wake of a massive wave of new hymnbooks for Unitarians, Presbyterians, Baptists, and Congregationalists (and the new Methodist books were not far off). In January 1846, the Unitarian magazine *Christian Examiner* reviewed several of these books, lamenting the sense of overwhelm they created while praising the ever-growing quantity and quality of hymn texts available through these collections.[19] When Ephraim Peabody reviewed *A Book of Hymns* for the *Examiner* in November of that same year, he lavished praise on the high quality and novelty of the poetry, and this proved to be both the great strength and the weakness of the book in his view. His opening sentence gave a key qualification for the book's achievement: "Regarded as a volume of devotional poetry for private reading, this collection is one of the best that we have ever seen."[20] The book worked very well as a reading book, but the problem of genre arose for Peabody when he considered it for church services, in which light he found that the book "contains altogether too large a proportion of pieces which are religious poems, but not hymns."[21] Peabody, pastor of the prestigious King's Chapel in Boston and the successor to Francis Greenwood, whose hymnbook was the main Unitarian champion that *A Book of Hymns* challenged, also found fault with the lack of penitentiary hymns; he was shocked at the lack of attention shown to sin in the volume. Yet the improving aesthetics gave Peabody cause for hope: "There is no department of literature in which there has been greater improvement than in that of devotional poetry. Formerly our hymn-books were crowded with the productions of men, who, though eminent as Christians, with few exceptions, were altogether undistinguished as poets. Now, the names of the first poets are familiar in our manuals of devotion. It is to be hoped that the change indicates improvement in the general spirit of literature, and gives omens of the coming of the time when the highest action of mind shall be hallowed by a religious consecration."[22] In other words, whether or not the book worked as a hymnbook for church use, it augured well for the future of literature.

Reviewers for the *Christian Register*, another Unitarian periodical, expressed similar reactions. Nathaniel Holmes Morison, a Harvard College classmate of Longfellow and a Baltimore pastor, opened with a head-shaking comment on the recent "mania for hymn book making" that "had taken possession of the public mind." The increased variety, however, was ultimately a good thing, allowing for the "peculiar wants and taste[s] of the [church] societies" to be more fully met than in previous years, and *A Book of Hymns* "is one of the best we have seen." As in Peabody's review, the aesthetic marks were high: "[The book] contains more excellent hymns and fewer dull, prosaic, uninspired, and uninspiring ones than any book with which we are acquainted." Morison credited this to the "qualities of mind and heart" that the "two young men" who compiled the work possessed: "devout feelings, refined tastes, and a just appreciation of poetic beauty." (Longfellow and Johnson found this particular part of the review amusing for their acquaintance's detached language.)[23] At the same time, Morison found that the compilers sometimes were mistaken about "the essential character of a Christian hymn—we mean its devotional character." Of the great religious poems included in the collection, the reviewer said: "We acknowledge their beauty and feel their power, but we cannot think them fitted for the devotional services of the sanctuary, when the soul is glowing with peculiar love, gratitude, and praise to God. . . . They do not come up to the soul's desire at a time of enthusiasm." Morison singled out Henry Longfellow's "A Psalm of Life" as a prime example of this; it was "not sufficiently *evangelical* in the true sense of that word for such a purpose [as corporate singing]." Morison insisted on a "wide distinction between sacred poetry and a hymn for Christian worship," closing his review with a call for *A Book of Hymns* to inspire a new and improved "Sabbath Recreations" volume—for home reading rather than congregational use.[24] A later, and crankier, anonymous reviewer for the *Christian Register* also singled out

"A Psalm of Life" as one of the bad choices, following this critique with a list of nearly 100 hymns in Greenwood's *Collection* and absent from Longfellow and Johnson's as a way of showing how far the volume had missed the mark as a congregational book. Though the reviewer agreed that the book "contains less bad poetry than any other Hymn Book that we know," it still lacked the texts—perhaps bad poems, in fact—"which we should very much prefer for the purposes of public worship."[25] Could good poetry and effective congregational use coincide?

Edward Everett Hale entered the conversation in January 1847 with an emphatic yes to that question. As the earliest adopter of the book for a church, Hale proposed a novel test for a hymnbook's quality. Rather than considering the contexts of private reading and corporate singing as the two most significant, Hale saw his own position as pastor as defining a crucial middle ground:

> Is it not worth remark, that if any one should note, for a series of years
> the hymns read by different preachers from one or another of the hymn
> books in general use, he would find that a quarter part of the hymns published there are perhaps never read at all? And is not this a decided fault
> in a hymn book? . . . In this view we suppose that the true test of one's
> opinion of a hymn book is this: "How many of the hymns in it would you
> refuse to read, were you officiating in religious worship?"[26]

For Hale the public reading, or giving out, of the hymn was the true test: What hymns would a preacher gladly place in his own mouth, inviting repetition from choir and congregation? This was a stricter test than private reading, while still acknowledging that the engagement of a single reader, the preacher, made the biggest difference in the use and success of a book. With *A Book of Hymns*, Hale argued, everything was good for the pulpit, making it good for the church. Indeed, the book had almost an addictive quality for Hale: "It is not a book which one glances over, selecting a good hymn here, and another there, while he omits or reads with an inattentive eye a number of unattractive hymns between. The reader is surprised perhaps to find himself reading hymn after hymn in succession, without occasion to turn hastily over any which he has dreaded to meet, for years. In many instances, we have found the first impression made on a reader, by the volume, to be surprise that he knew so little of the devotional poetry of our time." And this, for Hale, actually made the poems more hymnic than otherwise. Rather than emphasizing the divide between hymn and poem that Morison had, Hale found that the book was "strictly speaking a *hymn book*" because it was "not a manual of theology." It was the absence of didactic, preachy texts that made them hymns. Brushing aside Peabody's objections to the lack of penitential texts, Hale asserted that such emotions were more proper to prayer and silent reflection, while corporate singing favored the "cheerful, happy, and hopeful emotions," making a cheerful, praise-oriented hymnbook preferable to one that covered a wider range of spiritual experiences.[27] The cheerfulness of the collection was one of Hale's most powerful initial impressions of it; the book was still not titled when he ordered it, and the title he half-seriously recommended to Longfellow was "The Spiritual Songs of Our New England Zion, for Cheerful Churches and Happy Homes."[28] On this point, Hale was on the right side of history, for the didactic and penitential hymns continued to fade through the nineteenth century until by the 1890s even Presbyterian hymnody, under the guidance of hymnologist Louis Benson, was dominated by uplift, a trend that has only strenghtened since.[29]

Yet if Hale saw his classmates' book as "fitted for the sympathies of large congregations" by providing only "such poems . . . as we call hymns," the fact remained that the book was fundamentally a volume of poetry. Ticknor and Fields, in advertising the second edition in the *Christian Register*, quoted several reviews to that effect. From the *Literary World*: "As a collection of sacred poetry and appropriate Hymns, this book cannot be surpassed"; from the *Evening Gazette*: "It is probably the most poetical compilation of Christian poems adapted to the spiritual want of a community, that has been issued in our country"; the Boston *Daily Atlas* stated, "As a book of religious poetry, suited to the reading of a person of refined taste, it is superior to any collection that we have examined"; and the Boston *Courier* asserted, "A more valuable collection of devotional poetry we feel confident has never been issued." This ad appeared above those for Greenwood's *Collection* and Sewall's revised "New York Collection," where the large numbers of congregations adopting those books were the focus of the sales pitches. Ticknor and Fields, while mentioning that its book was "adopted by several churches," emphasized that its volume was a book of poetry.[30] And this emphasis helped to make the book as much a *read* book as a *sung* book.

Hale had already pointed out that such is the fate of a hymnbook to begin with, but reviewers' questions about how and why this book would be read led to the imagining of a new kind of hymnbook, one that would remain in the home and supply private reading exclusively. The *Christian Register*'s anonymous reviewer had proposed such a scenario: "We hardly know of a better collection of sacred poetry than this. We would gladly have it placed by the side of the Bible and Hymn Book in every family."[31] That placement in the home, alongside other genres of devotion, was already being seen in the emergence of what might be called the "private hymnbook." It is the story of that book to which I turn in the next chapter.

CHAPTER 12

The Return of the Private Hymnbook

As Longfellow and Johnson's *A Book of Hymns* (1846) went through reprint after reprint, the two pastor-compilers continued writing and collecting hymns, and as their theology moved further from Unitarianism to something like a broader theism during the 1850s, they found themselves increasingly dissatisfied with *A Book of Hymns*. By 1858, Johnson confessed to Longfellow, "I shudder to say that there are almost a half hundred hymns" in the book "which my tongue refuses to utter."[1] By 1860, both men were exhausted from their ministries, and they planned a vacation together in Europe to recuperate. The core of their new book, *Hymns of the Spirit*, came into being on that trip, which included a concentrated month of work in Nice, France; Longfellow later recalled that the rain kept them indoors and focused on their project.[2] The book's completion took a few more years, both men being preoccupied with the Civil War and home obligations upon their return to the States.

Longfellow in particular had a difficult and demanding reentry. Having learned of his sister-in-law Fanny's death from an English newspaper in Italy, Longfellow moved back to Craigie House to help his brother Henry care for his five children. Tensions ran high when the oldest boy, Charlie, ran away to enlist, and Sam stayed to watch the house and children when Henry took an emergency trip to Washington after learning that Charlie had been wounded in a cavalry skirmish.

Hymns of the Spirit finally appeared in 1864, again from Ticknor and Fields, but with decidedly less fanfare than the first book had enjoyed. The depression of the wartime book market was a factor; even among the massive Methodist, Presbyterian, and Episcopalian publishing houses, the most in-demand hymnbooks were tract-sized ones designed for troops in the field. But another reason was that the book was even more literary than its predecessor. Henry Vaughan, John Milton, and Harriet Beecher Stowe were included from *A Book of Hymns* contributors; William Cullen Bryant, Ralph Waldo Emerson, and the Renaissance poet George Sandys all had expanded roles. Connected with this increasingly literary source material was a God-as-Spirit theology that removed the historical person of Christ almost entirely, emphasizing instead God's transcendence in himself and his expression in nature and the human soul. This new focus held little attraction for more traditional Unitarian churches; Edward Everett Hale, whose Worcester church had been the first to receive *A Book of Hymns*, was now pastor of the South Congregational Church in Boston, and he reported that his congregation would not accept the new book because it lacked communion hymns.[3] At the same time, those more inclined to the theology of *Hymns of the Spirit* were also increasingly inclined to keep the Sabbath at home, as Emily Dickinson put it, leaving organized congregational life altogether. Longfellow and Johnson's work reflected and facilitated that shift to what may be called the "private hymnbook."

Of course, in the beginning, all hymnbooks were private hymnbooks. When Watts began publishing his System of Praise in the early eighteenth century, he hoped that congregations would use his books but assumed that, like previous hymnbooks made by Richard Baxter, George Wither, John Mason, and others in the seventeenth century, they would find their primary audience in relatively private settings: devotional reading and informal, social singing.[4] This was even more the case with John Donne's hymns and works like George Herbert's *The Temple* (1633), which were formatted and distributed as poetry—matter for devotional reading and occasionally adapted for singing, but designed primarily for individuals and small groups of readers. The growth of public, liturgical hymnody in English over the eighteenth century brought Watts's books, and those that came after, into the open, and by the turn of the nineteenth century, while many hymnbooks still served private, devotional purposes, it was expected that most popular hymnbooks would be suitable for public congregational song. Starting in the 1820s, new hymn collections, such as James Montgomery's *Christian Psalmist* (1825), John Keble's *Christian Year* (1827), and Reginald Heber's *Hymns* (1827), supplied texts for worship but were designed as initially for private consumption, often in ornate gift-book presentations or with the generous white space of contemporary poetry books.[5] The influence of these new collections was felt first in the burgeoning gift-book market, where devotional books with high production values (illustrations, fine bindings, gilt pages) enjoyed strong sales. By the mid-nineteenth century, the private hymnbook was established as a new—or, more accurately, reimagined—print genre that allowed for a wider scope of source material, increased attention to the devotional context of the home, and increased recognition of the female reader of hymns, especially the reader as compiler. Even as women's authoring of hymns increased at midcentury, few women hymnists enjoyed widespread name recognition, and even fewer saw much income from their hymns' popularity. The most successful compilers of private hymnbooks, however, were women, and their efforts helped to gradually reshape not only the canon of Anglophone hymnody but also readers' understandings of what a hymn could be.

The books of the 1820s shared a moment that saw two largely unrelated forces intersect: the growth of evangelical publishing and the Oxford movement. Montgomery's *Christian Psalmist*, discussed in chapter 10, followed not so much in the tradition of Watts's *Hymns*—a private hymnbook hoping to become public—as that of Newton and Cowper's *Olney Hymns*, which was meant more as a devotional collection than as a congregational singing book. *The Christian Psalmist* was meant for private reading and as a resource for compilers, who wielded great influence on the public reading and singing of hymns. It was part resource and part manifesto in its insistence on the importance of literary quality aligned with devotional fervor, and its influence went far beyond its several print runs.

Keble's *Christian Year* was a slightly different sort of book with a very different context. Keble was the rector of a small Oxfordshire parish, and by 1831 he had also become the professor of poetry at Oxford. The combination led to frequent comparisons with Herbert, whose departure from London's court life for a country parish was often seen as integral to his spiritual and poetic achievements. Unlike Herbert, however, Keble was politically and culturally involved, and his leadership in the reimagining of the Church of England in light of research into Anglo-Latin and ancient church sources made him one of the central figures of the Oxford movement. This movement did much to align British Protestant nationalism with High Church aesthetics and theology—the Gothic Revival in architecture and the translation of Latin hymns such as "All Creatures of Our God and King" were two of the lasting legacies of the movement—and caused controversy when High Church advocates, such as John Henry Newman, converted to Catholicism, inspiring many aesthetically minded students, such as Gerard Manley Hopkins, to follow suit and opening the movement to charges of corrupting British identity. Keble's ability to keep Catholicism at arm's length while displaying his own Anglo-Catholic sensibilities helped him remain at Oxford at a time when Catholics and other non-Anglicans were still barred from enrolling in the university. Yet if his famous tracts arguing his various doctrinal and aesthetic positions generated excitement in intellectual circles, his poetry connected quickly and profoundly with a much larger audience.

Keble's *Christian Year* was a series of poetic meditations on the Anglican Sunday lectionary through the course of the liturgical year. Many of these poems entered hymnbooks in the nineteenth century, particularly in England, but Keble did not write the poems explicitly as hymns, and they found their readiest audience among families and pious readers. One popular book of English country life described "the long quiet evening, when some of us gathered, as closely as possible, round the bright fire, and listened whilst one and another dear voice read some passage from Keble's *Christian Year*. Soothing, beautiful poetry!"[6] The first edition appeared in a most unhymnbook-like format, a two-volume presentation that could sit beside theological tomes on a private library shelf. The second and subsequent editions appeared generally in a smaller, one-volume format that fit much better the typical dimensions of a hymnbook. For Anglican conservatives who still resisted the innovation of hymn singing, Keble's book was a boon for the uniting of church liturgy with private devotional practice without resorting to a quasi-Catholic breviary, while hymn readers of nearly all denominations embraced Keble's lyricism, and many later hymn writers sought to emulate it.[7]

Reginald Heber, a fellow Oxfordian, predated the Oxford movement but also used the liturgical calendar to shape his devotional project. A prize-winning poet as an Oxford undergraduate, Heber settled into a country parish while continuing his literary pursuits part time as a reviewer for John Murray's *Quarterly Review*, a venue in which Heber shared page space with Sir Walter Scott, Lord Byron, Robert Southey, and other stars of the Murray catalog. Heber began writing hymns early in his clerical life, for which in retrospect he gave two competing reasons. The first was recreation, a personal hobby he wedged into his demanding schedule of sermon preparation and pastoral visits. The other reason was a counteroffensive in response to the Methodists who had begun competing for his parishioners; lively hymn singing was a known Methodist strength, and the Church of England had not yet adopted a hymnbook (indeed, it would not until decades after Heber's death). Like John Newton, Heber took matters into his own hands by providing original hymns for his congregants to sing in celebrating church feasts and seasons.

By 1811 Heber decided to seek wider attention to the matter of hymns, submitting his texts a few at a time to the *Christian Observer*, the Church of England's official magazine, while keeping his work with the *Quarterly Review* completely separate. Heber did privately share and discuss his hymns with Walter Scott and Henry Hart Milman, the latter another Murray author and Keble's predecessor as the Oxford professor of poetry; this was part of a lobbying effort Heber undertook to win official adoption of his hymns for church use, with the goal of completing an entire annual cycle of liturgically themed texts. By 1820 Heber had gained a considerable following in most of the major denominations, including in the United States, on the strength of his *Christian Observer* hymns, and that year he made a formal proposal to the bishop of London, who complimented Heber's writing but told him the church was not yet ready to consider adopting a hymnbook. Heber's best-known work, his missionary hymn "From Greenland's Icy Mountains," had gained for him a reputation as a champion of missions, and when he was offered the bishopric of Calcutta he accepted despite his delicate health. The massive Calcutta diocese required extensive travel in a tropical climate, and becoming its bishop was assumed tantamount to martyrdom. Heber, after several years' vigorous service, died suddenly in 1826, confirming his friends' fears for him and leaving his hymnbook incomplete and unpublished.[8]

Heber's widow, Amelia, quickly established herself as the keeper of her husband's memory, and while preparing his memoirs she took steps to publish Heber's hymns in a way that would bring together the two strands of his literary career, strands that Heber had purposely kept separate while he was alive. Amelia Heber recruited her husband's friend Milman, an acclaimed religious poet, to edit the hymns. Milman and Mrs. Heber arranged for *Hymns* to be published by John Murray, who had the first edition designed in the format of the works of Byron, Milman, and Southey: an octavo volume with high-quality paper, generous white space, a table of contents (but no first-line index), and Bishop Heber's name and title clearly displayed on the title page. Amelia Heber dedicated the book—identifying the volume as a collection of hymns written by her late husband—to the archbishop of Canterbury, thus continuing her husband's lobbying effort even as his works appeared in fine literary trappings. But the conventions of the single-authored volume of poetry that Murray used hid how odd the finished volume was. Since Heber had not written the complete cycle of hymns before he left for India, and he never returned to the project, Milman's editing involved filling the gaps in Heber's calendar with Milman's own works (including the Palm Sunday text "Ride On! Ride On in Majesty") and works by Walter Scott, John Dryden, Joseph Addison, William Cowper, Charles Wesley (listed as "anonymous"), and Isaac Watts (also not named, but identified by psalm number). Making these additions in order to fulfill Heber's original vision and to make the book more usable as a devotional work, Milman struggled to maintain that the book was indeed Heber's while acknowledging the various sources he'd drawn on, both in an editor's note and in the individual text attributions. Publishers of finely illustrated collections of religious poets quickly made use of Heber's *Hymns* as his "works," and a volume incorporating his hymns and other poems, such as his Oxford prize poem "Palestine," appeared soon. Most of these editions were careful to remove the non-Heber hymns, and later illustrated editions of *Hymns* alone did the same. However, the fact that Heber's *Hymns* accompanied by numerous steel engravings and a gilt binding was marketable in the 1860s (and now needed a first-line index) shows how much Heber and his hymns had become associated with private reading.

As gift books increasingly became the venue for reprints of Montgomery, Keble, and Heber, new collections began to emerge that claimed to focus not generally on sacred poetry (as the "works of Heber" volumes did) but rather on hymns in particular. While male authors and compilers had tended to dominate church collections, the most successful private hymnbooks of the 1850s and 1860s were edited by women, Caroline Snowden Whitmarsh foremost among them. Whitmarsh (later Guild) was a Boston Unitarian whose early education at the Ursuline Academy in Charlestown,

Massachusetts, likely influenced her ecumenical approach to religious verse.[9] Whitmarsh's first collection, *Hymns of the Ages*, was an immediate success upon its 1858 publication by Ticknor and Fields, despite her acknowledged reliance on antiquarian collections, such as *Lyra Catholica* (1849) and *Lyra Germanica* (1855) at a moment of high anti-Catholic sentiment in America notwithstanding.[10] Whitmarsh sought to bring a wider range of Christian thought and spirituality to American Protestant readers, and her approach enjoyed sales good enough for her publishers to urge her to compile two further volumes of *Hymns of the Ages*. Yet Whitmarsh was identified only by initials in her prefaces, alongside her collaborator, Anne Guild, and not at all on the title pages of her books. Frederic Dan Huntington, a Harvard professor and Amherst College graduate who would later become an Episcopalian bishop, wrote laudatory, signed prefaces for the volumes—which led to frequent attributions of the books to his editorship.

Hymns of the Ages was a popular gift book among highly educated and cultured readers, but Whitmarsh also produced another collection for a decidedly younger audience, *Hymns for Mothers and Children* (1861). As she stated in the preface, this was a very different project from the earlier one, due to the "sad lack of material." Her sources were not scholarly collections but rather small books she frequently had to borrow from the children who owned them as well as children's recitations she transcribed, "for there are no Athenaeum libraries of children's books, and this [book] has literally been gathered 'out of the mouths of babes.'"[11] Yet for all its editorial difficulties, *Hymns for Mothers and Children* succeeded, and the title was extended into a second series five years later, both books featuring engravings and gilt bindings. The engraved title pages and frontispieces depicted mothers reading to their children, but the construction of the collections made it clear that children were meant to do their share of reading in the books too. Sections for younger children and older children, poems voiced by children, and poems about play all were inviting to a flesh-and-blood child speaker-reader. With many poems on moral topics, family milestones (births, birthdays, deaths), and natural scenery, the collection ranged far from content suited to church services, but the line between hymn and poem had always been more permeable in children's collections. In her *Wayfaring Hymns* (1869), Anna Warner had faced a similar dilemma with a dose of philosophy: "Hymns they are not all, of course, strictly: I use the word because no better comes."[12]

Warner was another successful hymnbook compiler, her *Wayfaring Hymns* following her popular *Hymns of the Church Militant*, which appeared on the heels of *Hymns of the Ages* in 1858. Warner was the younger sister and collaborator of Susan Warner (whose novel *The Wide, Wide World* was discussed in interlude 1) and a hymnist in her own right; her most famous composition, "Jesus Loves Me, This I Know," appeared in the 1860 novel *Say and Seal* she and Susan cowrote.[13] *Hymns of the Church Militant*, as "simply a book of hymns for private use," stressed not only private reading but the private experience of writing the hymns: "For these are not assembly hymns, nor paraphrases, nor hymns written to order,—they are the living words of deep Christian experience." It was precisely the private, domestic space that provided a more universal view of the church than a congregational book could, and materials drawn from many denominations and centuries came together to "tell that the Church is one." Like Whitmarsh's ecumenical approach, the Presbyterian Warner reached beyond doctrine and affiliation to help her readers find in authentic, individual expressions the core of the true church; "look here at their hearts," she urged.[14]

This insistence on the universal message of her collection of individual voices allowed Warner to envision the church as a much larger, imagined community than the face-to-face experience in church tended to afford, but it also committed her to what was still a novel editing method for hymn texts. Lamenting the general tendency to revise hymns, Warner insisted: "I have tried to give the author's own words, and all of them." In other words, she assumed hymns to cohere as unified wholes much more along the lines of how we conceive of the modern lyric poem than as texts subject to the gravitational pull of creeds and community sensibilities that hymnbook compilers generally understood hymns to be. Warner used an organic metaphor to explain her choice: "There is always a fresh beauty in the free growth of a fine thing (even though it be a little unruly) which no strange hand can trim into better shape." This is an argument for the "natural" hymn, not the cultivated text. And yet so much editing had taken place for so long that Warner "long ago gave up the hope of finding *all* the lopped branches," and in a few instances she even found herself doing her own pruning of "objectionable verses." While she attempted to attribute each text, many were so indeterminate that she chose to leave the attribution blank. Anticipating the obsessive research of Louis Benson, John Julian, and other hymnologists of the late nineteenth century (and mirroring David Creamer's desire to get at the true Wesleyan texts), Warner offered a rare glimpse into the editorial labor behind her book's production: "Of well-known hymn writers, I could sometimes get an old edition and copy from that; but with the thousand nameless hymns, I could but compare and take which version I liked best. Often indeed . . . the original words asserted their own right without a question; and many times the hymn had to be *collected* from various book[s],—I have had twelve open before me at one time, for one hymn."[15] For the compiler who would arrive at an authentic text, then, reading was a remarkably demanding activity, requiring the acquisition, comparison, and critical assessment of many books for the sake of accessing the power of original, personal expression. Perhaps no step brought the hymn closer to the realm of literature than that of attempting the restoration of texts, and thus their authors' intent, a concern that had seldom been paramount for hymnbook compilers and that has still not prevailed as the highest principle in hymn editing (as it is in modern poetry editing) to the present day.

Clearly, the lives of hymnbook compilers were filled with professional labors and challenges. But what of the lives of the owners of private hymnbooks? A copy of the first edition of *Hymns for Mothers and Children* held at the American Antiquarian Society gives some insight into such a life. First of all, it bears the marks of a family history of gift giving. The first time it was gifted was to nine-year-old Fanny Chandler from her aunt Nancy Cushing Paine, with the inscription written on the front endpaper by Fanny's father, Dr. George Chandler, a psychiatric doctor and the genealogist for one of the oldest, most affluent families in Worcester, Massachusetts. Dr. Chandler's identification of the giver as "Mrs. Frederick Wm Paine of Lincoln Street" indicates the status of that family as well; the Paines, long connected by marriage and business relations with the Chandlers, lived on an affluent, although by 1861 old-fashioned thoroughfare. This was a high-end gift for high-end folks. Fanny, apparently years later (likely once she had become Fanny Lincoln, marrying into the family whose name her aunt's street bore), wrote another inscription on a flyleaf in the book, identifying herself as Fanny Chandler and the giver as "Aunt Nancy Paine." Above that, another inscription in the same hand indicates the book was later given to Dorothy Lincoln; the initials "D. L." were written in a younger hand above that inscription. Dorothy was born to Fanny and her husband, Waldo Lincoln, in 1890, and she died suddenly in Singapore while on a round-the-world vacation with her parents in 1909. The book was again Fanny's to give, and on October 25, 1912, she inscribed it to her granddaughter "dear little Louisa Dresser," the child of another daughter of Fanny and Waldo, Josephine. The occasion was Louisa's fifth birthday, making her most likely the youngest recipient of the book, but it does not seem that she kept it long, for her grandfather and Fanny's husband, Waldo, gave the book to the American Antiquarian Society (of which he was then president) in 1918. This book as gift had been not only for mothers and children but also for aunts, fathers, and grandchildren.

Beyond the inscriptions on the unprinted flyleaves, the young Fanny Chandler left a series of traces throughout her book. Check marks and notes indicate which hymns and hymn-poems she had memorized and recited at school, apparently taking advantage of elective choices of recitation texts to use a beloved home book for her school assignments. While this copy of *Hymns for Mothers and Children* has no trace of ever having been used in church—and its large size and highly illustrated style did not make it ideal for that setting—its history of moving from the Paines' home to the Chandlers' to the Lincolns' to the Dressers' demonstrates how widely hymns, and their use in private hymnbooks, could travel. Now a part of institutional memory and significant for the American Antiquarian Society's collection because of the Lincoln family's association with the society, *Hymns for Mothers and Children* offers a tantalizing view of what kinds of private, and not-so-private, spaces a private hymnbook could navigate in the nineteenth century.

CHAPTER 13

Emily Dickinson's Hymnody of Privacy

That Emily Dickinson's poetry engages with the meters, imagery, and tone of hymnody is a commonplace, and the starting point for almost every discussion of Dickinson and hymns has been Isaac Watts. Beginning with Thomas Johnson's statements that nearly all of Dickinson's poems "employ meters derived from English hymnology" and that these meters were "familiar to her from childhood as the measure in which Watts's hymns were composed,"[1] the equation of Watts and the hymn in Dickinson's world has gone virtually unquestioned. Dickinson's poetry shows her deep familiarity with Watts, from her use of "How Doth the Little Busy Bee" in a comic valentine (one of her first extant poems) to her parody of Watts's "Faith is the brightest evidence / Of things beyond our sight":

> "Faith" is a fine invention
> For Gentlemen who *see!*
> But Microscopes are prudent
> In an Emergency![2]

It requires little effort to imagine Dickinson as a private poet rejecting the values and demands of the publicly sung hymn, but practices of *reading* hymns were at the heart of Dickinson's interaction with hymnody, and they shed light on her place within a larger print culture and spiritual culture. The practices of devotional reading, liturgical performance, and using private hymnbooks that have been the subject of this book can lend new understanding of what Dickinson's commitment to "keep[ing] the Sabbath . . . at home" (Fr 236) entailed.

The Dickinsons kept copies of their church hymnbooks at home as well as in the family pew, judging by the multiple surviving copies of *Church Psalmody* and *The Sabbath Hymn Book* that bear the names of Edward

(Emily's father) or Austin Dickinson (her brother).[3] We can assume the Dickinsons did at least some hymn reading at home; they certainly sang hymns and played them on the piano, as Emily told one of her cousins she had been doing with her father the day before he died—years after she had stopped attending church.[4] Yet that does not necessarily mean that the Dickinsons sang in church. There was certainly music in First Church, Amherst; even during Emily's childhood there were instruments accompanying a quartet or choir, and an organ was added by the middle of the nineteenth century. However, the records of First Church indicate that pastor after pastor tried and failed, even as late as the 1920s, to convince the congregation to sing along with the hymns. When First Church adopted the *Sabbath Hymn and Tune Book* around 1860, the Dickinsons bought several copies of the alternative edition, the words-only *Sabbath Hymn Book*. It is known that at least some of the family read music, but music seems to have interfered with the reading of hymns too much for Edward's and possibly others' taste. Edward had opted for a words-only version of *Christian Psalmody*, a book used in connection with a singing school at First Church in 1817 that usually had an appendix of printed tunes with it, and the family's preferences changed little over time.

Understanding the Dickinson family's approach to hymnbooks and the liturgical realities of First Church provides new insight into the famous scene Emily Dickinson narrated to her friend and future sister-in-law, Susan Gilbert:

> When I was gone to meeting . . . when [the pastor] said "Our Heavenly Father," I said "Oh Darling Sue"; when he read the 100th Psalm, I kept saying your precious letter all over to myself, and Susie, when they sang— it would have made you laugh to hear one little voice, piping to the departed. I made up words and kept singing how I love you, and you had gone, while all the rest of the choir were singing Hallelujahs. I presume nobody heard me, because I sang so *small*, but it was a kind of a comfort to think I might put them out, singing of you.[5]

This has generally been interpreted as Emily quietly but daringly rebelling against the common practice of the church, seeming to join in the public worship while focusing on private affection instead. But the Dickinsons would have almost certainly sat silently reading from their hymnbooks while the choir sang, and there is no other evidence that Emily was ever a member of the First Church choir (though she sang in one at Mount Holyoke College during her studies there). What Emily was likely doing, then, was using the quiet, private space afforded by the customs of her family's church to escape from public worship into private fantasy and poetic composition. She may not have been supposed to do so, strictly speaking, but the realities of the church service gave her space to exercise her privacy, and she exercised it more than her fellow congregants knew.

Private hymn reading and, indeed, private hymnbooks were part of Susan Gilbert's lifestyle as well as the Dickinsons'. Gilbert had begun acquiring gift books of religious poetry while a student at the Utica Academy, where she received a "valentine" gift of Rufus Griswold's *Sacred Poets of England and America* from her classmates at Christmas 1848, and during her married life she built up a library of private hymnbooks to which Emily would have had ready access. Susan owned both series of *Hymns for Mothers and Children* and the first two volumes of *Hymns of the Ages*; the latter were presentation copies from her lifelong friend Frederic Dan Huntington, who wrote the prefaces. There is little direct evidence as to how, or if, the Dickinsons used these books, but several of Emily Dickinson's poetic choices suggest the influence, or at least her awareness, of Whitmarsh's books in particular. While it is not known when Susan acquired the *Hymns for Mothers and Children* volumes, it is quite plausible that the first series, published in 1861, was a gift on the occasion of the birth of her first child, Ned Dickinson, that same year.

Scholars have generally seen 1860–1861 as a time of tension, even of estrangement, between Emily and Susan Dickinson, but there has been little commentary on the effect of becoming an aunt on the poet's development. Emily Dickinson was close to all three of Susan's children; the death of her nephew Gilbert was arguably her most traumatic loss in her later years. Gilbert's death has been discussed at length by Dickinson scholars, but little if anything has been made of the births of the children as inspiration for Dickinson's works. The ephemerality of children's books, which Whitmarsh lamented, reflects the general lack of recording the history that passes between mother and child, from pregnancy and birth to care, early education, and the sharing of private reading from books precisely like Whitmarsh's hymn collections. Whitmarsh drew materials from the edge of oblivion in the ephemeral world of domestic print, and sent them back over that same edge. For the poet who wrote these lines in 1861, the silence and sacrifice of women's lives would not have been lost:

> Title divine, is mine.
> The Wife without the Sign -
> Acute degree conferred on me -
> Empress of Calvary - (Fr 194)

Among the other poems Dickinson wrote that year is the following, which I give here in its entirety:

> Baby -
> Teach Him - when He makes the names -
> Such an one - to say -
> On his babbling - Berry - lips -
> As should sound - to me -
> Were my Ear - as near his nest -
> As my thought - today -
> As should sound -
> "Forbid us not" -
> Some like "Emily." (Fr 198)

The speaker asks the receiver of the poem to teach a baby to say the name "Emily," which the speaker can already imagine hearing him say. This imagination takes the speech act into a curious subjunctive register, with the phrase "as should sound" repeated, and the sound only resembling "Emily." The request is an intimate one, and the imagined hearing is even more intimate, since the sound only sounds "some like 'Emily'" to the speaker. Amid these imaginings and directions appears a line that seems to surface from a separate train of thought, "Forbid us not," a reference to one of Christ's most famous statements: "Suffer the little children to come unto me, and forbid them not: for of such is the kingdom of God" (Mark 10:14). This statement is quoted in epigraphs and verse lines in several places in *Hymns for Mothers and Children*, but Dickinson would not have had to read it there to know it was a commonplace in religious writings about children.

More interesting than the question of where she found the phrase is what she did with it, changing "them" to "us." In the midst of the connection between the speaker/listener and the child saying "Emily," a spontaneous prayer arises that unites them as children before Christ, asking that they not be forbidden. One way of understanding this move relates to the tensions between the poet and her sister-in-law during this period; the two cryptic notes that survive from 1861, one by each woman, suggest struggles, perhaps both internal and external, that separate the women and their mourning of that separation. "Forbid us not" could be read as a plea to Susan to see Emily as needing her love just as Ned did and to not turn either of them away. Another, more radical reading is also possible. The first line of the poem is a single word, "Baby," and if we take this to be the person whom the speaker addresses, we might then interpret "teach Him" as referring to the baby teaching Christ how to say "Emily." As Christ's statement suggests that infants have the right to assume they will not be turned away, the speaker calls on the baby as an advocate with Christ or, possibly, the more judgmental "Father" that Dickinson repeatedly portrays in her poems. The birth of a new Dickinson baby, like the presence of private hymnbooks, is significant for understanding the imagery and imagined exchanges in Dickinson's poetry during her most productive years, and both have been largely overlooked precisely because of their place in the everyday domesticity of the home, although that context provided much of Dickinson's raw material alongside her expansive reading.

The persona of the speaker in the "Baby" poem, like those of her most famous poems today—"My Life Had Stood a Loaded Gun," "Because I Could Not Stop for Death," "This Is My Letter to the World"—can be read as steeped in autobiography, and yet they are not Emily Dickinson's direct voice. Virginia Jackson's study of Dickinson's "lyric address" helps to explain the strategies of abstraction and fictionalizing that were available to Dickinson within the nineteenth-century tradition of the poetess (exemplified by Felicia Hemans),[6] but Dickinson also had access to a form of address not previously identified. In chapter 10, I used the phrase "dramatic hymn" to describe some of Hemans's poems, texts that read like hymns but used a descriptive title to create a narrative frame, thus moving the work into the realm of imagination rather than collapsing speaker and reader, as in the usual devotional reading. Examples of the dramatic hymn were plentiful in Dickinson's time, in periodicals and gift books especially.

Perhaps the quintessential dramatic hymn was Henry Longfellow's "A Psalm of Life." Reprinted in school texts, anthologies, magazines, and newspapers with astonishing frequency, Longfellow's poem was perhaps his best-known lyric during his lifetime, contributing the phrase "foot-steps on the sands of time" to the idiom of the English language. Its message of up-lift and determination ("Let us then be up and doing") was a key reason for its popularity, but its flexibility of address was phenomenal. The opening couplet strikes a note of defiance: "Tell me not, in mournful numbers, / Life is but an empty dream!"[7] But to whom is the speaker saying this? And who is he? The subtitle Longfellow originally included explains: "What the Heart of the Young Man Said to the Psalmist." The speaker is voicing the internal monologue—the deep-seated response—of a cheerful youth to someone identified as "the Psalmist." Could this be the Moses of Psalm 90, who remarks that humans "spend our years as a tale that is told"? Quite pos-sibly. Andrew Higgins's examination of the text of "A Psalm of Life" and its early printing history demonstrated that the poem was composed as a re-sponse to the "Coplas de Manrique," an elegy by a famous Spanish courtier-poet who indeed claimed that life was but an empty dream in the wake of his father's death.[8] But few readers who skipped the group of translated texts in the back of Longfellow's *Ballads and Other Poems* (1842), which included the poet's rendition of Manrique's "Coplas," would easily see the connection. Longfellow seems to have hidden the intertext in plain sight, using the "psalmist" moniker to let the reader imagine who the young man and his morose interlocutor might be. In many reprintings, the subtitle was left off—one example is its inclusion in Samuel Longfellow and Samuel Johnson's *Book of Hymns*, the first of dozens of times "A Psalm of Life" appeared in a hymnbook—leaving the rhetorical situation even more to the reader's imag-ination. The speaker could be construed as Longfellow, but when he pub-lished the poem he was hardly young: in his mid-thirties and mourning the loss of his first wife, Mary. As a poem celebrating the richness and meaning-fulness of life, complete with a call to action, "A Psalm of Life" could be a rousing read, either alone or while singing in public. It would have been quite feasible for readers in either context to collapse their identity with the speak-er's, particularly if the "young man" characterization of the subtitle were dropped. And yet it can just as easily be taken as addressing the reader, the speaker pointing a finger out of the text in a second-person exhortation. This kind of slippage of identity, of address, of hymn-poem classification, would have been a ready model for Dickinson's experiments.

Some of Dickinson's early poems seem especially engaged with this role playing; Fr 231 begins, "We dont cry - Tim and I - / We are far too grand - ." Tim and the speaker lock themselves away for fear of death, torn by a sense of helplessness and a longing for a final home, which leads to a frightened crisis:

> Then - we shake - Tim and I -
> And lest I - cry -
>
> Tim - reads a little Hymn -
> And we both pray,
> Please, Sir, I and Tim -
> Always lost the way!

The prayer has a distinctly Dickensian ring to it, an expression of an orphan's voice longing for comfort while fearing abandonment, and it comes after the turning point of the poem: hymn reading.[9] At this point, actions of shutting in and out give place to reaching out into the unknown. While Tim reads the hymn merely to stave off tears, the reading inspires language, prayer, and poetry—the connection between soul and God that hymns had been developed to foster. Yet this is not a binary scene; the close of Fr 231 is the prayer "Take us simultaneous - Lord - / I - 'Tim' - and - me!"

For Dickinson, the hymn was always about greater connection, both horizontally and vertically, and she learned how to use its stance while moving between the highly theatrical persona in Fr 231 and a voice much closer to the blending of speaker and reader typical of the dramatic hymn:

> At least - to pray - is left - is left -
> Oh Jesus - in the Air -
> I know not which thy chamber is -
> I'm knocking - everywhere -
>
> Thou settest Earthquake in the South -
> And Maelstrom, in the Sea -
> Say, Jesus of Nazareth -
> Hast thou no arm for Me? (Fr 377)

Here the speaker's desperate attempt to find God's saving help—and the unusual specifying of Jesus as the addressee in a Dickinson poem—brings

Dickinson's spiritual quest much more in line with that of Cowper, strug-
gling with fears of damnation while hoping that the search for God will not
be finally empty. The Dickinson poems that work best as dramatic hymns
tend to be expressions of abandonment, anxiety, and hope: not the stuff of
congregational hymnbooks, but a stance much more easily recognized in
one's private reading as an authentic spiritual experience, whether Christian
or otherwise.

This raises the question of whether we can call any of Dickinson's
poems "hymns." One source of confusion over Dickinson's use of the term
is that the poems she thus designated almost always focus on secular subjects:
a hummingbird, the seasons, patriotism. All these topics featured in *Hymns
for Mothers and Children*; nature and patriotism boasted their own sections.
But why call these "hymns" to begin with? Dickinson's letters suggest an
answer. When she called poems hymns, it was when her work was under
threat of being cut short or misunderstood. The most significant of these
works were three pieces donated to an 1880 fundraiser at First Church for
children's missions abroad, and she asked Thomas Wentworth Higginson
"if they were faithful." He agreed to read the poems, and Dickinson sent
him four, "lest one of them you might think profane."[10] Dickinson was concerned that her poems did not fit their new context, or might be judged so
because she offered them as commodities; they were gifts, but meant to fetch
a price. These poems were destined for the market, however local, and by
referring to them as "hymns," Dickinson claimed a very particular kind of
social life for what critics have generally considered her private poetry. The
connections to God and to others must hold in order to keep these poems
faithful, even as they moved out of old contexts and into something the
poet could not foresee. These hymns were envisioned as "letters to the
world" that required considerable doses of privacy to reach their particular public, but Dickinson repeatedly insisted that reaching their public is
what hymns do.

Dickinson described one such public in a letter comforting her sister,
Lavinia, after she kept vigil over the death of their aunt for whom she
was named, Lavinia Norcross: "Well, she is safer now than 'we know or
even think.' . . . Tuneful little aunt, singing, as we trust, hymns than
which the robins have no sweeter ones."[11] This is the hymn of the faithful
martyr, music that stretches across the chasms of death, "Clear strains of

Hymn / The River could not drown - " (Fr 323). It stands out not for its content but for its supernatural beauty, outdoing the hymns that the robins sing.

For birds also sing hymns. In a famous letter, Dickinson shared an anecdote of finding a bird singing hidden in a bush: "Wherefore sing, I said, since nobody *hears*? . . . '*My* business is to *sing*'—and away she rose! How do I know but cherubim, once, themselves, as patient, listened, and applauded her unnoticed hymn?"[12] This story immediately followed the poet's declaration, "*My* business is to love," emphasizing the parallels between poet and bird, loving and singing. The bird sings despite a lack of a visible audience and rises to follow its song, which is (or may be) heard by angels. What Dickinson imagined her aunt doing in the heavenly presence of angels and a bird doing among the same angels on earth, she also imagined herself doing. Dickinson understood the hymn as a form of hopeful communication, in which the lack of an evident audience is offset by faith in a spiritual reception. Hymns are not simply poems that are spiritually received; the reception is what makes the hymn.

An episode of the Dickinson-Higginson correspondence dramatized this hymning of a poem. In May 1874, Higginson sent Dickinson his Memorial Day poem "Decoration," and she thanked him for the "Poem,"[13] which identifies the unmarked grave of a bereaved woman as that of the bravest soul in a soldiers' cemetery. "Decoration" appeared in *Scribner's* in June; that same month, Dickinson's father, Edward, died suddenly. When she next wrote to Higginson in response to his condolences, she closed the letter with a new mention of "Decoration": "Your beautiful Hymn, was it not prophetic? It has assisted that Pause of Space which I call 'Father.' "[14] What had been a poem in May was now a hymn with "prophetic" importance, honoring a woman's bravery in the face of loss and negotiating the "Space" of an earthly father's absence and an ongoing struggle with a heavenly Father. Higginson's sentimental, occasional poem was transformed through Dickinson's grief into a gateway to the luminous. It became a hymn in Dickinson's situated reading of it.

Dickinson imagined a similar, and gendered, power for hymns in Fr 454, narrating a presumably female speaker sustaining a declining male character; it begins:

I rose - because He sank -
I thought it would be opposite -
But when his power dropped -
My Soul grew straight.

This is one of Dickinson's most metrically complex poems, and several
scholars have noted the broken quatrains and the inclusion of a pentameter
line in the final stanza.[15] Yet little has been said about what the "Hymn" is
that the speaker wields twice in the poem. In the second stanza, an incomplete verse relates the speaker's power: "I cheered my fainting Prince - / I
sang firm - even - Chants - / I helped his Film - with Hymn - ." The chants'
firmness and evenness have little to do with meter, though the dashes give
a sense of restraint and deliberation to the line; the hymn's strength is not
in its content or its form, but lies deeper. The hymn that the speaker chants
here is of death and the afterlife:

I told him Best - must pass
Through this low Arch of Flesh -
No Casque so brave
It spurn the Grave -

I told him Worlds I knew
Where Emperors grew -
Who recollected us
If we were true - (Fr 454)

Death is inevitable but, as Dickinson continually insists, it is not the
end; if armor (the "Casque," or helmet) cannot ensure immortality, truth
can. And this turns out to be a truth that surprises its teller, a truth not
consciously known before it is voiced:

And so with Thews of Hymn -
And Sinew from within -
And ways I knew not that I knew - till then -
I lifted Him - (Fr 454)

As the male body and its armor both fail, the "Hymn" has its own "Thews"
and "Sinew"; this is brawn, but not male brawn, as Michael Manson pointed

out.[16] Nor does strength conquer another, but instead sustains and connects with him. The hymn that Dickinson's speaker wields here is not Watts's common-meter quatrain but rather the deeper spiritual power that animates that form, power not reducible to metrical form or propositional knowledge. The power and pleasure of the hymn does not inhere solely in the stanza. If it begins there—in the hymn heard in church, or read by a child at home or at school, or recalled in mourning a loved one—it reaches beyond form into spirit, and in so doing constitutes a peculiar interpersonal force that Dickinson acknowledged, celebrated, and wielded in her writings.

Yet Manson was right to insist that "Dickinson works mostly with meters that either realized or partially realized stanzaic form," a commitment that "suggests that something about the experience of this kind of rhythmic completion spoke to her."[17] If the music she longed to listen to was "not Hymn from Pulpit read" (Fr 229), reading from the pulpit, in the classroom, or in the closet could very well lead to such music. The power of hymns for Dickinson was fundamentally spiritual, but it also had a certain embodiment—or, perhaps more precisely, an articulation. The poems in which Dickinson dealt directly with "Hymn" do not settle into regular metrical patterns, but a number of her poems do, and when this regular metrics combines with theological subject matter, it can be difficult *not* to see Dickinson reaching back to Watts. And yet, Watts is hardly the whole story, or even the most relevant part of the story, when it comes to understanding Dickinson's relationship to hymnody. She engaged deeply with later hymnists, like Anna Letitia Barbauld and James Montgomery, and she also reached back past Watts to older traditions as her brother, Austin, did with his favorite, "Jerusalem, My Happy Home," an English Renaissance translation of a text by St. Augustine—and the only hymn Dickinson quoted more than once in her correspondence. When Martha Winburn England stated that Dickinson "wrote nineteenth-century hymns,"[18] she seemed to be gesturing toward this blend of read tradition and formal freedom that animated Dickinson's, Hemans's, and others poets' work in the mid-nineteenth century.

One final example can help put a finer point on what it means to think of Dickinson as a reader as well as a writer of hymns:

My period had come for Prayer -
No other Art - would do -
My Tactics missed a rudiment -
Creator - Was it you? (Fr 525)

Prayer is here one of many "Arts," the one that a certain "period" calls for. As in other arts, an effort to succeed by technique fails, and the failure brings forth a disarming question to God, "Was it you?" The subsequent stanzas trace the speaker's quest up to "Horizons" and "the North," but instead of finding the house of the Lord or the celestial city, only "Vast Prairies of Air / Unbroken by a Settler" appear—the agoraphobic defeat of a pioneering effort to track down God. Another, more perplexed question arises: "Infinitude - Had'st Thou no Face / That I might look on Thee?" The otherness of God has stymied the speaker, and only in this moment of recognized failure and anguished questioning does a way forward present itself:

The Silence condescended -
Creation stopped - for me -
But awed beyond my errand -
I worshipped - did not "pray" - (Fr 525)

It is ultimately God's silence that speaks in a transforming way, enacting a classic Dickinsonian courtesy in "stopp[ing] for me." The experience takes the speaker beyond the mere technique or art of praying into something much more authentic and meaningful, clearly related but not mere "prayer." Works such as Fr 525 fit well Anna Warner's description of the contents in her private hymnbook, *Hymns of the Church Militant*: "These are not assembly hymns, nor paraphrases, nor hymns written to order,—they are the living words of deep Christian experience."[19] Dickinson's experience was indeed deeply Christian, though with an unorthodox approach to church. She sought to connect with her readers through the silence of the page, finding a way to speak to the divine without "praying," to believe and find assurance without the "faith" she sends up in Fr 202. She indeed found ways to write "Hymn," but only by absorbing and moving beyond hymns.

The Hymnological Decade

Living abroad in the 1860s, Philadelphia educator Charles Dexter Cleveland noticed that the British had little knowledge of the progress of American hymnody. He also noticed that a few people had made recent efforts to close that knowledge gap. In the preface to his own contribution to the cause, *Lyra Sacra Americana* (1868), Cleveland saw these efforts as part of what he declared to be the "hymnological decade." A steady flow of treatises, anthologies, biographical dictionaries, and other books was appearing on both sides of the Atlantic, organizing the now venerable history of Anglophone hymns and offering context for interpreting the continually accelerating production of hymns in and beyond denominations. Hymns were ubiquitous, plentiful, and varied enough to warrant a field of study: hymnology. This field was by no means an 1860s invention, but it became much more visible then. Key contributing factors were the rise of the private hymnbook, which drew on and popularized the antiquarian and cosmopolitan collections of *lyra* and other hymnody; the conception of the hymn as an authored, lyrical poem, which brought hymnody more into the realm of literary history; and the rise of the hymnal.

This last point may inspire some surprise. Why would including music in hymnals lead to a spike in the scholarly treatment of hymns? The printed music's disruption of earlier reading practices, an obstacle Henry Ward Beecher faced in bringing out *The Plymouth Collection*, was a central problem. As hymnals became less legible and less amenable to home study, hymns became increasingly the property of the church and its clergy. Works of hymnology catered to the specialist, the interested party, rather than the general reader. Hymnology gave ministers new context—and new avenues of study—for understanding the sources and histories of the texts they used in public worship, while distilling that context into the paratextual shorthand that graced the headers and footers of hymnal pages in the later nineteenth century: tune titles; names of authors, composers, and translators; and dates of composition. Those paratexts echoed the extensive annotations provided in companion volumes to denominational hymnals, a print genre inspired by David Creamer's annotations in the 1848 *Methodist Hymnology*. Indeed, hymnology often constituted a defense of the emerging hymnal format as well as a guide for negotiating the new set of affordances those books offered to congregations and their leaders. Louis Benson identified the first American hymnological treatise as *Hymns and Choirs*, largely written by the compilers of *The Sabbath Hymn Book*, Austin Phelps and Edwards A. Park.

The depth and range of topics in *Hymns and Choirs* were impressive. The first section, by Phelps, traced the history of Christian hymnody, developed a taxonomy of hymn genres, and offered critical assessments of each genre's fitness for modern hymnals. The second section, by Park, presented a remarkably thorough theory of editing hymn texts, and the final section, by Daniel Furber, detailed the best practices for using choirs and hymnbooks to facilitate congregational singing. Deeply shaped by the work of Lowell Mason and William Bradbury, the book presented a learned, holistic vision for the ideal content and use of hymnody from a "better music" perspective. It also served as a 400-page-long advertisement for *The Sabbath Hymn Book* series, compiled by Phelps, Park, and Mason. The preface to *Hymns and Choirs* explained that the book grew out of a theory formulated during the making of the hymnal, and all three sections made numerous observations on *The Sabbath Hymn Book*'s exemplary success in carrying a key principle into practice. Indeed, the book, especially the third section, could be read as a companion to *The Sabbath Hymn Book* and a guide for how to use it. The creation of a companion volume had been the launching point of modern hymnology, and those books continue to be the central goal of hymnological research to the present day; companion volumes to guide pastors and music directors have been standard for at least a century in most denominations. Landmark scholarly works, such as John Julian's *Dictionary of Hymnology* (1892) and Benson's *The English Hymn* (1915), have mainly served to feed these companions.

As this approach expanded the scholarly resources available to those interested in hymns, however, it also contributed to a fundamental shift in the place of hymnody in the lives of individuals, families, and congregations. As tune-filled hymnals grew in size and cost, they disrupted older reading practices, making private hymnbooks necessary for those wanting access to hymn reading at home. Churches began to install pew racks and to provide hymnals for congregants, decisively shifting the economics as well as the uses of hymnody by the turn of the twentieth century. Implicit in this shift was a greater assertion of clergy control over worship. While the move from hymnbook to hymnal was meant to empower congregational singing, and it did indeed contribute to the improvement of singing, it began as a pastoral movement, not a lay one. Despite the importance of ritual for baptism, communion, and other elements of worship, clergy's standard understanding of Protestant worship in the eighteenth and nineteenth centuries was based on a three-part division: preaching, prayer, and praise or song. Ministers were to provide knowledge and leadership in all three areas, and only the third category actually involved active congregational participation. This had always made singing in church a highly emotional and fraught element of worship for Protestants in particular, and moving the books permanently into church ensured greater uniformity, and thus greater control, of praise.

Phelps insisted that praise was fundamentally no different from preaching and prayer, an argument that would have been news to millions of hymn-reading worshipers, many of whom used their hymnbooks as retreats from the pain of boring sermons. Phelps also marked devotional hymns as inferior to the more public sung hymns: "Even brilliant and forceful poems may be open to so many of the objections we have enumerated, that, with all their virtues, they must pass out of our hymn-books for public praise, and remain in collections of devotional poetry for private meditation."[1] As hymnody feminized during the mid-nineteenth century, not least through the women who compiled private hymnbooks, the public practice of hymnody became increasingly the purview of men, to the point that one reviewer of the 1874 *Presbyterian Hymnal* quipped: "It takes an able-bodied man to stand and hold the average modern hymn-book through the singing of a long hymn."[2] These were books designed by powerful men, for powerful men, and apparently it took a powerful man to use it.

The clergy's increasing control of hymn use and the concomitant emphasis on practical application in hymnological scholarship were reinforced by practices of collecting hymnbooks and moving them into institutional libraries. Creamer's collection, the product of a layman's obsession with Wesleyan origins, is the earliest known major American collection of hymnbooks, and, like most that followed, it was a working collection and was treated accordingly. Creamer heavily annotated his books, tracking textual variants and sources and recording bibliographic cross-references. When he was on the brink of financial ruin following the Civil War, he sold his collection to the newly founded Drew University in New Jersey; it was accompanied by a carefully prepared list of all the books. The university cataloged the books following Creamer's list, but the collection, now held in the Methodist Library at Drew, has generally drawn attention from scholars interested in worship practices, not historians, bibliographers, or literary scholars.

Lowell Mason's collection, which he bequeathed to Yale's theology department, has fared worse than the Creamer collection. Mason's vision for his gift was for his library to help train ministerial candidates in hymnology to aid them in offering better liturgical leadership to their churches, but there is no evidence that the theology department ever used the collection for that purpose. Mason's collection was massive (some 10,000 items) and therefore difficult to house; it also bore the traces of his prolific compiling of hymns, with many books, even rare early editions, having been heavily annotated and clipped for the construction of the dummy books that facilitated Mason's editing process, scrapbook-style. When the music department opened Sprague Hall in 1917, the theology department removed the Mason collection from its basement home and gave it to the music department, which quickly discovered that the collection outstripped the department's storage capacity. When the Divinity School opened in 1933, the music department removed all the books not containing music (in other words, the hymnbooks) and gave them to the Divinity School; upon the Beinecke Rare Book and Manuscript Library's opening in 1963, the music department moved all the pre-1850 print material there. Remaining at the music department's library were Mason's post-1850 printed music scores, manuscripts, and the sole handwritten catalog of the entire collection, compiled by Joel Sumner Smith in the 1870s. Yale music librarian Eva J. O'Meara wrote a helpful article on the history and scope of the collection, but accessing the material, never a star feature of Yale's library holdings, is a challenge.[3]

By contrast, the Louis F. Benson Collection at Princeton Theological Seminary has been carefully preserved and cataloged, and it is accessible through both the library's online catalog and Benson's own handwritten card catalog. Benson's collection began in earnest when he was editing the Presbyterian Church (USA)'s *Hymnal* (1895), and though it eventually included such prestigious items as previously unknown first editions of Watts's *Hymns*, it too was a working collection. Unlike Mason, Benson was careful to acquire duplicate copies of the volumes he wished to cut up for his dummy books, but his books are still extensively annotated. While collections such as the Harris Collection of Poetry at Brown University's John Hay Library and the Berg Collection of Literature at the New York Public Library found their way to institutions with fellowship support to attract visiting scholars, hymnbook collections have generally passed to seminaries with scant research or even cataloging funds. Hymnbook collections have been directed to the keepers of the church rather than to the keepers of culture, and there have been few incentives to engage those collections instead of institutional and theological holdings. Little wonder it has taken so long for a book like this to appear, or that hymnbooks and their place in daily and institutional life have not been more widely studied.

Yet we can recognize today the echoes of hymnbook culture if we listen for them. In addition to Anglican Books of Common Prayer and Roman Catholic missals, hymnals remain fixtures in many Christian and Jewish worship spaces. Intriguingly, the availability of computer-based audiovisual technologies has led many congregations back around to the hymnbook as large projection screens display the words of hymns and praise songs free of musical notation; congregants, reading these words as they sing together, may very likely leave the bulky hymnals in the pew racks in front of them, preferring the simpler presentation that harks back to an earlier time through present-day tech solutions. More fundamentally, even in a poetry world seemingly dominated by free verse, many poetry readers' and listeners' expectations as to what poems sound like and what they do come from the hymn stanza. While popular music lyrics in a range of genres have retained the common-meter stanza as their formal signature, children the world over still learn "Twinkle, Twinkle, Little Star" and "Mary Had a Little Lamb," once staples of children's hymnbooks, written by authors dedicated to blending the delight of poetry with the uplift of hymnody—and who contributed significantly to the diffusion of hymn material into the larger poetic world. Even my beginning literature students almost to a person tend to prefer Henry Wadsworth Longfellow to Walt Whitman on a first encounter in a college classroom; they see the measured lines of "The Village Blacksmith" and "Paul Revere's Ride" as more poetic, even more engaging, than the expansive effusions of "Song of Myself."

Of course, much of hymnbook culture has been lost to history—or has become historic rather than being seen as widely lived experience. Worshipers may very well connect their private Bible reading with the lectionary or sermon text of Sunday services, but the musical dimension of public worship once had a similar counterpart in the private reading, memorization, and singing of hymn texts through the medium of the personally owned hymnbook. As these books traveled with their owners and users, they enabled forms not only of reading but of living with books, keeping a book in a pocket or bag for easy reference in a free moment. Books that lived not as much on shelves as on people's tables, desks, and nightstands created a remarkably robust, widespread set of reading and book-use practices that helped fuel the rise of mass literacy, as children became owners of hymnbooks as rewards for and aids to the process of learning to read. These highly portable, inexpensive, easily concealable books facilitated child literacy, slave literacy, Native literacy, and poor adult literacy. And in so doing, hymnbooks contributed powerfully to the development of a mass poetic culture anchored by print literacy *and* by performative aurality.

Dichotomies between traditional ballads and written poetry fail to account for the role of the hymn in bringing two poetic worlds together, contributing to and drawing from what we think of as folk culture while also providing the poetic cues for generations of poets, from Emily Dickinson to Sharon Olds, many of whom freely acknowledged their literary formation by hymns. The picture of hymnbook culture reflected in this book is not merely one of a reader sitting, alone and absorbed, with a book. It is a picture of a reader surrounded by other readers, in motion and in development, looking at and carrying and using their books in an increasingly diverse and inescapable print world. Life did not pause for the hymnbook as we generally assume it does for the leisure reading of a novel. Rather, life happened in and through the hymnbook, pushing the bounds of defined spiritual and domestic spheres, of sacred and secular time and space.

Some of the hymnbook's shape lives on today in a curious place, in part owing to the particular problems of curating Emily Dickinson's work. By editor Ralph Franklin's count, there are more than 1,800 Dickinson poems, plus variants—with no obvious organization or titles from the author. A solution to these difficulties in the first editions of Dickinson's work, beginning with the 1890 *Poems* edited by Mabel Loomis Todd and Thomas Wentworth Higginson, was to create titles and to organize the poems into broad thematic clusters: "life," "love," "nature," and "time and eternity"— headings that could have been taken straight from a private hymnbook such as *Hymns for Mothers and Children*. This approach helped to assimilate Dickinson's work to expectations as to what hymn-inflected poetry should look like and say, and based on that it is now generally rejected by more recent editors trained in a scholarly tradition that holds up the author's latest expression (e.g., a last known revision of a text) as authoritative. The difficulties that this later approach runs into are several: determining which version of a poem was latest can be nearly impossible, even after painstaking analysis; and choosing an organizational system where there was no one unifying system to begin with seems presumptuous. Both Thomas Johnson in the 1950s and Franklin in the 1990s used a chronological ordering to solve the latter problem, though they dated the poems very differently based on their views of the evidence and their analysis. As to solving the first problem, Johnson and Franklin both did the best they could, demonstrating rather impressive feats of scholarship in the process.

But how does one navigate poems in a non-intuitive sequential order? Surely readers of Dickinson could not be expected to memorize the chronology of her works. This problem was resolved with a solution that now seems quite intuitive to modern readers without considering why it should be so intuitive: the poems are designated in both modern editions with sequential numbers from earliest to latest (with undated poems following) and indexed by first line at the back of the book. The first-line index is arguably necessary because of the lack of titles, but it is viable because many Dickinson poems were already quite well known by the time of Johnson's 1955 edition, and references to those poems in scholarship by their first lines served to reinforce the first-line index as a useful path to specific Dickinson works. This type of index, developed by Watts for the peculiar kind of oral memory–directed intensive reading he imagined for his hymnbooks, now

214 *Epilogue*

guides readers of a poet who has long been seen as a wry, secular interlocutor of Watts. Editors have taken similar approaches with the works of Whitman, whose lifelong habit of revising and retitling his poems made identification by first line necessary for ease of locating textual versions in a standard collection; again, the recalling of first lines makes the use of such an index convenient, since so many of Whitman's opening lines are known to students of his poetry.

In the 1980s, the Library of America began collecting the poetry of Whitman, Edgar Allan Poe, and other writers alongside novels, short stories, and nonfiction. In the Whitman (1982) and Poe (1984) volumes, separate indexes for titles and first lines appeared in the back; for all subsequent poetry collections in the series, a combined index of titles and first lines became the norm, so much so that the header "Index of Titles and First Lines" was replaced simply by "Index." For the Library of America, a publication project that has always made use of the thin Bible paper also used in school collections like *The Norton Anthology*, the index offers a way into the various volumes by making use of previous familiarity, memory, sound, and perhaps even devotion. As monuments of American literature, the Library of America volumes are the heirs of a print heritage stretching back to a new kind of poetry book, one that was able to reach worlds of public performance and private intimacy. If we keep the Sabbath at home with our poetic ancestors, it is only because hymnbooks helped to teach us how to do so.

blind-stamping: The pressing of a design into a book binding without adding other material, such as *gilding*.

codex: What is considered a "book" in the West: a text made up of turnable pages bound together on only one side.

duodecimo (12mo): A book format formed by folding a printed sheet into two groups of six leaves; this is one of the two most common hymnbook formats. See *octodecimo*.

endpaper: A folded paper, plain or decorated, half of which is glued to the book's inside cover while the other half is left free to turn; the free endpaper is often called a *flyleaf*.

flyleaf: Unprinted page at the front or rear of a book.

fore-edge painting: An illustration technique in which the edge of the *page block* opposite the book's spine has an image drawn or painted on, usually so that it is only visible when the *page block* is bent slightly.

frontispiece: An illustrated *verso* page facing the book's title page.

gilding/gilt: Gold-leaf decoration that may be applied to designs on the cover, a name stamped onto a cover, or the edges of the *page block*. When used on a cover, it is called gilt-stamping.

morocco: A fine grade of imported leather, initially named for its place of origin during the Renaissance and later used as a more generic term for any high-grade, strongly colored leather binding.

octavo (8vo): A book format (large for a hymnbook) formed by folding a printed sheet in half twice, thus producing an eight-leaf *signature*.

octodecimo (18mo): A book format formed by folding a printed sheet into three groups of six leaves, resulting in a book smaller than a 12mo; this is one of the two most common hymnbook formats. See *duodecimo*.

page block: The collection of *signatures* sewn or glued together to form the complete printed contents of a book, minus its cover.

panel binding: A binding produced by building up geometrical designs on regular book boards, using materials ranging from pieces of wood to papier-mâché.

paratexts: Printed material in a book beyond the main body of the text, including title pages, prefaces, notes, indexes, headers, and images.

quarter-calf: A binding in which the leather on the book's spine covers only a small portion of the cover boards compared to half-calf or full-calf.

recto: The right-hand page in a typical two-page spread in a book; the page one is supposed to read first in unbound manuscripts.

sextodecimo (16mo): A book format (large for a hymnbook) formed by folding a printed sheet in half three times, thus producing a sixteen-leaf *signature*.

signature: A single printed sheet folded into the appropriate number of leaves for the final book form.

verso: The left-hand page in a typical two-page spread in a book; the page one is supposed to read second in unbound manuscripts.

vicesimo-quarto (24mo): A pocket-size book format formed by folding a 12mo *signature* in half.

wallet binding: A leather binding in which the cover wraps around the *page block* and closes by inserting a leather tongue into a loop or strap.

Note: I have relied for many of these definitions on John Carter, *ABC for Book Collectors*, 7th ed. (New Castle, DE: Oak Knoll Press, 1995).

NOTES

Preface

1. Louis F. Benson, *The English Hymn: Its Development and Use in Worship* (New York: George H. Doran, 1915); J. R. Watson, *The English Hymn: A Critical and Historical Study* (New York: Clarendon, 1999).

2. Wesley Kort, *Take, Read: Scripture, Textuality, and Cultural Practice* (University Park: Pennsylvania State Univ. Press, 1996); Paul J. Griffiths, *Religious Reading: The Place of Reading in the Practice of Religion* (New York: Oxford Univ. Press, 1999); Paul Ricoeur, *Essays on Biblical Interpretation*, ed. Lewis S. Mudge (Philadelphia, PA: Fortress, 1980); Charles Taylor, *Modern Social Imaginaries* (Durham, NC: Duke Univ. Press, 2004); Misty G. Anderson, *Imagining Methodism in Eighteenth-Century Britain: Enthusiasm, Belief, and the Borders of the Self* (Baltimore, MD: Johns Hopkins Univ. Press, 2012); Giorgio Agamben, *The Highest Poverty: Monastic Rules and Form-of-Life*, trans. Adam Kotsko (Stanford, CA: Stanford Univ. Press, 2013); Jean-Luc Marion, *The Crossing of the Visible*, trans. James K. A. Smith (Stanford, CA: Stanford Univ. Press, 2003); John Henry Cardinal Newman, *An Essay in Aid of a Grammar of Assent* (1870; repr., South Bend, IN: Univ. of Notre Dame Press, 1979).

3. Claudia Stokes, *The Altar at Home: Sentimental Literature and Nineteenth-Century American Religion* (Philadelphia: Univ. of Pennsylvania Press, 2014); Mary De Jong, " 'With My Burden I Begin': The (Im)Personal 'I' of Nineteenth-Century Hymnody," *Studies in American Spirituality* 4 (1993): 196–208; David Music, "Isaac Watts in America before 1729," *Hymn* 50.1 (Jan. 1999): 29–33; Music, "Jonathan Edwards and the Theology and Practice of Congregational Song in Puritan New England," *Studies in Puritan American Spirituality* 8 (2004): 103–33; Music, "Jonathan Edwards's Singing Lecture Sermon," *Studies in Puritan American Spirituality* 8 (2004): 135–47; Dennis Dickerson, *African Methodism and Its Wesleyan Heritage: Reflections on AME Church History* (Nashville, TN: AMEC Sunday School Union, 2009); Dickerson, "Heritage and Hymnody: Richard Allen and the Making of African Methodism," in *Sing Them Over Again to Me: Hymns and Hymnbooks in America*, ed. Mark A. Noll and Edith L. Blumhofer (Tuscaloosa: Univ. of Alabama Press, 2006), 175–94.

4. Anthony Giddens, *The Constitution of Society: Outline of the Theory of Structuration* (Malden, MA: Polity, 1984), is the foundational work in this line of theory. See also Elizabeth Shove, *The Design of Everyday Life* (New York: Berg, 2007); Shove et al., eds., *Time, Consumption and Everyday Life: Practice, Materiality and Culture* (New York: Berg, 2009); Shove et al., *The Dynamics of Social Practice: Everyday Life and How It Changes* (Los Angeles, CA: Sage, 2012). This strand of social practice theory gestures toward actor-network theory, associated most centrally with the work of Bruno Latour, and it is largely independent of Pierre Bourdieu's notion of practice as a kind of embodied knowing. See Latour, *Reassembling the Social: An Introduction to Actor-Network-Theory* (New York: Oxford Univ. Press, 2007); Bourdieu, *The Logic of Practice*, trans. Richard Nice (Stanford, CA: Stanford Univ. Press, 1990). Bourdieu's concept, while it is invested in embodiment, tends to focus on human actors, ideas, and institutions, not on objects. Latour's ideas have been debated and reinterpreted many times, and the tendency, particularly in the "new materialism," is to assign a greater agency to objects, as in Jane Bennett's work. While I ascribe grammatical agency to hymnbooks throughout my book, I'm less interested in the argument that things have agency than in the idea that they are implicated at a deep level in the social practices of humans.

5. Matthew P. Brown, *The Pilgrim and the Bee: Reading Rituals and Book Culture in Early New England* (Philadelphia: Univ. of Pennsylvania Press, 2007); Patricia Crain, *Reading Children: Literacy, Property, and the Dilemmas of Childhood in Nineteenth-Century America* (Philadelphia: Univ. of Pennsylvania Press, 2016); M. O. Grenby, *The Child Reader, 1700–1840* (New York: Cambridge Univ. Press, 2011); H. J. Jackson, *Marginalia: Readers Writing in Books* (New Haven, CT: Yale Univ. Press, 2001); Leah Price, *How to Do Things with Books in Victorian Britain* (Princeton, NJ: Princeton Univ. Press, 2012); Lauren F. Winner, *A Cheerful and Comfortable Faith: Anglican Religious Practice in the Elite Households of Eighteenth-Century Virginia* (New Haven, CT: Yale Univ. Press, 2010); Candy Gunther Brown, *The Word in the World: Evangelical Writing, Publishing, and Reading in America, 1789–1880* (Chapel Hill: Univ. of North Carolina Press, 2004); Colleen McDannell, *Material Christianity: Religion and Popular Culture in America* (New Haven, CT: Yale Univ. Press, 1995); McDannell, ed., *Religions of the United States in Practice*, 2 vols. (Princeton, NJ: Princeton Univ. Press, 2001); David D. Hall, *Cultures of Print: Essays in the History of the Book* (Amherst: Univ. of Massachusetts Press, 1996); Hall, ed., *Lived Religion in America: Toward a History of Practice* (Princeton, NJ: Princeton Univ. Press, 1997); Michael Cohen, *The Social Lives of Poems in Nineteenth-Century America* (Philadelphia: Univ. of Pennsylvania Press, 2015); Edward Whitley, *American Bards: Walt Whitman and Other Unlikely Candidates for National Poet* (Chapel Hill: Univ. of North Carolina Press, 2010); Virginia Jackson, *Dickinson's Misery: A Theory of Lyric Reading* (Princeton, NJ: Princeton Univ. Press, 2005); D. F. McKenzie, *Bibliography and the Sociology of Texts*, rev. ed. (New York: Cambridge Univ. Press, 1999).

Prologue: Looking for Hymns

1. Gary Macy, "Thirty Ways You Use Your Hymnal!" *Hymn* 29.3 (July 1978): 165.

2. Throughout this volume I use the word "hymnbook" to refer to a book without interlined, printed music, and "hymnal" to refer to a book with interlined music.

3. Colleen McDannell, *The Christian Home in Victorian America, 1840–1900* (Bloomington: Indiana Univ. Press, 1986).

4. Garett Stewart, *The Look of Reading: Book, Painting, Text* (Chicago: Univ. of Chicago Press, 2006).

Introduction: A Reader's Hymnbook

1. Charles H. Bell, *History of the Town of Exeter, New Hampshire* (Exeter, NH, 1888), 307–8.

2. Meredith McGill, *American Literature and the Culture of Reprinting, 1834–1853* (Philadelphia: Univ. of Pennsylvania Press, 2002).

3. Richard F. Hixson, *Isaac Collins: A Quaker Printer in Eighteenth-Century America* (New Brunswick, NJ: Rutgers Univ. Press, 1968), 180–82.

4. Isaac Watts, *The Psalms of David, Imitated in the Language of the New Testament* [with *Hymns and Spiritual Songs*] (Exeter, NH, 1819), front flyleaf, in author's collection.

5. Ann Taylor and Jane Taylor, *Hymns for Infant Minds, with an Analysis to Each* (Worcester, MA, 1831), [5], in author's collection.

6. Taylor and Taylor, *Hymns for Infant Minds*, 18.

7. Taylor and Taylor, *Hymns for Infant Minds*, front flyleaves.

8. Isaac Watts, *Divine and Moral Songs for the Use of Children* (London, 1848), flyleaf, in author's collection.

9. M. O. Grenby, *The Child Reader, 1700–1840* (New York: Cambridge Univ. Press, 2011).

10. Charles West Cope, *Reminiscences of Charles West Cope* (London, 1891), 174.

11. Wilbur Macey Stone, *The Divine and Moral Songs of Isaac Watts: An Essay Thereon and a Tentative List of Editions* (New York: Triptych, 1918), 33.

12. Watts, *Divine and Moral Songs*, vi.

Interlude 1. The Wide, Wide World of Hymns

1. Susan Warner, *The Wide, Wide World*, ed. Jane Tompkins (New York: Feminist Press, City Univ. of New York, 1987), 74–75. Future references will be given parenthetically in the text.

2. Matthew P. Brown, *The Pilgrim and the Bee: Reading Rituals and Book Culture in Early New England* (Philadelphia: Univ. of Pennsylvania Press, 2007).

3. Paul J. Griffiths, *Religious Reading: The Place of Reading in the Practice of Religion* (New York: Oxford Univ. Press, 1999).

Chapter 1. How Hymnbooks Made a People

1. Quoted in Louis F. Benson, *The English Hymn: Its Development and Use in Worship* (New York: George H. Doran, 1915), v.

2. Joshua Smith and Samuel Sleeper, comps., *Divine Hymns, or Spiritual Songs: For the Use of Religious Assemblies and Private Christians* (Exeter, NH, 1793). While no extant copy prior to 1793 is known, evidence points to editions as early as 1784; see Benson, *English Hymn*, 202.

3. *The African Union Hymn Book* (Wilmington, DE, 1822), 4.

4. African Methodist Episcopal Church, *The Doctrines and Discipline of the African Methodist Episcopal Church* (Philadelphia, 1817), 94.

5. Jon Michael Spencer, *Black Hymnody: A Hymnological History of the African-American Church* (Knoxville: Univ. of Tennessee Press, 1992), 201.

6. African Methodist Episcopal Church, *The African Methodist Pocket Hymn Book* (Philadelphia, 1818), n.p.

7. On the history of the AME Church and Richard Allen's hymnbooks, see Dennis Dickerson, *African Methodism and Its Wesleyan Heritage: Reflections on AME Church History* (Nashville, TN: AMEC Sunday School Union, 2009); Dickerson, "Heritage and Hymnody: Richard Allen and the Making of African Methodism," in *Sing Them Over Again to Me: Hymns and Hymnbooks in America*, ed. Mark A. Noll and Edith L. Blumhofer (Tuscaloosa: Univ. of Alabama Press, 2006), 175–94. On the struggles between Wesley and American Methodists over hymnody, see Benson, *English Hymn*, 280–98.

8. On the structure and history of the Big Quarterly, see Lewis V. Baldwin, *"Invisible" Strands of African Methodism: A History of the African Union Methodist Protestant and Union American Methodist Episcopal Churches, 1805–1980* (Metuchen, NJ: ATLA/Scarecrow, 1983), 126–51.

9. Eileen Southern and Josephine Wright, comps., *African-American Traditions in Song, Sermon, Tale, and Dance, 1600s–1920: An Annotated Bibliography of Literature, Collections, and Artworks* (New York: Greenwood, 1990), 42.

10. The book carries a date of 1835 but a comparison of the type used in the hymnbook and in settings of hymns in the *Latter-Day Saints' Messenger and Advocate* in early 1836 has led scholars to assign the later date for the book. See Linda King Newell and Valeen Tippetts Avery, *Mormon Enigma: Emma Hale Smith*, 2nd ed. (Urbana: Univ. of Illinois Press, 1994), 57, 317n15; Mary Dennis

Poulter, "The First Ten Years of Latter-Day Saint Hymnody: A Study of Emma Smith's 1835 and Little and Gardner's 1844 Hymnals," master's thesis, Univ. of Massachusetts, Lowell, 1996, 7.

11. Emma Smith, ed., *A Collection of Sacred Hymns of the Church of Jesus Christ of Latter Day Saints*, 2nd ed. (Nauvoo, IL, 1841), [iii].

12. Poulter, "First Ten Years," 24.

13. Minute book, 1838–1843, Kahal Kadosh Beth Elohim Records, 204, 206, MS 1047, College of Charleston, SC.

14. The best account of Moïse's life and writings is Shira Wolosky, "The First Reform Liturgy: Penina Moise's Hymns and the Discourses of American Identity," *Studies in American Jewish Literature* 33.1 (2014): 130–46.

15. Minute book, 1838–1843, 204, 206–8, 227.

16. Jeon A. Jick, "The Reform Synagogue," in *The American Synagogue: A Sanctuary Transformed*, ed. Jack Wertheimer (Hanover, NH: Brandeis Univ. Press/Univ. Press of New England, 1987), 85–110, 86.

Chapter 2. How to Fight with Hymnbooks

1. For instance, see James Carley, "Religious Controversy and Marginalia: Pierfrancesco Di Piero Bardi, Thomas Wakefield, and Their Books," *Transactions of the Cambridge Bibliographical Society* 12.3 (2002): 206–45. H. J. Jackson has argued that a shift occurred between the sixteenth and eighteenth centuries in marginal annotation practices, moving from an emphasis on aiding study to more interpretive, including argumentative, responses. See Jackson, *Marginalia: Readers Writing in Books* (New Haven, CT: Yale Univ. Press, 2001), 50–56.

2. John Wesley, ed., *A Collection of Hymns, for the Use of the People Called Methodists* (London, 1780), iv.

3. *A Collection of Hymns for the Use of the Protestant Church of the United Brethren* (Bath, England, 1801), flyleaves, Library Company of Philadelphia.

4. *Collection of Hymns . . . United Brethren*, xvii, xxiii, title page.

5. *Extracts from the Minutes of the General Assembly of the Presbyterian Church in the United States of America: From A.D. 1817, to A.D. 1820, Inclusive* (Philadelphia, 1817–1820), 173, 313–15, 387–88.

6. Archibald Alexander, ed., *A Selection of Hymns, Adapted to the Devotions of the Closet, the Family, and the Social Circle* (New York, 1831), xiii–xiv.

7. *Psalms and Hymns for Public Worship: Comprising the Entire Selection Authorized by the General Assembly of the Presbyterian Church, with Titles Prefixed to Each, Directions for Musical Expression, and the Hymns Arranged according to Subjects* (Carlisle, PA, 1834), [iii].

8. Fleming published a book, paid for by Duffield's supporters in the congregation, defending him in the wake of the trial: *The Principle of Presbyterian Discipline,*

Unfolded and Illustrated in the Protests and Appeals of the Rev. George Duffield (Carlisle, PA, 1835).

9. *Minutes of the General Assembly of the Presbyterian Church in the United States of America* (Philadelphia, 1836), 34–35.

10. The most thorough treatment of the doctrinal and cultural issues involved in the schism is George M. Marsden, *The Evangelical Mind and the New School Presbyterian Experience: A Case Study of Thought and Theology in Nineteenth-Century America* (New Haven, CT: Yale Univ. Press, 1970).

11. *Minutes of the General Assembly of the Presbyterian Church in the United States of America* (Philadelphia, 1839), 163–64.

12. Minutes of the Committee on Psalmody, 1838–1843, Presbyterian Church in the United States of America (Old School), Record no. 090226, n.p., Presbyterian Historical Society, Philadelphia.

13. Benson found "the amazing total of 888,650 copies" in the board of publication's records, despite the Old School's communicants totaling only 159,137 in the period. Louis F. Benson, *The English Hymn: Its Development and Use in Worship* (New York: George H. Doran, 1915), 383.

14. Benson, *English Hymn*, 383–85.

15. Benson, *English Hymn*, 553.

16. Richard M. Cameron et al., "The Church Divides, 1844," in *The History of American Methodism*, 3 vols., ed. Emory Stevens Bucke et al. (New York: Abingdon, 1964), 2:11–85, 34–35.

17. Cameron et al., "Church Divides," 2:42–44.

18. Cyrus Prindle, comp., *A Collection of Hymns, for the Use of the Wesleyan Methodist Connection of America*, new ed. (New York, 1845), iii, iv. The 1843 edition from which this book was derived already had a section of several pages marked "Anti-Slavery," and a miscellaneous collection of hymns in the back was rearranged to expand that section and add the temperance section in the 1845 book.

19. Methodist Episcopal Church, South, *A Collection of Hymns for Public, Social, and Domestic Worship* (Charleston, SC, 1847), 3, 4.

20. John R. Tyson, "The Methodist National Anthem: 'O for a Thousand Tongues to Sing' and the Development of American Methodism," in *Sing Them Over Again to Me: Hymns and Hymnbooks in America*, ed. Mark A. Noll and Edith L. Blumhofer (Tuscaloosa: Univ. of Alabama Press, 2006), 20–42.

21. On the Book Concern controversy, see Arthur E. Jones Jr., "The Years of Disagreement, 1844–61," in *The History of American Methodism*, 3 vols., ed. Emory Stevens Bucke et al. (New York: Abingdon, 1964), 2:144–205, 177–81; Richard Sutton, ed., *The Methodist Church Property Case* (New York, 1851) (the MECS published an edition of this book in Richmond, Virginia, in 1851).

22. "The New Hymn Book," *Quarterly Review of the Methodist Episcopal Church, South* 2.1 (Jan. 1848): 69–131, 69.

23. "The New Hymn Book," 126–27.

24. Lucius C. Matlack, *The History of American Slavery and Methodism, from 1780 to 1849, and History of the Wesleyan Methodist Connection of America; in Two Parts, with an Appendix* (New York, 1849), 260.

25. *Minutes of of the General Assembly of the Presbyterian Church in the United States* (Augusta, GA, 1865), 353–54.

26. *Minutes of the General Assembly of the Presbyterian Church in the Confederate States of America* (Columbia, SC, 1864), 307.

Chapter 3. Hymnbooks at Church

1. *Book of Common Prayer* (New York, 1829), American Antiquarian Society, Worcester, MA.

2. Francis W. P. Greenwood, comp., *A Collection of Psalms and Hymns for Christian Worship*, 10th ed. (Boston, 1833), American Antiquarian Society, Worcester, MA.

3. Martineau's copies of *Hymns for the Christian Church and Home*, 5th ed. (London, 1846), and *Hymns of Praise and Prayer*, 2nd ed. (London, 1877), both bearing his date entries, are in the Harris Manchester College Library, Oxford.

4. Samuel Longfellow and Samuel Johnson, comps., *A Book of Hymns for Public and Private Devotion*, 2nd ed. (Boston, 1848), Andover-Harvard Theological Library.

5. *Psalms and Hymns Adapted to Social, Private, and Public Worship in the Presbyterian Church in the United States of America* (Philadelphia, 1843), 69 (hymns section) (16mo Onderdonk copy at American Antiquarian Society, Worcester, MA).

6. *Psalms and Hymns Adapted to Social, Private, and Public Worship in the Presbyterian Church in the United States of America* (Philadelphia, 1843), front flyleaf (12mo Onderdonk copy at American Antiquarian Society, Worcester, MA).

7. 1900 US Census, Kings County, NY, Population Schedule, Brooklyn Ward 9, p. 3b; and "Elizabeth Onderdonk," Find a Grave Index, both Ancestry .com (accessed Feb. 14, 2017).

8. Daniel S. Lamson, *History of the Town of Weston, Massachusetts, 1630–1890* (Boston: George Ellis, 1913), 159, appendixes IV and V.

9. This is apparently quoted from memory from Boston Unitarian Ezra Stiles Gannett's 1840 essay "The Church and the World." The transcriber (possibly Nathan Hagar) misattributed the essay to Horatio Alger Sr., another Unitarian minister, whose son was the famous rags-to-riches novelist of the later nineteenth century.

10. Francis W. P. Greenwood, comp., *A Collection of Psalms and Hymns for Christian Worship*, 23rd ed. (Boston, 1837), front and rear flyleaves, American Antiquarian Society, Worcester, MA.

11. Francis W. P. Greenwood, comp., *A Collection of Psalms and Hymns for Christian Worship*, 27th ed. (Boston, 1839), front and rear flyleaves, American Antiquarian Society, Worcester, MA.

12. *Hymns for the Use of the Methodist Episcopal Church* (New York, [1849]), 321, American Antiquarian Society, Worcester, MA.

13. Francis W. P. Greenwood, comp., *A Collection of Psalms and Hymns for Christian Worship*, 29th ed. (Boston, 1840), front endpaper, Longfellow House–Washington's Headquarters National Historic Site.

14. Edward S. Ninde, *The Story of the American Hymn* (1921; repr., New York: AMS Press, 1975), 201.

15. Lucy Larcom, *A New England Girlhood, Outlined from Memory* (Boston, 1889), 58.

16. Julius Melton, *Presbyterian Worship in America: Changing Patterns since 1787* (1967; repr., Eugene, OR: Wipf and Stock, 2001), 22–23.

17. On the tunebook's role in connecting singing schools and choirs, see Richard Crawford, "Introduction," in *American Sacred Music Imprints, 1698–1810: A Bibliography* by Allen Perdue Britton, Irving Lowens, and Richard Crawford (Worcester, MA: American Antiquarian Society, 1990), 1–54, 20–21. For a full account of the practice and theology of singing schools, see David Music, "Jonathan Edwards and the Theology and Practice of Congregational Song in Puritan New England," *Studies in Puritan American Spirituality* 8 (2004): 103–33.

18. Christanne Miller, *Reading in Time: Emily Dickinson and the Nineteenth Century* (Amherst: Univ. of Massachusetts Press, 2012), 54.

19. Samuel Joseph May, *Memoir of Samuel Joseph May* (Boston, 1876), 73–74.

20. Francis W. P. Greenwood, comp., *A Collection of Psalms and Hymns for Christian Worship*, 36th ed. (Boston, 1843), rear flyleaf, American Antiquarian Society, Worcester, MA.

21. Samuel Longfellow to Samuel Johnson, January 19, 1846, Samuel Longfellow Papers, Longfellow House–Washington's Headquarters National Historic Site, Cambridge, MA.

22. *A Collection of Hymns for the Use of the Methodist Episcopal Church* (New York, 1842), front flyleaf, American Antiquarian Society, Worcester, MA.

Chapter 4. Giving Hymnbooks, and What the Hymnbook Gives

1. Nathan Beman, comp., *The Church Psalmist; or, Psalms and Hymns for the Public, Social, and Private Use of Evangelical Christians*, 40th ed. (New York, 1856), front endpaper, American Antiquarian Society, Worcester, MA.

2. The inscription is undated, so it is unclear whether the gift predated her literary fame, though with a second edition of the *Collection* appearing in 1827, it almost certainly preceded that date.

3. Catharine Maria Sedgwick, annotation written in Henry Devereaux Sewall, ed., *A Collection of Psalms and Hymns, for Social and Private Worship* (New York, 1820), 107, Jay Fliegelman Collection, Stanford University, Stanford, CA.

4. Sedgwick in Sewall, *Collection*, front flyleaf.

5. Anonymous writer in Sewall, *Collection*, front endpaper.

6. See, for example, Caroline M. Kirkland, *The Helping Hand: Comprising an Account for the Home, for Discharged Female Convicts, and an Appeal in Behalf of That Institution* (New York, 1853), 126; *Report of the Prison Association of New York*, vol. 4 (New York, 1849), 199.

7. John Lord Taylor, *Memoir of His Honor Samuel Phillips, LL.D.* (Boston, 1856), 298–302.

8. On the bonds of gift giving and charity, see Lewis Hyde, *The Gift: Creativity and the Artist in the Modern World*, 2nd ed. (New York: Vintage, 2007); Jacques T. Godbout with Alain Caillé, *The World of the Gift*, trans. Donald Winkler (Montreal: McGill-Queen's Univ. Press, 1998).

9. Caroline Levine's discussion of "affordances of form" traces a helpful history of the term from J. J. Gibson's work in the 1970s to Donald Norman's *Design of Everyday Things* (Garden City, NY: Doubleday, 1990). See Levine, *Forms: Whole, Rhythm, Hierarchy, Network* (Princeton, NJ: Princeton Univ. Press, 2015), 152n15.

10. *The African Methodist Episcopal Church Hymn Book* (Philadelphia, 1861), American Antiquarian Society, Worcester, MA.

11. *The Sunday School Hymn Book* (Philadelphia, 1828), Library Company of Philadelphia.

12. William Cowherd, *Select Hymns for the Use of Christian Worship* (Manchester, England, 1823), Huntington Library, San Marino, CA.

13. John Inglesby, *A Selection of Free-Grace Hymns, Carefully Chosen and Revised by Eben-Ezer Baptist Church* (New York, 1807), American Antiquarian Society, Worcester, MA.

14. First Presbyterian Church (Scranton), Records, 1849–1981, Presbyterian Historical Society, Philadelphia, PA.

15. *Psalms and Hymns Adapted to Social, Private, and Public Worship in the Presbyterian Church in the United States of America* (Philadelphia, 1843), Library Company of Philadelphia.

16. *Psalms and Hymns Adapted to Public Worship* (Philadelphia, 1841), Presbyterian Historical Society, Philadelphia, PA.

17. *A Collection of Psalms, Hymns, Anthems . . . for Use in the Catholic Church . . . in the United States* (Washington, DC, 1830), American Antiquarian Society, Worcester, MA.

18. *Family Hymns* (New York, 1838), American Antiquarian Society, Worcester, MA.

19. James Edmeston, "On Singing from the Hymnbook of a Departed Sister," in *The Christian Keepsake and Missionary Annual* (Philadelphia, 1840), 196.

20. Nathan Strong, Abel Flint, and Joseph Steward, comps., *The Hartford Selection of Hymns, from the Most Approved Authors*, 8th ed. (Hartford, CT, 1831), Library Company of Philadelphia.

21. *The Psalms and Hymns . . . of the Reformed Dutch Church in North America* (Philadelphia, 1847). This copy is owned by the American Antiquarian Society; unfortunately, nothing is known about its provenance, or when the book was ornamented, before the AAS acquired it in 2013.

22. David H. Battenfeld, "The Source for the Hymn in *Moby-Dick*," *American Literature* 27.3 (Nov. 1955): 393–96, claims the 1847 *Psalms and Hymns* as Melville's precise source. Steven Olsen-Smith has updated Battenfeld's work, concluding that the 1831 and 1832 versions cannot be ruled out as possible sources. Olsen-Smith, "The Hymn in *Moby-Dick*: Melville's Adaptation of Psalm 18," *Leviathan* 5.1 (Mar. 2003): 29–47.

23. Louise L. Foster, "The Nineteenth-Century American Pocket Diary," in *Suave Mechanicals: Essays on the History of Bookbinding*, vol. 3, ed. Julia Miller (Ann Arbor, MI: Legacy Press, 2016), 280–99.

Chapter 5. Devotion and the Shape of the Hymnbook

1. Nathan Beman, *Church Psalmist; or, Psalms and Hymns, for the Public, Social, and Private Use of Evangelical Christians* (Philadelphia, 1843), 6.

2. Matthew P. Brown, "Hand Piety; or, Operating a Book in Early New England," in *Cultural Narratives: Textuality and Performance in American Culture before 1900*, ed. Sandra M. Gustafson and Caroline F. Sloat (Notre Dame, IN: Univ. of Notre Dame Press, 2010), 14–33.

3. Allan Westphall's excellent case study of the devotional reading of Thomas Connary in nineteenth-century New Hampshire illuminates certain parallels to Craft's practices of interleaving books, cross-references, and so on. It intrigues me that Connary, an Irish Catholic immigrant, seems to have owned no hymn-books—or, at least, none survive for Westphall to analyze. See Westphall, *Books and Religious Devotion: The Redemptive Reading of an Irishman in Nineteenth-Century New England* (University Park: Pennsylvania State Univ. Press, 2014).

4. Isaac Watts and Joel Barlow, *Psalms Carefully Suited to the Christian Worship in the United States* (Philadelphia, 1788), Special Collections, Princeton Theological Seminary Library, Princeton, NJ.

5. On the Americanization of Watts after the Revolutionary War, see Rochelle A. Stackhouse, *The Language of the Psalms in Worship: American Revisions of Watts' Psalter* (Metuchen, NJ: Scarecrow, 1997).

6. Only five copies of this particular imprint are listed in WorldCat. After inspecting the Craft copy at Princeton Theological Seminary and the copy at the American Antiquarian Society, I found that catalog descriptions of the copies at the Free Library of Philadelphia and the University of Minnesota do not indicate that a first-line index was included. The Virginia Historical Society's catalog does not record a copy of this book, despite a record existing for it in WorldCat.

7. Tate and Brady's *New Version of the Psalms of David* first appeared in London in 1696, and it was generally considered a more genteel, urban alternative to Thomas Sternhold and John Hopkins's *Whole Booke of Psalmes, Collected into English Meter* (1562). From the mid-eighteenth century onward, New England editions of Tate and Brady included anonymously compiled hymn supplements, a practice that unevenly extended to Books of Common Prayer, Bay Psalm Books (New England church psalters), and Bibles.

8. The fullest account of Watts as an educator is chapter 6 of Arthur Paul Davis, *Isaac Watts: His Life and Works* (New York: Dryden, 1943), which I have relied on for my account of Watts's career.

9. Hoxie Neale Fairchild, *Religious Trends in English Poetry*, vol. 1: *1700–1740: Protestantism and the Cult of Sentiment* (New York: Columbia Univ. Press, 1939), 130; Harry Escott, *Isaac Watts, Hymnographer: A Study of the Beginnings, Development and Philosophy of the English Hymn* (London: Independent Press, 1962), 121.

10. Barton's *Century* did not have a table when it first appeared in London in 1659, but his *Two Centuries* (London, 1672) did.

11. This element of hymnbook design has received scant attention. In giving an account of the history of hymnbooks' subject indexes, Mary Louise VanDyke offers a brief discussion of the different alphabetization and typography used in modern first-line indexes but no earlier history of the form. Ann Blair's helpful anatomy of indexing techniques in scholarly books of the Renaissance era gives no mention of first-line indexes. See VanDyke, "Indices: More than Meets the I," in *Sing Them Over Again to Me: Hymns and Hymnbooks in America*, ed. Mark A. Noll and Edith L. Blumhofer (Tuscaloosa: Univ. of Alabama Press, 2006), 122–51; Blair, *Too Much to Know: Managing Scholarly Information before the Modern Age* (New Haven, CT: Yale Univ. Press, 2010), 137–44.

12. I have adapted the idea of a hymn being "handed down" from Donald Davie, *A Gathered Church: The Literature of the English Dissenting Interest, 1700–1930* (New York: Oxford Univ. Press, 1978), 20–21.

13. Isaac Watts, *Hymns and Spiritual Songs*, 2nd ed. (London, 1709), xiv.

14. Cotton Mather, *The Diary of Cotton Mather*, 2 vols., ed. W. C. Ford (1911–1912; repr., New York: Frederick Ungar, 1957?), 2:142.

15. Richard Baxter, *The Poor Man's Family Book* (London, 1674).

16. According to David D. Hall and Russell L. Martin, Mather is the author of 335 imprints of the 3,519 in the North American Imprints Program, while Watts accounts for 98, the same as for George Whitefield. However, Hall and Martin do not include Watts's version of the psalms in that count, and they acknowledge that if it were possible to take edition sizes into account, "the relative weighting of authors and titles would change considerably: For example, the press run of a single edition of Isaac Watts's *Hymns and Spiritual Songs* equaled the press run of four or five Cotton Mather sermons." Hall and Martin, "Appendix Two: A

Note on Popular and Durable Authors and Titles," in *The Colonial Book in the Atlantic World*, ed. Hugh Amory and David D. Hall (New York: Cambridge Univ. Press/American Antiquarian Society, 2000), 519–21.

17. George M. Marsden, *Jonathan Edwards: A Life* (New Haven, CT: Yale Univ. Press, 2003), 170–73.

18. Earlier, in his *Warnings from the Dead* (Boston, 1693), Mather included an unattributed hymn (possibly written by him) in the middle of one of the two sermons included in the pamphlet. Preaching against giving in to the temptation to lust, Mather offered several practical suggestions for overcoming the temptation, the last resort being to "set your selves to *Sing* unto the Lord a proper *Hymn*, that may be a special Antidote against the Infestations of the *Fiery Flying Serpents*" (64). To illustrate the point, Mather offered an example of a hymn ("Oh! Glorious God, who dost Improve"), saying, "Such a *Shield* as *this*, has been sometimes held up against such *Fiery Darts*" (64). Here we see Mather using hymns as personal weapons of spiritual warfare, a striking instance of the extraliturgical importance of hymns for the Boston divine.

19. Cotton Mather, *Christian Thank-Offering* (Boston, 1696); *Everlasting Gospel* (Boston, 1700); *Companion for the Afflicted* (Boston, 1701).

20. Cotton Mather, *The Wonderful Works of God Commemorated* (Boston, 1690), 16.

21. George Herbert, *The Complete English Works*, ed. Ann Pasternak Slater (New York: Knopf, 1995), 9. Herbert's *The Temple* was in the library at Harvard College, Mather's alma mater, as early as 1636; see Ramie Targoff, *Common Prayer: The Language of Public Devotion in Early Modern England* (Chicago: Univ. of Chicago Press, 2001), 118.

22. Charles E. Hambrick-Stowe, *The Practice of Piety: Puritan Devotional Disciplines in Seventeenth-Century New England* (Chapel Hill: Institute for Early American History and Culture and Univ. of North Carolina Press), 117–18; Meredith Marie Neuman, *Jeremiah's Scribes: Creating Sermon Literature in Early New England* (Philadelphia: Univ. of Pennsylvania Press, 2013).

23. Marsden, *Jonathan Edwards*, 244–45.

24. *The African Union First Colored Methodist Protestant Hymn Book* (Wilmington, DE, 1871), Schomburg Center for Research in Black Culture, New York.

Interlude 2. Philadelphia, 1844

1. On the history of the 1844 Philadelphia riots and the events leading up to them, see Michael Feldberg, *The Philadelphia Riots of 1844: A Study in Ethnic Conflict* (Westport, CT: Greenwood, 1975); Ray Allen Billington, *The Protestant Crusade, 1800–1860: A Study of the Origins of American Nativism* (New York: Macmillan, 1938), 220–37. Mary Ann Meyers gives an excellent account of the events of the 1840s leading to the riots through the context of coverage and

commentary in the *Philadelphia Catholic Herald*. Meyers, "The Children's Crusade: Philadelphia Catholics and the Public Schools, 1840–1844," *Records of the American Catholic Historical Society of Philadelphia* 75.2 (June 1964): 103–27.

2. "Riot," *Catholic Herald* 12.19 (May 9, 1844), 149; "A New Prayer-Book," *Catholic Herald* 12.19 (May 9, 1844), 152.

3. "Cheap Sunday School Hymn Book," *Catholic Herald* 12.5 (Feb. 1, 1844), 40.

4. "A Catholic Sunday School Hymn Book," *Catholic Herald* 12.9 (Feb. 29, 1844), 69.

5. Edwin F. Hatfield, comp., *The Chapel Hymn Book, with Tunes, for the Worship of God* (New York, 1873), 283.

Chapter 6. Hymnbooks and Literacy Learning

1. Isaac Watts, *Hymns and Spiritual Songs: In Three Books* (Exeter, NH, 1819), 160–61.

2. Janet Duitsman Cornelius, *"When I Can Read My Title Clear": Literacy, Slavery, and Religion in the Antebellum South* (Columbia: Univ. of South Carolina Press, 1991), 70–71.

3. Arthur Paul Davis, *Isaac Watts: His Life and Works* (New York: Dryden, 1943), 73.

4. E. Jennifer Monaghan, *Learning to Read and Write in Colonial America* (Amherst: Univ. of Massachusetts Press, 2005), 30.

5. Monaghan, *Learning to Read*, 13.

6. Isaac Watts, *Divine Songs Attempted in Easy Language for the Use of Children*, ed. J. H. P. Pafford (Oxford: Oxford Univ. Press, 1971), 145–46.

7. Patricia Crain, *Reading Children: Literacy, Property, and the Dilemmas of Childhood in Nineteenth-Century America* (Philadelphia: Univ. of Pennsylvania Press, 2016).

8. On the early Sunday school movement, see Philip B. Cliff, *The Rise and Development of the Sunday School Movement in England, 1780–1980* (Nutfield, England: National Christian Education Council, 1986), 1–70; Anne M. Boylan, *Sunday School: The Formation of an American Institution, 1790–1880* (New Haven, CT: Yale Univ. Press, 1988), 6–13.

9. Boylan, *Sunday School*, 22–26.

10. *Original Hymns, for the Use of Adult Scholars in Sunday Schools* (New York, 1818), verso of title page.

11. The Union Church's text shows that the New York book was their source, though another variant had also appeared in the Philadelphia Sunday and Adult School Union's supplement for adult learners to their *Sunday School Hymn Book* (Philadelphia, 1819).

12. Monaghan, *Learning to Read*, 241.

13. Samuel Davies, *Letters from the Rev. Samuel Davies, &c. Shewing the State of Religion in Virginia, Particularly among the Negroes*, 2nd ed. (London, 1757), 9.

14. Davies, *Letters*, 11, 12.

15. Davies, *Letters*, 12.

16. Davies, *Letters*, 13, 16.

17. Isabel Rivers, "The First Evangelical Tract Society," *Historical Journal* 50.1 (2007): 1–22, 6–9.

18. "Review: The Religious Instruction of Negroes in the United States," *Biblical Repertory and Princeton Review* 15.1 (Jan. 1843): 22–41, 26–27.

19. Virginia banned teaching slaves to read in 1831. Cornelius, *When I Can Read*, 32–33.

20. William T. Dargan, *Lining Out the Word: Dr. Watts Hymn Singing in the Music of Black Americans* (Berkeley: Univ. of California Press, 2006).

21. Margaret V. Ray, introduction, in James Evans, *Cree Syllabic Hymn Book*, ed. Margaret V. Ray (Toronto: Bibliographical Society of Canada, 1954), 7–9.

22. Peter Jones, comp., *Collection of Ojebway and English Hymns, for the Use of Native Indians* (Toronto, 1830?).

23. Donald B. Smith, *Sacred Feathers: The Reverend Peter Jones (Kahkewaquonaby) and the Mississauga Indians* (Lincoln: Univ. of Nebraska Press, 1987).

24. James Evans, *The Speller and Interpreter, in Indian and English, for the Use of the Mission Schools, and Such as May Desire to Obtain a Knowledge of the Ojibway Tongue* (New York, 1837).

25. James Evans and George Henry, comps., *A Collection of Chippeway and English Hymns, for the Use of the Native Indians* (New York, 1837).

26. Smith, *Sacred Feathers*, 153, 185.

Chapter 7. How Hymnbooks Made Children's Literature

1. Two prominent examples of this narrative are F. J. Harvey Darton, *Children's Books in England: Five Centuries of Social Life*, 3rd ed., rev. Brian Alderson (New Castle, DE: British Library/Oak Knoll Press, 1999); and Gillian Avery, *Behold the Child: American Children and Their Books, 1621–1922* (Baltimore, MD: Johns Hopkins Univ. Press, 1994).

2. Based on the number of editions Wilbur Macey Stone identified and his estimates of the total number of copies sold vis-à-vis *The New-England Primer*, it may be claimed (as I do in this book) that Watts's *Divine Songs* was the most-reprinted children's book in the eighteenth century *and* the nineteenth. See Stone, *The Divine and Moral Songs of Isaac Watts: An Essay Thereon and a Tentative List of Editions* (New York: Triptych, 1918), esp. 9–10 for his estimates.

3. On the economic importance of, and the potential psychological resistance to, books given as rewards in the nineteenth century, see Kimberley Reynolds, "Rewarding Reads? Giving, Receiving and Resisting Reward and Prize Books,"

in *Popular Children's Literature in Britain*, ed. Julia Briggs, Dennis Butts, and M. O. Grenby (Burlington, VT: Ashgate, 2008), 189–207.

4. Quoted in James d'Alté A. Welch, *A Bibliography of American Children's Books Printed prior to 1821* (Worcester, MA: American Antiquarian Society and Barre, 1972), xxiii.

5. On the book's role in the rise of the Christmas gift market, see Leigh Eric Schmidt, *Consumer Rites: The Buying and Selling of American Holidays* (Princeton, NJ: Princeton Univ. Press, 1995), 110–23.

6. Margaret Spofford, "Women Teaching Reading to Poor Children in the Sixteenth and Seventeenth Centuries," in *Opening the Nursery Door: Reading, Writing and Childhood, 1600–1900*, ed. Mary Hilton, Morag Styles, and Victor Watson (New York: Routledge, 1997), 47–62, 48; Gilbert H. Muller, *William Cullen Bryant: Author of America* (Albany: State Univ. of New York Press, 2010), 10; Lucy Larcom, *A New England Girlhood, Outlined from Memory* (Boston, 1889), 58.

7. Quoted in Norma Clarke, " 'The Cursed Barbauld Crew': Women Writers and Writing for Children in the Late Eighteenth Century," in Hilton, Styles, and Watson, *Opening the Nursery Door*, 91–103, 91.

8. Two especially helpful rejoinders to Lamb and his supporters are Clarke, "The Cursed Barbauld Crew"; and Lissa Paul, *The Children's Book Business: Lessons from the Long Eighteenth Century* (New York: Routledge, 2011), esp. 100–103.

9. I rely for my account of Barbauld's background and career on William McCarthy's excellent biography, *Anna Letitia Barbauld: Voice of the Enlightenment* (Baltimore, MD: Johns Hopkins Univ. Press, 2008).

10. Anna Letitia Barbauld, *Hymns in Prose for Children* (London, 1781), 1, 43.

11. Walt Whitman, *Complete Poetry and Collected Prose*, ed. Justin Kaplan (New York: Library of America, 1982), 31.

12. Anna Letitia Barbauld, *Gl'inni giovenelli*, trans. Pietro Bachi (Boston, 1832).

13. On Newbery's publishing practices and the seeming impossibility of determining the authorship of his children's books, see John Rowe Townsend, "A Man of Parts," in *John Newbery and His Books: Trade and Plumb-Cake for Ever, Huzza!*, ed. John Rowe Townsend (Metuchen, NJ: Scarecrow, 1994), 1–22, 14–19.

14. The attribution of texts to specific Taylor sisters and other bibliographical information on the Taylors' works are drawn from Christina Duff Stewart, *The Taylors of Ongar: An Analytical Bio-Bibliography*, 2 vols. (New York: Garland, 1975).

15. Joyce Irene Whalley and Tessa Rose Chester, *A History of Children's Book Illustration* (London: John Murray/Victoria and Albert Museum, 1988), 18–19, 23.

16. Lewis Carroll, *Alice in Wonderland* (Norton Critical Edition, 3rd ed.), ed. Donald J. Gray (New York: Norton, 2013), 16.

17. Carroll, *Alice in Wonderland*, 80–81.

18. Angela Sorby, *Schoolroom Poets: Childhood, Performance, and the Place of American Poetry, 1865–1917* (Hanover, NH: Univ. Press of New England/Univ. of New Hampshire Press, 2005), xxix–xxxiii; see also Joan Shelley Rubin, *Songs*

of Ourselves: The Uses of Poetry in America (Cambridge, MA: Belknap, 2007). For a comparative study of British and American poetry recitation techniques, see Catherine Robson, *Heart Beats: Everyday Life and the Memorized Poem* (Princeton, NJ: Princeton Univ. Press, 2012).

19. Carroll, *Alice in Wonderland*, 16.

Chapter 8. How Hymns Remade Schoolbooks

1. Shirley Brice Heath, "Child's Play; or, Finding the Ephemera of Home," in *Opening the Nursery Door: Reading, Writing and Childhood, 1600–1900*, ed. Mary Hilton, Morag Styles, and Victor Watson (New York: Routledge, 1997), 17–30, 17.

2. Reward of merit, Boston, 1820, American Antiquarian Society, Worcester, MA.

3. Isaac Watts, *The Art of Reading and Writing English*, 2nd ed. (London, 1722), xi–xii.

4. Arthur Paul Davis, *Isaac Watts: His Life and Works* (New York: Dryden, 1943), 84–85.

5. Barbara M. Benedict argued for Watts's book-reading strategies in *Art of Reading* as representative of eighteenth-century adult book reading generally; see Benedict, *Making the Modern Reader: Cultural Mediation in Early Modern Literary Anthologies* (Princeton, NJ: Princeton Univ. Press, 1996), 186–88.

6. See, for instance, E. Jennifer Monaghan, *Learning to Read and Write in Colonial America* (Amherst: Univ. of Massachusetts Press, 2005), chap. 8. However, it is worth pointing out that Lawrence A. Cremin argued in his foundational *American Education* trilogy that evangelical publishers in the early United States created an integrated curriculum of piety and literacy, which "secular" textbook producers like William McGuffey followed closely; Cremin, *American Education: The National Experience, 1783–1876* (New York: Harper and Row, 1980), 69–73.

7. This point has been compellingly demonstrated in Kyle B. Roberts, "Rethinking *The New-England Primer*," *Papers of the Bibliographical Society of America* 104.4 (Dec. 2010): 489–523.

8. Percival Merritt, "The Royal Primer," in *Bibliographical Essays: A Tribute to Wilberforce Eames*, ed. George P. Winship (Cambridge, MA: Harvard Univ. Press, 1924), 35–60.

9. Merritt, "Royal Primer," 35.

10. John Newbery, ed., *The Royal Primer* (Philadelphia, 1753), 48–51. The only known copy of this title is in the Rosenbach Collection at the Free Library of Philadelphia.

11. Lindley Murray, *The English Reader; or, Pieces in Prose and Poetry, Selected from the Best Writers* (New York, 1799), vii.

12. On the interplay between theater and oratory in Murray's time, see Jay Fliegelman, *Declaring Independence: Jefferson, Natural Language and the Culture of Performance* (Stanford, CA: Stanford Univ. Press, 1993).

13. Murray, *English Reader*, iv.

14. Watts, *Art of Reading*, xii–xiii.

15. While previous biographers demurred on the question of who recommended McGuffey to Smith, Quentin R. Skrabec Jr. identified Catharine Beecher as the recommender and claimed she was involved as a consultant as the books were produced. See Skrabec, *William McGuffey: Mentor to American Industry* (New York: Algora, 2009), 71–72.

16. Harvey C. Minnich, *William Holmes McGuffey and His Readers* (New York: American Book, 1936), 23.

17. Minnich is the only source I have found that mentions Amanda Mariah Wilson as Obed's collaborator on the 1853 revisions; see Minnich, *William Holmes McGuffey*, 86.

18. John H. Westerhoff III, *McGuffey and His Readers: Piety, Morality, and Education in Nineteenth-Century America* (Nashville, TN: Abingdon, 1978), 19, 102–5.

19. William H. McGuffey, *McGuffey's Newly Revised Eclectic Second Reader* (Cincinnati, OH, 1853), 13–14.

20. Charles Dexter Cleveland, comp., *Hymns for Schools, with an Appropriate Selection of Tunes* (New York, 1850). One such inscribed copy is at the American Antiquarian Society, Worcester, MA.

Chapter 9. *Singing as Reading; or, A Tale of Two* Sacred Harps

1. The best treatment of Lowell Mason's life and career, and the one that I rely on throughout this chapter, is Carol A. Pemberton, *Lowell Mason: His Life and Work* (Ann Arbor, MI: UMI Research Press, 1985).

2. The Masons' contemporary Nathaniel D. Gould claimed sales of 75,000 copies for the patent-note edition in its first year, and the round-note edition sold 85,000 in its first two years. See Gould, *Church Music in America: Its History and Peculiarities at Different Periods* (Boston, 1853), 140.

3. The bibliography of the Masons' *Sacred Harp* books is far more complex than previous commentators have acknowledged. Several scholars, including Carol Pemberton and George Pullen Jackson, have referred to an "Ohio Sacred Harp" that they assumed predated the 1834 Cincinnati *Eclectic Harmony*, but the two books are almost certainly the same. The Boston editions began in 1836 with the subtitle *Eclectic Harmony*, then changed to *Beauties of Church Music* by 1840, possibly as early as 1838, although *Eclectic Harmony* copies published by Shepley and Wright in Boston were still produced in, and possibly after, 1840. The second volume of *Beauties* appeared in 1840, which suggests that *Eclectic Harmony* was

renamed in that year—in Boston, but not in Cincinnati—to match the new book. Each of the books was revised at least once, multiplying the complexity of identifying *Sacred Harp* editions. More work needs to be done on these titles to establish bibliographic certainty. On the "Ohio Sacred Harp" confusion, see Pemberton, *Lowell Mason: A Bio-Bibliography* (New York: Greenwood, 1988), 54; Jackson, *White Spirituals in the Southern Uplands: The Story of the Fasola Folk, Their Songs, Singings, and "Buckwheat Notes"* (Chapel Hill: Univ. of North Carolina Press, 1933), 18.

4. Lowell Mason and Timothy Mason, comps., *The Sacred Harp; or, Eclectic Harmony* (Cincinnati, OH, 1834), [4].

5. Lowell Mason and Timothy Mason, comps., *The Sacred Harp; or, Eclectic Harmony* (Cincinnati, OH, 1837), no. 222. As with many of the Masons' attributions to the European masters, including Beethoven, Handel, and Mendelssohn, it is difficult to determine whether the tune does connect with an authentic composition. In at least some cases, it seems that the Masons were appealing to a tradition, and seeking prestige, by naming a famous composer.

6. Lowell Mason and Timothy Mason, comps., *The Sacred Harp; or, Eclectic Harmony*, rev. ed. (Cincinnati, OH, 1847), no. 164.

7. The earliest instance I have found of the variant opening stanza is in *The Brick Church Hymns, Designed for the Use of Social Prayer Meetings and Families* (New York, 1823), 163. To my knowledge, it never appeared in Britain.

8. William Walker, ed., *The Southern Harmony, and Musical Companion* (Spartanburg, SC, 1835). As with White and King's *Sacred Harp*, many later printings of this title were produced in Philadelphia, where shape-note type was in better supply.

9. This diary, now in the possession of Mason's descendant Ellen Dunlap, has been made available to me by Dunlap's gift of a transcript she produced. I am deeply grateful to Ms. Dunlap for sharing this remarkable source.

Interlude 3. Henry Ward Beecher Takes Note

1. Much of my account of Beecher's hymnbook production is drawn from William C. Beecher and Samuel Scoville, *A Biography of Rev. Henry Ward Beecher* (New York, 1888), 363–64.

2. On the history of American music printing, see Richard J. Wolfe, *Early American Music Engraving and Printing: A History of Music Publishing in America from 1787 to 1825 with Commentary on Earlier and Later Practices* (Urbana: Univ. of Illinois Press/Bibliographic Society of America, 1980), esp. 10–11 on music type. On the process and history of music type, see "Music Composition," in *American Dictionary of Printing and Bookmaking: Containing a History of the Arts in Europe and America* (New York, 1894), 383–87.

3. Beecher and Scoville, *Biography*, 364.

4. For an overview of electrotyping and its relationship to stereotyping, see Michael Winship, "Printing from Plates in the Nineteenth-Century United States," *Printing History* 5.2 (1983): 15–26.

5. For a typical account of singing at Plymouth Church during Beecher's time as its pastor, see Lyman Abbott, ed., *Henry Ward Beecher: A Sketch of His Career* (New York, 1883), 401.

Chapter 10. Did Poets Write Hymns?

1. On the history of psalm paraphrases during the Elizabethan era, see Rivkah Zim, *Metrical Psalms: Poetry as Praise and Prayer, 1535–1601* (New York: Cambridge Univ. Press, 1987).

2. Samuel Johnson, *The Lives of the English Poets*, vols. 21–23 of *The Yale Edition of the Works of Samuel Johnson* (New Haven, CT: Yale Univ. Press, 2010), 21:314–15.

3. Johnson, *Lives*, 23:1306–7.

4. Later editions of Cowper's writings often incorporated a hymn he wrote for the Olney Sunday school, which Newton did not include in *Olney Hymns*, bringing the total to sixty-eight hymns in those later editions.

5. James Montgomery, "Introductory Essay," in John Newton and William Cowper, *Olney Hymns*, 5th ed. (Glasgow, 1843), v–xliii, xxv–xxvi.

6. John Newton and William Cowper, *Olney Hymns* (London, 1779), vii.

7. For a history of Collins's Select Library of Christian Authors and his involvement with Montgomery, see David Keir, *The House of Collins: The Story of a Scottish Family of Publishers from 1789 to the Present Day* (London: Collins, 1952).

8. Montgomery, "Introductory Essay," xxx, xiv.

9. Andrew Piper gives a helpful account of the history and theory of the collected editions that proliferated in Britain and continental Europe in the early nineteenth century, including the impulse to incorporate increasing amounts of material. See Piper, *Dreaming in Books: The Making of the Bibliographic Imagination in the Romantic Age* (Chicago: Univ. of Chicago Press, 2009), 54–82.

10. William Cowper, *The Miscellaneous Works*, ed. John Smythe Memes, 3 vols. (Edinburgh, 1834), 3:485.

11. Montgomery's biography has not been studied nearly on the level of Cowper's, but a helpful overview is John H. Johansen, "The Hymns of James Montgomery," *Transactions of the Moravian Historical Society* 16.1 (1954): 14–29.

12. James Montgomery, *Poetical Works*, 5 vols. (Boston, 1858), 5:xvii–xviii.

13. Isobel Armstrong, "Anna Letitia Barbauld: A Unitarian Poetics?" in *Anna Letitia Barbauld: New Perspectives*, ed. William McCarthy and Olivia Murphy (Lewisburg, PA: Bucknell Univ. Press, 2014), 59–81.

14. Catherine Robson devoted one of her three case studies to "Casabianca" in *Heart Beats: Everyday Life and the Memorized Poem* (Princeton, NJ: Princeton Univ. Press, 2012).

15. Felicia Hemans, *Hymns on the Works of Nature, for the Use of Children* (Boston, 1827), [iii].

16. Felicia Hemans, *Scenes and Hymns of Life, with Other Religious Poems* (London, 1834), vii.

17. Rufus W. Griswold, *Sacred Poets of England and America* (Philadelphia, 1849), 326, 338.

18. Griswold, *Sacred Poets*, 461.

19. On Griswold and women writers, see Judy Myers Laue, "Rufus Wilmot Griswold's 'The Female Poets of America': The Politics of Anthologizing," PhD diss., Univ. of Southern California, 1988.

20. Griswold, *Sacred Poets*, 398.

Chapter 11. How Poems Entered the Hymnbook

1. Samuel Longfellow and Samuel Johnson, comps., *A Book of Hymns for Public and Private Devotion* (Cambridge, MA, 1846), American Antiquarian Society, Worcester, MA.

2. William Wordsworth, *Poems in Two Volumes, and Other Poems, 1800–1807*, ed. Jared Curtis (Ithaca, NY: Cornell Univ. Press, 1983), 165.

3. Charles Nutt, *History of Worcester and Its People*, 4 vols. (New York: Lewis Historical Publishing, 1919), 2:885–86.

4. Samuel Longfellow, "Memoir," in Samuel Johnson, *Lectures, Essays, and Sermons*, ed. Samuel Longfellow (Boston, 1883), 1–142, 30.

5. Samuel Johnson to Samuel Longfellow, July 31, 1846, Samuel Longfellow Papers, Longfellow House–Washington's Headquarters National Historic Site, Cambridge, MA (hereafter Longfellow Papers).

6. Samuel Longfellow to Samuel Johnson, [September 1863], Longfellow Papers.

7. Samuel Longfellow to Samuel Johnson, February 17, 1846, Longfellow Papers.

8. The correspondence indicates that they met in several other places for their work as well: Sam Johnson's home in Salem, Frank Appleton's home in Peabody, and even the Old Corner Bookshop.

9. Samuel Longfellow to Anne Longfellow Pierce, April 24, 1845, Longfellow Papers.

10. Longfellow, "Memoir," 30.

11. Johnson to Longfellow, July 31, 1846.

12. Samuel Longfellow to Samuel Johnson, October 27, 1846, Longfellow Papers.

13. Samuel Longfellow to Samuel Johnson, January 17, 1848, Longfellow Papers.

14. Ticknor and Fields's cost books give a date of "June 1848" for the second edition and a date of "June X 1848" for the third. Warren S. Tryon and William Charvat, eds., *The Cost Books of Ticknor and Fields and Their Predecessors, 1832–1858* (New York: Bibliographical Society of America, 1949), 124, 127.

15. Tryon and Charvat, *Cost Books*, 125–26, 110–11.

16. Tryon and Charvat, *Cost Books*, 245.

17. Tryon and Charvat, *Cost Books*, 290.

18. Samuel Johnson to Samuel Longfellow, June 17, 1859, Longfellow Papers.

19. N. L. F., "New Hymn Books," *Christian Examiner* 40.1 (Jan. 1846): 29–47.

20. Ephraim Peabody, "New Hymn Book," *Christian Examiner* 41.3 (Nov. 1846): 422–26, 422.

21. Peabody, "New Hymn Book," 423.

22. Peabody, "New Hymn Book," 423–24, 426.

23. Samuel Johnson to Samuel Longfellow, December 8, 1846, Longfellow Papers.

24. Nathaniel Holmes Morison, "New Publications," *Christian Register* 25.39 (Sept. 26, 1846): 155.

25. "Hymns and Sacred Poetry," *Christian Register* 25.49 (Dec. 5, 1846): 194.

26. Edward Everett Hale, "Hymns and a Book of Hymns," *Monthly Religious Magazine* 4.1 (Jan. 1847): 40–46, 40.

27. Hale, "Hymns and a Book," 41, 42.

28. Samuel Longfellow to Anne Longfellow Pierce, April 21, 1846, Longfellow Papers.

29. Benson noted with approval the late nineteenth-century transition in Protestant churches generally from didactic to devotional hymnody. Louis F. Benson, *The English Hymn: Its Development and Use in Worship* (New York: George H. Doran, 1915), 573–74.

30. "New Hymn Book," *Christian Register* 28.2 (Jan. 13, 1849): 8.

31. "Hymns and Sacred Poetry," 194.

Chapter 12. The Return of the Private Hymnbook

1. Samuel Longfellow, "Memoir," in Samuel Johnson, *Lectures, Essays, and Sermons*, ed. Samuel Longfellow (Boston, 1883), 53.

2. Longfellow, "Memoir," 58–62.

3. Samuel Longfellow to Samuel Johnson, [April 1867], Samuel Longfellow Papers, Longfellow House–Washington's Headquarters National Historic Site, Cambridge, MA.

4. Isaac Watts, *Hymns and Spiritual Songs* (London, 1707), xiii.

5. Louis F. Benson, *The English Hymn: Its Development and Use in Worship* (New York: George H. Doran, 1915), 435–42.

6. Elizabeth Emra Holmes, *Scenes in Our Parish*, 1st and 2nd ser. (New York, 1833), 22.

7. On the literary history of the Oxford movement and its importance to the history of British poetry in particular, see G. B. Tennyson, *Victorian Devotional Poetry: The Tractarian Mode* (Cambridge, MA: Harvard Univ. Press, 1981).

8. Heber's most recent biography is Derrick Hughes, *Bishop Sahib: A Life of Reginald Heber* (Worthing, England: Churchman, 1986). Much of Hughes's account of Heber's hymnody and other literary pursuits relies on Amelia Shipley Heber, *The Life of Reginald Heber, D.D., Lord Bishop of Calcutta*, 2 vols. (London, 1830).

9. "Whitmarsh, Caroline Snowden," in *Appleton's Cyclopaedia of American Biography*, 6 vols. (New York, 1887–1889), 6:486.

10. On American Protestants' attitudes toward Catholicism in the 1850s, see Jenny Franchot, *Roads to Rome: The Antebellum Protestant Encounter with Catholicism* (New York: Cambridge Univ. Press, 1994).

11. Caroline Snowden Whitmarsh, ed., *Hymns for Mothers and Children*, 1st ser. (Boston, 1861), iii, iv.

12. Anna Warner, ed., *Wayfaring Hymns* (New York, 1869), vi.

13. Susan Warner and Anna Warner, *Say and Seal*, 2 vols. (Philadelphia, 1860), 2:115–16.

14. Anna Warner, ed., *Hymns of the Church Militant* (New York, 1858), iv.

15. Warner, *Hymns of the Church Militant*, v–vi.

Chapter 13. Emily Dickinson's Hymnody of Privacy

1. Thomas H. Johnson, *Emily Dickinson: An Interpretive Biography* (1955; repr., New York: Atheneum, 1972), 84.

2. Emily Dickinson, *The Poems of Emily Dickinson: Reading Edition*, ed. R. W. Franklin (Cambridge, MA: Belknap, 1999), Fr 202. Future references to Dickinson's poems will be given parenthetically in the text, using Franklin's numbering in this edition.

3. Lowell Mason and David Greene, comps., *Church Psalmody: A Collection of Psalms and Hymns Adapted to Public Worship, Selected from Dr. Watts and Other Authors* (Boston, 1831); Edwards A. Park, Austin Phelps, and Lowell Mason, comps., *The Sabbath Hymn Book* (New York, 1858). Nearly all of the surviving books are at the John Hay Library at Brown University. There are a copy of Watts owned by Emily Norcross Dickinson (the poet's mother) and two early "Watts and select" volumes owned by Edward Dickinson at the Houghton Library, Harvard University.

4. Emily Dickinson, *Letters*, 3 vols., ed. Thomas H. Johnson (Cambridge, MA: Belknap/Harvard Univ. Press, 1958), 2:526.

5. Dickinson, *Letters*, 1:201.

6. Virginia Jackson, *Dickinson's Misery: A Theory of Lyric Reading* (Princeton, NJ: Princeton Univ. Press, 2005).

7. Henry Wadsworth Longfellow, *Poems and Other Writings*, ed. J. D. McClatchy (New York: Library of America, 2000), 3–4.

8. Andrew Higgins, "Longfellow's Conversations: *Weltliteratur* as Aesthetic in the Early Poetry," in *Reconsidering Longfellow*, ed. Christoph Irmscher and Robert Arbor (Madison, NJ: Fairleigh Dickinson Univ. Press, 2014), 11–32.

9. On the Dickensian dimension of Tim and Dickinson's other alter ego, Dollie, see Rise B. Axelrod and Steven Gould Axelrod, "Dickinson's Dickens: 'Tim' and 'Dollie,'" *Emily Dickinson Journal* 11.1 (2002): 21–32.

10. Dickinson, *Letters*, 3:680, 3:681.

11. Dickinson, *Letters*, 2:362.

12. Dickinson, *Letters*, 2:419.

13. Dickinson, *Letters*, 2:525.

14. Dickinson, *Letters*, 2:528.

15. Michael L. Manson, "'The Thews of Hymn': Dickinson's Metrical Grammar," in *A Companion to Emily Dickinson*, ed. Martha Nell Smith and Mary Loeffelholz (Malden, MA: Blackwell, 2008), 368–90, 382–85; Annie Finch, *The Ghost of Meter: Culture and Prosody in American Free Verse* (Ann Arbor: Univ. of Michigan Press, 1993), 26–27.

16. Manson, "Thews of Hymn," 384–85.

17. Manson, "Thews of Hymn," 389–90.

18. Martha Winburn England and John Sparrow, *Hymns Unbidden: Donne, Herbert, Blake, Emily Dickinson and the Hymnographers* (New York: New York Public Library, 1966), 119.

19. Anna Warner, ed., *Hymns of the Church Militant* (New York, 1858), iv.

Epilogue: The Hymnological Decade

1. Austin Phelps, Edwards A. Park, and Daniel L. Furber, *Hymns and Choirs; or, The Matter and Manner of the Service of Song in the House of the Lord* (Andover, MA, 1860), 126.

2. "The Presbyterian Hymnal," *Independent* 26 (Nov. 12, 1874): 9. On the feminizing of nineteenth-century hymnody, see Claudia Stokes, *The Altar at Home: Sentimental Literature and Nineteenth-Century American Religion* (Philadelphia: Univ. of Pennsylvania Press, 2014), chap. 2; June Hadden Hobbs, *"I Sing for I Cannot Be Silent": The Feminization of American Hymnody, 1870–1920* (Pittsburgh, PA: Univ. of Pittsburgh Press, 1997), chap. 1.

3. Eva J. O'Meara, "The Lowell Mason Library," *Notes*, 2nd ser., 28.2 (Dec. 1971): 197–208.

Page numbers in *italics* refer to figures.